WHO WAS JOHN?

Who Was John?

The Fourth Gospel debate after
Pope Benedict XVI's
Jesus of Nazareth

ST PAULS

JOHN REDFORD

Who Was John?

The Fourth Gospel debate after
Pope Benedict XVI's
Jesus of Nazareth

To Bishop William

From John

With this for your kind visit
here prayers for your ministry
in the Archdiocese.

ST PAULS

The version of the Bible used throughout is *The New Jerusalem Bible*, (hence NJB) except when an author is quoted with a biblical text included, in which case the version used by that author remains in place.

Front cover: *Crucifixion of Our Lord* from a sixteenth century icon in the National Museum, Lviv, Ukraine.

Nihil Obstat: The Reverend Father John J. Henry, M.Th, LSS Ph.D.

Imprimatur: The Right Reverend John Hine, Ph.L., Auxiliary Bishop in Southwark.

The Nihil Obstat and Imprimatur are official declarations that a book or publication is free of doctrinal or moral error. No implication is contained therein that those who have granted the imprimatur agree with the contents, opinions, or statements expressed.

ST PAULS Publishing
187 Battersea Bridge Road, London SW11 3AS, UK

Copyright © ST PAULS UK 2008

ISBN 978-0-85439-746-4

Set by Tukan DTP, Stubbington, Fareham, UK
Printed in Malta by Progress Press Company Limited

ST PAULS is an activity of the priests and brothers of the Society of St Paul who proclaim the Gospel through the media of social communication.

CONTENTS

COMMENDATION

I warmly recommend this fine work on the authorship of the Fourth Gospel by Father John Redford, Reader in Biblical Hermeneutics at the Maryvale Institute, Birmingham. It is a competent and stimulating response to the request put out by the Holy Father to begin a debate that he hoped to initiate with the publication of his best-selling book *Jesus of Nazareth*. Redford strongly supports the case that the Fourth Gospel, contrary to much scholarly opinion was written by John the Apostle, Son of Zebedee, who is none other than the enigmatic "beloved disciple". While Redford asserts the substantial reliability of the Gospel of John, he deals carefully with the complex issues relating to the process of the writing of this most controversial of Gospels. I find his conclusions fascinating, and hope that this book will stimulate further discussion in keeping with the desire of Pope Benedict.

Avery Cardinal Dulles, S.J.
Laurence J. Professor of Religion and Society
Fordham University

DEDICATION

To His Holiness Pope Benedict XVI, in grateful thanks for the wisdom and inspiration of his theological writings, and in his courageous oversight as pastor throughout my priestly and academic life.

FOREWORD

Much of the study involved in writing this book was put together during a six month sabbatical in Paris at the turn of the millennium, studying at the excellent biblical library at L'Institut Catholique. For that sabbatical, I thank the late *emeritus* Archbishop of Birmingham, Maurice Couve de Murville, who arranged it with his numerous French connections. It was my privilege to know him earlier as a fellow priest, as a fellow member of the Society of Old Testament Studies, and finally with myself as a member of Staff of the new Maryvale Institute of Higher Education which he vigorously promoted as its first President. *Requiescat in Pace.*

The Catholic Church needs a debate about scripture in this first decade of the new millennium. Catholic biblical scholars in general have accepted the post-Bultmannian scepticism about the Gospels, at least as a hermeneutical principle. One who argues for their substantial reliability is seen as putting the clock back to the "fundamentalist" days before the papal encyclical of Pius XII: *Divino Afflante Spiritu.*

It could be argued that Catholic scholarship has not yet come fully to terms with biblical criticism. In simply following current trends rather than challenging them, the vital contribution of Catholic theology in an ecumenical context is lacking in a world which more and more has attempted to undermine the historical authenticity of Christian origins.

This was surely in the Pope's mind as he wrote and published his important book *Jesus of Nazareth.* This present book is an offering to what is hopefully the beginning of a debate initiated by the Pope on scripture, history, and theology, and about the relationship between them.

In writing this book, I am particularly grateful to prestigious scholars of the Evangelical tradition who have written excellent commentaries and monographs on St John's Gospel. In following sceptical trends, recent Catholic scholarship has tended to favour Liberal Protestant interpretation, often it seems without question. Good Evangelical scholarship is by no means fundamentalist, but in my opinion presents the evidence fairly, including the evidence for the tradition as well as against it.

As with my two previous books *Bad, Mad or God? Proving the Divinity of Christ from St. John's Gospel* and *Born of a Virgin: Proving the Miracle from the Gospels,* I thank once more my noble assistant, Mary Bull, who has read through the text with her especially sharp eye; also my secretary Mrs Ann Weston. I thank also my colleagues on the Maryvale Staff, who have been as ever most supportive of my work. Finally, once again, I thank Annabel Robson, the Commissioning Editor of St Pauls, for her wise counsel; Teresa Rees our typesetter; and Maria Yatsiv for the wonderful book of Ukrainian icons, together with the author of that book for the cover page icon of the beloved disciple at the foot of the cross.

Part One
What Debate?

Having published his book *Jesus of Nazareth*, Pope Benedict XVI implicitly challenges the world of biblical scholarship to reopen the debate as to whether or not the Gospel of John is a substantial eye-witness source for the Life of the historical Jesus, in particular for his self-consciousness of his own being and mission.

The Pope contends that it is.

CHAPTER ONE

THE POPE WRITES A BOOK

> - **Pope Benedict XVI in *Jesus of Nazareth,* wishes to affirm as theologian that the Life of the historical Jesus was truly the revelation of the Word become flesh for our salvation.**
> - **He sees modern historical Jesus research as an obstacle to writing such a life, because of what he sees as an illicit distinction between the "historical Jesus" and the "Christ of faith".**
> - **On the contrary, the Pope affirms that in particular the four Gospels are historically reliable when they tell us that Jesus declared his divinity during his life on earth.**

For a Pope to write and publish a scholarly book is itself a major publishing event. The fact that the English edition of *Jesus of Nazareth*[1] has been published by Bloomsbury, the publishers of the *Harry Potter* books, indicates that the publishing world is confident of a best seller; a hope which, according to reports, has been well vindicated.[2]

The previous occupant of the See of Peter, Pope John Paul II, Karol Wojtyla, was probably the most prolific writer of all the Popes in the two-thousand-year history of the Church. Encyclicals, homilies, the new Code of Canon Law, addresses to the millions on his jet-setting trips around the world, even an Apostolic Constitution, the new *Catechism of the Catholic Church,* kept the Vatican publishing house frantically busy throughout his twenty-six years as the first Polish Pope. He even produced a more informal book *Crossing the Threshold of Hope,* the result of a series of conversations the Pontiff had with the journalist Vittorio Missori;[3] and *Memory and Identity,*[4] his own personal reflections at the eventide of his life.

But during his long pontificate, John Paul II published no work specifically of academic scholarship. Certainly he was competent to do so. During his career as a Polish priest and bishop, Karol Wojtyla lectured and wrote works on philosophy and sexual ethics,[5] and indeed, his encyclical *Faith and Reason*,[6] while written in the *genre* of a papal document, was acclaimed widely by reviewers of all persuasions as the product of one of the greatest thinkers of the twentieth century.

Why do Popes in general not publish works for academia? It is possibly not only a question of time in a crushing daily agenda, but also that the Pope might feel that his white cassock gives him an unfair advantage in scholarly debate over his academic peers.

The Professor Pope

But the present Pope, Joseph Ratzinger, has now published a scholarly work on Jesus. Of all the occupants of Peter's chair in recent centuries, Pope Benedict is most of all qualified to write academic theology. He is a professional theologian of the first rank, perhaps in his own right the foremost theologian in the world today of any Christian denomination.

He is indeed a Professor Pope.[7] In 1953 he obtained his doctorate in theology with a thesis entitled "People and House of God in St Augustine's Doctrine of the Church". After lecturing on dogmatic and fundamental theology at the Higher School of Philosophy and Theology in Freising, he went on to teach at Bonn, from 1959 to1963; at Münster from 1963 to 1966 and at Tübingen from 1966 to 1969. During this last year he held the Chair of dogmatics and history of dogma at the University of Regensburg, where he was also Vice-President of the University. From 1962 to 1965 he made a notable contribution to Vatican II as a *peritus,* "expert"; being present at the Council as theological advisor to Cardinal Joseph Frings, Archbishop of Cologne. It was from these prestigious academic appointments that he eventually became Archbishop of Munich, then in 1981 the Prefect of the Vatican Congregation for the Doctrine of the Faith, and finally on 19 April 2005 being elected Pope by the College of Cardinals after the death of Pope John Paul II.

The number and theological depth of his publications is

awesome, books which are scholarly and which have reached a large readership. Ignatius Press, his publisher in the USA, lists thirty-six titles by him they have published.[8] His literary output did not diminish while, appointed by John Paul II, he headed the Congregation for the Doctrine of the Faith, the Church's doctrinal overseer. It was in that post that he earned for himself both the reputation of being what the media called the Church's Rottweiler, and his unpopularity with liberal Catholics.

But Joseph Ratzinger would have seen no contradiction between writing books of great theological creativity, and in disciplining those whom he considered had transgressed the boundaries of orthodoxy. His specific expertise was as a dogmatic theologian; that is to say, he explored theological issues presupposing the faith of the Church, particularly as expressed in the Creed.

"Dogma" is today a dirty word. "Party dogma" would be a derogatory reference to ideas within a political party which were unable to change, or even "an arrogant declaration of opinion".[9] Originally, the Greek word *dogma* meant "opinion" or "judgement". It was used especially with reference to a decree of the Roman Senate, and meant more generally "a positive ordinance, emanating from a distant and unquestionable authority".[10] In the New Testament, it referred to decrees of Roman rulers [Luke 2:1, Acts 17:7], of the Jewish law [Ephesians 2:15], and also of the decrees of the apostles and elders of the Church [Acts 16:4.].[11]

The Church teaches that the doctrines of the faith, the Trinity, the Incarnation, and other teachings related to that central doctrine, were revealed by Christ while on earth and expressed by his apostles in their teaching and in their writing, particularly in the scriptures. They are dogmas of faith. They cannot be changed. Only their understanding can and will be developed. The Christian Creed which is recited in church every Sunday, in essence goes back to the second century.[12] Dogmatic theology as a branch of theology can only develop if those doctrines are accepted as a starting point in its investigations, and accepted as a criterion of true development. Ratzinger would have seen himself as the appointed guardian

15

of the faith once declared to the saints, and representing the magisterium. That is the teaching authority of the Church, consisting of the Catholic bishops in union with the Pope, the successor of Peter, which has the assistance of the Holy Spirit throughout the centuries to express and maintain the truth of Christian revelation.[13]

In the shoes of the fisherman

In being elected Bishop of Rome, Ratzinger would then have seen himself as not only as *representing* the magisterium, but nothing less than himself as office-holder of the magisterium, with the commission of Christ himself. The word *magisterium*, "teaching office", derives from *magister*, teacher, and in the Middle Ages could simply refer to the office of a qualified *magister* of academic theology. After his election to the chair of the fisherman become apostle Peter, Ratzinger would have correctly seen himself, according to Catholic theology, as *magister* of the universal church. He has succeeded to the most important professorship in the world.

The Catholic Church, with a billion members worldwide, could be seen as a vast empire of teaching and of practice stemming from that teaching. In the second half of the century before Christ, only a few decades before Jesus was born, a Latin poet named Virgil composed his famous *Aeneid*, a mythical tale in praise of the origins of the city of Rome.[14] Jupiter, "the Father of Gods and Men",[15] prophesies concerning the Romans that "On them I impose no limits of time or place. I have given them an empire that will know no end".[16]

That prophecy in the *Aeneid* was strangely fulfilled, not by the mighty Roman Empire, which by the fifth century of our era was terminally in decline, but by the papacy, a spiritual empire which now has its centre in a nation state occupying Vatican City, a square mile of the modern City of Rome. After two thousand years this spiritual empire is still growing, even though its end is being constantly predicted. When it loses strength in one part of the world, as in present day

Western Europe, it burgeons in other zones of our planet, as now in Africa, Asia, and the Philippines.

In the new millennium, we are becoming used to empires being built not based upon country, but upon the diffusion of ideas. As I am preparing this book, Rupert Murdoch, the head of a vast media empire, has just acquired ownership of *The Wall Street Journal*, with its massive influence on the world of finance. Owning one hundred newspapers in many parts of the world, and satellite television networks, Murdoch is truly an emperor. The financial assets of his operations are more than that of most countries; and his influence on ideas makes him more powerful than most heads of state.

Catholics today tend to downplay as triumphalist overmuch emphasis on the authority of the Pope, using his own preferred title "servant of the servants of God". The Second Vatican Council, meeting in the Vatican from 1961-65, was a great reforming Council. The four thousand bishops who attended wanted to balance Catholic emphasis on the authority of the Pope with a more collegial vision. The Church had always taught that the worldwide College of Bishops succeeded the Twelve Apostles appointed by Christ himself. This was written well into the foundation document of the Council *Lumen Gentium*, ("Light of the Nations"), the Dogmatic Constitution on the Church.[17]

But this in no way contradicted the teaching of the First Vatican Council (1869-70), cut short by the Franco-Prussian War, which stated firmly:

> 1. We teach and declare that, according to the gospel evidence, a primacy of jurisdiction over the whole Church of God was immediately and directly promised to the blessed apostle Peter and conferred on him by Christ the Lord.[18]

This "gospel evidence" refers to Matthew 16:19, where Jesus tells the fisherman disciple Peter, in response to his confession of faith in Jesus as Son of God that he is to be the rock on which Jesus will build his church.[19] In the teaching of the Catholic Church, the Bishop of Rome, as the successor of Peter, succeeds to this primacy of authority in the Shoes of the Fisherman. *Lumen Gentium* does not reduce this claim of primacy, but rather sets the authority of the Pope within the context of the authority of the College of Bishops:

> This Sacred Council, following closely in the footsteps of the First Vatican Council, with that Council teaches and declares that Jesus Christ, the eternal Shepherd, established His holy Church, having sent forth the apostles as He Himself had been sent by the Father;(136) and He willed that their successors, namely the bishops, should be shepherds in His Church even to the consummation of the world. And in order that the episcopate itself might be one and undivided, He placed Blessed Peter over the other apostles, and instituted in him a permanent and visible source and foundation of unity of faith and communion. And all this teaching about the institution, the perpetuity, the meaning and reason for the sacred primacy of the Roman Pontiff and of his infallible magisterium, this Sacred Council again proposes to be firmly believed by all the faithful.[20]

During discussions in the Council, theologians (especially bishops!) had complained that pre-Vatican II thinking had diminished the role of bishops rather to being legates of the Pope, rather than successors of the apostles in their own right in their own dioceses. *Lumen Gentium* addressed this problem, asserting that bishops were truly successors of the apostles. But the Council also had in its sights what it saw as the opposite danger, that of "Conciliarism": that the authority of the Pope was dependent on the collective authority of the bishops.[21] It wanted to go much further than the view of Eastern Orthodox Christians, that the Pope had primacy of *honour* rather than primacy of *jurisdiction*. Rather, Vatican II asserted that the Bishop of Rome had authority over the other bishops, just as Jesus in his own day "placed Blessed Peter over the other apostles, and instituted in him a permanent and visible source and foundation of faith and communion".

We live in an age where democracy is viewed as the only legitimate form of secular government. But in a new millennium of mass communication, the perceived importance of the role of the single leader of any given organisation or community, however democratically that leader has been elected, has not diminished, only rather increased. The media want to know "who is in charge?" in order to bring to book some individual who is responsible in this or that community.

It is not my intention in this book to defend the Catholic view of the role of the Bishop of Rome as the successor of Peter, which I have attempted to do briefly in a previous little work to which I have already referred.[22] My only intention here is to attempt to understand the context in which a religious leader of such supreme importance writes a best-selling book. Why did Pope Benedict break with usual tradition and write a book which he submits to the world, indeed particularly to the academic world, not as a work in which he exercises his papal authority but as a work of scholarship?

Why write *Jesus of Nazareth*?

Initially of course, we must understand that the Pope is not writing purely an academic work, but has a spiritual intent:

> It goes without saying that this book is in no way an exercise of the magisterium, but is solely an expression of my personal search "for the face of the Lord" (cf. Psalm 27:8). Everyone is free, then, to contradict me. I would only ask my readers for that initial goodwill without which there can be no understanding.[23]

However, the occupant of the See of Peter cannot make such a search purely individual, particularly if he attains a readership of millions, nor could he ever expect it to remain purely individual, in the nature of his office. *Jesus of Nazareth* is clearly also a work of scholarship, not limited to being a set of personal spiritual reflections. As we shall see, the Pope expresses firm academic opinions, and counters what he sees as inadequate academic views. I would suggest therefore immediately that the Pope, in writing *Jesus of Nazareth*, is using his influence to exercise his *magisterium* in the more general mediaeval meaning of the term, precisely as a *magister,* a *magister sacrae doctrinae,* a "Master of Sacred Doctrine".[24] The Professor Pope is exercising his professorial role, a role for which as we have seen he is uniquely qualified.

A distinguished theology professor in his lectures and in his writings will include not only dogmas of faith, but opinions which he holds as most likely, and most beneficial to understand the questions at hand. He will propose those opinions precisely as opinions and as nothing more, even though he might hold some opinions strongly. But those opinions will be the more carefully considered by his students because of the weight of his own scholarship and of his own insights. And part of the intention of his presentation will be to institute a fruitful debate, to further the work of theological reflection.

Even if *Jesus of Nazareth* is not a formal exercise of the papal magisterium, I would submit that it is a work where the Pope is intending to exercise a teaching role, and using the weight of his papal office not in order to conclude discussion – *Roma locutus est, causa finita est,* "Rome has spoken, the case is closed" – but entirely the opposite, to reopen the debate about Jesus, and a debate which he will submit needs to take on board entirely new perspectives.

A Life of Jesus

Half a century ago, it was a popular *genre* in theological studies to write a "Life of Jesus". A student for ordination once asked his bishop, "My Lord, can you recommend a good *Life of Jesus?*" The good bishop replied, "Have you tried the one by St Luke?"

That reply was smart, but not entirely fair. The four canonical Gospels, Matthew, Mark, Luke and John, while sharing much in common about the life, death, and resurrection of Jesus, are in many ways different from each other. The infancy of Jesus is described only in Matthew 1-2 and Luke 1-2, and none of the incidents recounted are the same; for example, the story of the Magi is told only in

Matthew [2:1-12], while the shepherds feeding their flocks by night are only recounted in Luke [2:8-15].

Admittedly, similarities in the telling of the adult life of Jesus are striking. Matthew, Mark, and Luke are called the "Synoptic Gospels" (from the Greek *synopsis* "seen together") because they are so similar, so much so that one seems to have been the literary source for the other two for the adult life of Jesus. Traditionally, Matthew was considered the source of Mark and Luke; but since the nineteenth century, the common view has been that Mark's was the first Gospel to have been written, and Matthew and Luke used Mark.[25] Much of Mark is in Matthew and Luke from the baptism of Jesus, his miracles, his parables, and finally his passion.

But Mark has little of the teaching of Jesus, as contained in Matthew's "Sermon on the Mount" [Matthew 5-7]. Luke alone has the superb parables of the Good Samaritan [Luke 10:22-29] and the Prodigal Son [Luke 14:11-32]. Only Luke also, with his obvious human sympathy, tells the story of the Good Thief on the cross, to whom Jesus answered, "In truth I tell you, today you will be with me in paradise" [Luke 23:43]. Only Matthew 27 recounts the strange story that, after Jesus had died on the cross, "[52] the tombs opened and the bodies of many holy people rose from the dead, [53]and these, after his resurrection, came out of the tombs, entered the holy city and appeared to a number of people".

The accounts of the appearances of the risen Jesus to his astonished disciples in the Synoptic Gospels are as dissimilar as are the accounts of the infancy. Mark even has no account whatsoever of the appearances of Jesus, apart from the ending of his Gospel [Mark 16:9-20], which probably was not part of the original edition of Mark.[26] Only Luke recounts the appearance of Jesus to his disciples on the road to Emmaus [Luke 24:13-52]. And only Matthew has Jesus commissioning his disciples to preach the Gospel to the whole world [Matthew 28:18-20].

Finally, the Fourth Gospel, that of John, is the most dissimilar of all. John consists of long discourses by Jesus and of dialogues with either his opponents or his disciples, as contrasted with the short and pithy sayings which we find in the Synoptics. Only in the Fourth Gospel does the Baptist call Jesus the "Lamb of God who takes away the sins of the world" [John 1:36]. There are only seven miracles recounted in the whole of John's Gospel,[27] including the turning of water into wine [John 2:1-11], and the raising of Lazarus [John 12:41-44], which are not included in the Synoptic account. Most of what is contained in the account of the passion and death of Jesus in John and his resurrection appearances are not to be found at all in the Synoptics. In fact, chapters 7-21, two-thirds of the content of the Fourth Gospel, narrates events taking place only in the last six weeks of Jesus' life that is his final visit to Jerusalem, his trial, crucifixion and death, and his resurrection.

Even taking a straightforward, even superficial view, of the four Gospels, therefore, it would seem at first sight a feasible project for an individual to attempt to synthesise the four accounts into a "Life of Jesus" from that individual's own perspective. After all, the Fourth evangelist has to admit at the end of his Gospel: " There was much else that Jesus did; if it were written down in detail, I do not suppose the world itself would hold all the books that would be written" [John 21:25]. Each of us could in theory present the life of Jesus, using material from the four Gospels, from the insights we have gained from our reading of those Gospels, just as the evangelists themselves wrote their Gospels from the material they had to hand.

This is precisely what Pope Benedict has done in *Jesus of Nazareth*. But, as we shall now see, writing such a *Life of Jesus* raises theological and historical problems of which the Pope was clearly aware.

Why no *Lives of Jesus*?

It would seem therefore at first sight that the writing of a *Life of Jesus* could be a fruitful exercise, and the Pope in his book quotes notable scholars who attempting such an exercise inspired him in his early years by using such a genre.[28] A *Life of Jesus* would first attempt to synthesise the four gospel accounts into a coherent presentation of Jesus' life from his infancy to his resurrection. The writer of such a *Life* would also add knowledge of the background of the Gospels, such as the political situation in the Holy Land at the time of Christ. Above all, as the Pope says, such a theologian would "present him (Jesus) as a man living on earth who, fully human though he was, at the same time brought God to men, the God with whom as Son he was one. Through the man Jesus, then, God was made visible, and hence our eyes were able to behold the perfect man".[29]

Unfortunately, the Pope states regretfully, such *Lives of Jesus* as by Guardini and Daniel-Rops are no longer a common *genre* among biblical scholars and theologians. That this has happened, the Pope argues, is because biblical scholars have followed a "reductionist" methodology. No longer is the life of Jesus presented as God become man for our salvation, as the Gospels present him. That, as the Pope explains, for modern critical scholarship, is not "the historical Jesus" but rather "the Christ of faith".

Rather, the Pope is aware that today in biblical scholarship, Jesus is presented in purely human terms, as a Jewish prophet of the first century who followed the prophet John the Baptist and then set out on his own, had a reputation for performing miracles, proclaimed the kingdom of God, called God his Father, gathered disciples around him, welcomed prostitutes and sinners to follow him, whose message angered the Jewish authorities of his day, and who was put to death by crucifixion after condemnation by the Roman governor of the day, Pontius Pilate.[30]

Naturally, modern scholars differ as to detail regarding what they consider to be the historically verifiable facts concerning the life of Jesus.[31] But nearly all seem to agree in stating that Jesus did not explicitly claim to be the divine Son of God, nor do they think that it can be proven that he proclaimed his divinity to his astonished fellow Jews, saying "Before Abraham was, I AM", as John's Gospel said he did [John 8:58].

For modern scholarship, it was only after the resurrection that Christians understood Jesus to be the divine Son of God.

The Gospels, it is claimed, were documents of faith, soaked through with an overlay of the beliefs of the first Christians. They read back their own faith retrospectively into the narratives of the life of Jesus; so, for M. Casey, a Jewish prophet becomes a Gentile God.[32] For the Pope, this is a disastrous situation:

> All these attempts have produced a common result: the impression that we have very little certain knowledge of Jesus and that only at a later stage did faith in his divinity shape the image we have of him. This impression has by now penetrated deeply into the minds of the Christian people at large. This is a dramatic situation for faith, because its point of reference is being placed in doubt: Intimate friendship with Jesus, on which everything depends, is in danger of clutching at thin air.[33]

The Pope makes the obvious point that "far from uncovering an icon that has become obscured over time, they are much more like photographs of their authors and the ideals they hold".[34] To quote John P. Meier's summary of such modern subjective opinions: "Whether one looks at the more serious works of writers like John Dominic Crossan and Burton L. Mack or the sensationalistic popular works of authors like Robert W. Funk, one finds Jesus the Cynic philosopher or Jesus the generic Mediterranean peasant or Jesus the religious iconoclast largely overshadowing if not obliterating the specific first-century Palestinian Jew named Jesus".[35]

It is hardly surprising that the Pope, schooled as he was from the beginning in the richness of Christian theological thought, is not inspired similarly by such pathetic "Lives", which, like the rock film *Jesus Christ Superstar,* lead us rather to feel sorry for Jesus than to believe in him. These lives of Jesus can in no way inspire to genuine Christian faith. The Pope now wishes to inspire us to faith in Jesus by recounting Jesus' life in his own way. He can do this because, as he says, "I believe that this Jesus – the Jesus of the Gospels – is a historically plausible and convincing figure".[36]

The life of the Word become Flesh

The *Jesus of Nazareth,* which the Pope presents is no reductionist image, no purely human Jesus.

Beginning his account with the baptism of the adult Jesus by John the Baptist, the Pope focuses on the divine voice of the Father, "This is my beloved Son" [Luke 3:21], which is both a revelation of Jesus' divine nature, and a prophecy of the baptism of his death for the "sins of humanity".[37] The baptism of Jesus, then, for the Pope, is the revelation in history of the being and the meaning of Jesus of Nazareth the "Word become flesh" [John 1:14].

Focussing next on the temptations of Jesus in the desert [Luke 4:1-13\\], the Pope sees the devil quoting scripture to tempt Jesus as a parable of the modern misuse of scripture:

> The common practice today is to measure the Bible against the so-called modern worldview, whose funda-mental dogma is that God cannot act in history – that everything to do with God is to be relegated to the domain of subjectivity. And so the Bible no longer speaks of God, the living God; no, now we alone speak and decide what God can do and what we will and should do. And the Antichrist, with an air of scholarly excellence, tells us that any exegesis that reads the Bible from the perspective of faith in the living God, in order to listen to what God has to say, is fundamentalism; he wants to convince us that only *his* kind of exegesis, the supposedly purely scientific kind, in which God says nothing and has nothing to say, is able to keep abreast of the times.[38]

Then, going on to discuss the "kingdom of God", the initial proclamation of Jesus, accompanied by his miracles of healing and of exorcism, the Pope refuses to accept the common view in modern scholarship, following the Catholic modernist Loisy that "Jesus preached the kingdom of God, and what came was the Church".[39] Rather, by this phrase "kingdom of God" that means for the Pope "God's being-Lord, of his Lordship",[40] Jesus is drawing attention to the fact that, by his casting out demons "by the finger of God" [Luke 11:20], "the Kingdom of God becomes present here and now, that it is 'drawing near'".[41]

Far, therefore, from Jesus implicitly denying his divinity by focussing on the "kingdom of *God*", for the Pope, this phrase on the contrary is an implicit Christological claim on Jesus' part: "...God is always at the centre of the discussion, yet precisely because Jesus himself is God-the Son – his entire preaching is a message about the mystery of his person..."[42]

For the Pope, this comes over especially strongly in the Beatitudes, [cf. Matthew 5:11] "Blessed are you when people abuse you and persecute you and speak all kinds of calumny against you falsely on my account". The Pope explains:

> The "I" of Jesus himself, fidelity to his person, becomes the criterion of righteousness and salvation. In the other Beatitudes, Christology is present, so to speak, in veiled form; here, however, the message that he himself is the centre of history emerges openly. Jesus ascribes to his "I" a normative status that no teacher of Israel – indeed, no teacher of the Church – has a right to claim for himself. Someone who speaks like this is no longer a prophet in the traditional sense, an ambassador and trustee of another; he himself is the reference point of the righteous life, its goal and centre.[43]

Again, for the Pope, this means that, furthermore, the Church was not a post-Easter creation of the disciples of Jesus, perverting a simple message of a Jewish prophet about the kingdom of God to a dogma about the Son of God and his infallible Church. Rather, in his calling of the Twelve apostles, which "Twelve – the number of the tribes – is at the same time a cosmic number that expresses the comprehensiveness of the newly reborn People of God. The Twelve stands as the patriarchs of this universal people founded on the Apostles".[44]

Only in this way, the Pope argues, can the crucial event of the transfiguration [Matthew 17:1-9\\] be understood:

> On the mountain they (the disciples Peter, James and John) – in the conversation of the transfigured Jesus with the Law and the Prophets (i.e. with Moses and Elijah) – they realise that the true Feast of Tabernacles has come.

On the mountain they learn that Jesus himself is the living Torah, the complete Word of God. On the mountain they see the "power" (*dynamis*) of the Kingdom that is coming in Christ.[45]

Thus *Jesus of Nazareth* comes to its climax with chapter 10 entitled *Jesus Declares his Identity*.[46] Clearly, once more against a great deal of modern Gospel scholarship, the Pope ascribes to Jesus rather than to the primitive church the claim in Mark 2:25 that the Son of Man has power to forgive sins.[47] "If Jesus ascribes this authority to the Son of Man, then he is claiming to possess the dignity of God himself and to act on that basis".[48] Even more, the Pope sees the response of Jesus to the terrified disciples in the boat during the storm: "Take heart, it is I [I am he]; have no fear" [Mark 6:50] as not simply Jesus saying "Do not worry, fellows, it is only me"; but rather truly a "theophany": "the sort of fear that overwhelms man when he finds himself immediately exposed to the presence of God himself".[49]

NOTES – CHAPTER ONE

1 Ratzinger, J. Pope Benedict XVI, *Jesus of Nazareth: From the Baptism in the Jordan to the Transfiguration*. Transl. Adrian A. Walker. London, Bloomsbury, 2007.

2 "Pope Benedict's book has been released in six different languages and has sold more than 1.5 million copies, according to the Vatican". *The Tablet*, 2 June, 2007.

3 Messori, Vittori, ed. *Crossing the Threshold of Hope, by His Holiness John Paul II*. Transl. McPhee, J. and M. London, Jonathan Cape, 1994.

4 John Paul II, *Memory and Identity; Personal Reflections*. London, Weidenfeld and Nicholson, 2005.

5 Buttiglione, R. *The Thought of the Man who Became Pope John Paul II*. Transl. Paulo Guietti and Francesca Murphy. Eerdmans, Cambridge, 1997.

6 Pope John Paul II: Encyclical Faith and Reason: Of the Supreme Pontiff, To the Bishops of the Catholic Church on the Relationship between Faith and Reason. http://www.catholic-ew.org.uk/resource/fandr01/index.htm

7   http://www.vatican.va/holy_father/benedict_xvi/biography/
    documents/hf_ben-xvi_bio_20050419_short-biography_en.html
8   http://www.ignatiusinsight.com/authors/
    cardinalratzinger.asp#ratzingerbooks
9   COD, 346.
10 VGT, 166.
11 AS, 119.
12 Machen, 1958, 3.
13 I deal with the whole question of the authority of the Church in
    matters of doctrine in my book *What is Catholicism? Hard Questions,
    Straight Answers*. Huntington, Indiana, Our Sunday Visitor Publishing
    Division, 82-135, Chapter 3 entitled *Infallibility, Primacy, and
    Episcopacy.*
14 "It is therefore clear that Virgil wrote and wrote acceptably in praise
    of his patron, the ruler of Rome", i.e. of Emperor Augustus. Virgil,
    The Aeneid, Translated with an Introduction by David West. London,
    Penguin Classics, 1991, ix.
15 *Ibid.,* 10.
16 *Ibid.,* 11.
17 http://www.vatican.va/archive/hist_councils/ii_vatican_council/
    documents/vat-ii_const_19641121_lumen-gentium_en.html
18 Session 4: 18 July 1870, First dogmatic constitution on the Church of
    Christ. http://www.ewtn.com/library/COUNCILS/V1.HTM
19 The interpretation of this text is, of course, disputed. For my own
    explanation of the interpretation, cf. *Op.cit.*, 97-102. For an ecumenical
    discussion on this topic, cf. Brown R.E., *et al,* ed., *Peter in the New
    Testament.* London, Geoffrey Chapman, 1974.
20 Tanner, 863.
21 The debate regarding Conciliarism was particularly acute on the eve
    of the Reformation, J.H. Burns, ed., *Conciliarism and Papalism.
    Cambridge Texts in the History of Political Thought.* University of
    London, January, 1998.
22 *Op. Cit.* 82-135.
23 JN, xxiii-xxiv.
24 In the mediaeval universities, a student would become first a *Magister
    Sacrae Paginae*, a "Master of the Sacred Page", and then after more
    years of teaching a *Magister Sacrae Doctrinae*, a "Master of Sacred
    Doctrine". For a discussion of the nature of *Sacra doctrina.* cf. Thomas
    Aquinas, *Summa Theologica*, Part 1, Question 1. http://www.ccel.org/
    a/aquinas/summa/FP/FP001.html#FPQ1OUTP1
25 Before the eighteenth century, the traditional and most widely
    accepted view was that Matthew's Gospel was first. The great
    similarities of the three "synoptic" Gospels was explained, following
    Augustine, by the theory that Mark copied Matthew, and then Luke
    copied both Mark and Matthew, The chronological sequence was
    therefore Matthew®Mark®Luke. NJBC, **40:5**, 587. Towards the

end of the eighteenth century and the beginning of the nineteenth, Griesbach's hypothesis became popular, which proposed the order Matthew®Luke®Mark. Orchard, Longstaff, ed. 1978, 51. But following the studies of Lachmann, Wilke, Weisse, and above all Heinrich Julius Holtzmann, NTHIP, 146-155, by the middle of the nineteenth century the pendulum was swinging towards Mark®Matthew®Luke, where basically it has stayed ever since, thus becoming the "critical orthodoxy". The acceptance of Marcan priority further necessitates a hypothetical document "Q" (for the German *Quelle*, Source) to explain the existence of the "Double Tradition" of material in Matthew and Luke not already in Mark, for example the Lord's Prayer [Matthew 6:9b-13,// Luke 11:2-4]. NJBC, **40:13**, 590. This theory is sometimes called the "Two Document" hypothesis, those two documents being Mark and Q as the basic source of the other two Synoptic Gospels Matthew and Luke; although this theory also has to provide explanations for the existence of material in Matthew and not in Luke, which has been named the source "M" and of material in Luke and not in Matthew which has been named the source "L"; for example the Infancy Narratives in Matthew 1-2 and Luke 1-2 respectively.

26   Taylor, Mark, 610. I discuss Mark 16:9-20, in the context of the significance of manuscript variations in *Born of a Virgin: Proving the Miracle from the Gospels.* London, St Pauls Publishing, 2007, 50.

27   2:1-11, 3:46-54, 5:1-15, 6:1-15, 6:16-21, 9:1-7, 12:41-44.

28   JN, xi.

29   *Ibid.*

30   For a typical presentation of a reductionist *Life of Jesus*, cf. *Retrospect: A Short Life of Jesus.* A summary of the argumentation of HJCG, 569-572.

31   Cf. MJ3, 3.

32   Casey, 1991.

33   JN, xii.

34   JN, xii.

35   MJ3, 3.

36   JN, xxii.

37   JN, 18.

38   JN, 36

39   JN, 48.

40   JN, 56.

41   JN, 60.

42   JN, 63.

43   JN, 90.

44   JN, 171.

45   JN, 317.

46   JN, 319-355.

47   E.g. Bultmann is certain that "Mark 2.5b-10 has manifestly been

given its place because the Church wanted to trace back to Jesus *its* own right to forgive sins". HST.*15-*16. For him, therefore, the whole of 2:5b-10 is a later insertion by the Tradition. Cf. BMG, 36.

48 JN, 331.
49 JN, 351-2.

CHAPTER TWO

THE POPE AND RUDOLF BULTMANN

- This conviction of the Pope, that the historical Jesus understood himself and declared himself to be God, has been unpopular with New Testament scholars in particular since the massive influence in the twentieth century of Rudolf Bultmann.
- Bultmann sees revelation as not from a supernatural intervention in history, but only from existential experience. Thus for Bultmann, the history of Jesus cannot itself be a manifestation of the Word become flesh.
- The origin of Bultmann's view of revelation is to be found in the philosophy of Immanuel Kant who denied that the human mind could obtain objective knowledge about God. Pope Benedict insists upon this capability in particular as expressed in the encyclical *Fides et Ratio* issued by his predecessor Pope John Paul II, in which the present Pope co-operated as Prefect for the Congregation of the Doctrine of the Faith.
- On the contrary, the Pope affirms, the Christian revelation is historical in its essence.

St John's Gospel in *Jesus Of Nazareth*

In *Jesus of Nazareth* the Pope has presented the life of Jesus from his baptism through to his transfiguration as a series of events which manifest Jesus as truly the Word become flesh. Jesus, precisely as an historical figure, is truly the revelation of God.

But when the Pope turns to the Fourth Gospel in *Chapter 8: the Principal Images of John's Gospel,* he interrupts this sequence of Jesus' adult life:

1. Baptism
2. The Temptations of Jesus
3. The Gospel of the Kingdom of God
4. The Sermon on the Mount

Nine of the ten chapters present some kind of historical sequence, which the Pope interprets as the progressive revelation by the historical Jesus of who he is, what he teaches, and what he has come to do. Chapter 8 interrupts this sequence, because the Fourth Gospel neither structures its narratives as do the three Synoptic Gospels, nor does it contain the teaching of Jesus and the Kingdom, the Temptations, the Our Father, or the Parables.

The Pope treats Chapter 8 as a kind of Johannine Interlude, but not without purpose. As we shall see, he wishes first to insist that the Fourth Gospel was based upon eye witness testimony, that it intends to present the historical Jesus, and is not just a "Jesus poem" as claimed Martin Hengel.[1] The Pope then proceeds to outline the *Principal Johannine Images,* i.e. Water, Vine and Wine, Bread, and The Shepherd.[2] These key themes in John, to be found in the long discourses and dialogues, the Pope admits, while they "do not simply transmit a stenographic transcript of Jesus' words and ways", "yet" the Gospel "remains faithful to what really happened and is not a 'Jesus poem', not a violation of the historical events".[3] For the Pope these Johannine discourses go to the heart of what the historical Jesus claimed to be, to teach, and to do.

But, before we go on to discuss more in detail the Pope's particular interest in the Fourth Gospel it is worth while pausing to consider his very particular way of describing the life of Jesus, using material mainly from the Synoptic Gospels. As we shall now see, his way is entirely the opposite from the way in which Gospel studies have been conducted during the past two hundred years and more.

The Hermeneutic of suspicion

A traveller in Ireland had lost his way. Walking through a village, he met one of the inhabitants, and asked him "Could you tell me the way to Dublin?" to which the local replied, "If I was going to Dublin, I wouldn't start from here."

In my book *Bad, Mad or God?*, I trace briefly the history of the so-called *Quest of the Historical Jesus* from its beginnings in Hamburg, 1778, with the publication of Herbert Samuel Reimarus' *The Aims of Jesus and His Disciples*, right through to the beginning of this new millennium.[4]

I argue that, from the beginning, it was *A Blinkered Quest*, because it began from the wrong starting point. Those who began the Quest were closed to the possibility that Jesus might have been truly the Word become flesh, God become Man. They were deists, like Reimarus, and Lessing who publicised Reimarus' work, or pantheists, like David Friedrich Strauss, who shattered German Lutheranism by his *Life of Jesus Critically Examined*, not believing that miracles or the incarnation were possible, because their God could not work beyond secondary causes.

Albert Schweitzer, who wrote the classical account of the history of the Quest at the beginning of the twentieth century, freely admits that what motivated Reimarus, Strauss and the early Questers was nothing less than hatred of the Christian dogma that Jesus was God become Man.[5]

I argue that this bias has never left historical Jesus scholarship, in fact right up to the very present. The "Critical Minimum",[6] the set of facts described below which in general scholars now agree about the historical Jesus, present a de-supernaturalised picture of him. A prophet who was reputed as a miracle worker, who preached the coming kingdom of God, who taught in parables, who was unpopular with the religious establishment of his day, who was put to death by a nervous Roman governor Pontius Pilate because he feared insurrection, is an account of a person strictly within the parameters of a non-miraculous history. But, as I submitted in *Bad, Mad or God?* this anti-supernaturalist bias was never proved, only assumed.

33

The massive figure of Rudolf Bultmann, who bestrides the twentieth century from beginning to end (1884-1976), only reinforced and further developed this scepticism about the Gospels. The Pope acknowledges the decisive importance of Bultmann in shaping the study of St John's Gospel, attributing its view of Jesus not to the historical Jesus himself, but rather to Gnosticism.[7] We must consider this view later.

But Bultmann was equally disastrous in his influence on Synoptic studies. In his *History of the Synoptic Tradition* [8] he reduced the methodology of studying the Gospels of Matthew, Mark and Luke to analysing the individual "pericopes", miracle stories or sayings of Jesus. The miracles of Jesus generally are treated as "legends",[9] and the sayings of Jesus are judged to be inauthentic if they imply that Jesus was a *theos anér,* a "divine man".[10]

This meant that the writing of the Gospel narratives was a matter of putting the pericopes together into a sequence of events by the three evangelists Matthew, Mark and Luke. But this sequence, for Bultmann, was not an *historical* sequence. Rather, it was the result of the creative work of the *redactors,* the Gospel editors, who put the legends together into a continuous story which itself had little or no historical value. For Bultmann, the Gospel writers were not the apostolic individuals so named testifying to events related by eye-witnesses, but imaginative editors who put the miracle stories and so-called sayings of Jesus into a continuous narrative to edify the primitive Christian community. For Bultmann, all three evangelists based their writing of the Gospel on Mark; and Mark put together his Gospel as itself a legend to prove that Jesus was a Greek style divine man:

> It is in Mark that *the Gospel type* is first to be met.[11] In no way is any one of his sources to be called a Gospel. Of course we cannot prove that there was no one alongside him, or before him, whose work could, like his, be termed a Gospel; but it is hardly likely. For neither Matthew nor Luke has used such a work; both take the outline of Mark as basic. At all events the Gospel is the product of the Hellenistic Church. Its origin thus rests on two factors:

(1) On the Hellenistic Church taking over the Palestinian tradition. (2) On new motives in the Hellenistic Church which produced the shaping of the traditional material into a Gospel.[12]

Bultmann held to the view first propounded by Willhelm Bousset (1865-1920)[13] that the primitive Christian community began with a belief that Jesus was just a Rabbi; but under the influence of Greek Gentile converts began more and more to see Jesus as a *Kurios*, a Hellenistic God. Paul's use of *kurios* in Philippians 2:9-10, for Bousset, would be prime evidence of early Hellenistic Christianity's Kurios worship.

On the contrary, I argue with the Cambridge theologian C.F.D. Moule,[14] and with Michael Green,[15] that the early Palestinian Christians did not just see Jesus as a Rabbi but rather as *Mara* [1 Corinthians 16:22], the Aramaic word for Lord, i.e. the divine Lord, God. Thus Mark, in putting together his Gospel, was not superimposing Hellenistic categories on the life of a Jewish religious teacher, but witnessing to the stupendous events in the life of a completely Jewish Messiah who in fact was even more than a Messiah; he was the Son of God. That is Mark's true story, his history.[16]

Mark's Gospel outline

Mark's Gospel has an inner coherence precisely as a narrative, which is in fact matched only by the Fourth Gospel:[17]

- Mark announces "the beginning of the good news about Jesus, Son of God".[18]
- This "supernatural being" is declared to be Son of God by the divine voice at his baptism by John [Mark 1:11].
- He begins by calling disciples and then performing miracles, declaring to the paralytic that his sins are forgiven, the bystanders think he is blaspheming [Mark 2:5].
- The unclean spirits scream out "You are the Son of God" [Mark 3:11].

35

- The disciples are terrified to find out that even the winds and the sea obey Jesus [Mark 4:41].
- Jesus is declared "Son", once again, by the heavenly voice at the transfiguration: "This is my Son the Beloved, listen to him" [Mark 9:7].
- Jesus tells the Parable of the Wicked Tenants, the son being sent by the owner of the vineyard only to be killed by the tenants [Mark 12:1-12].
- Jesus denies that the Messiah is the Son of David, surely implying that he is rather the Son of God [Mark 12:35-37].[19]
- Finally, Jesus proclaims before the Sanhedrin that he is the Son of the living God [Mark 14:61-62] and at his crucifixion, the centurion at the foot of the cross says "Truly that man was God's Son" [Mark 15:39].[20]
- "And the women", having found the tomb of the crucified Jesus empty, "came out and ran away from the tomb because they were frightened out of their wits; and they said nothing to anyone, for they were afraid" [Mark 16:8].

As compared with the Pope's plan of his chapters in *Jesus of Nazareth*, there is the same emphasis in Mark's outline on Jesus as divine Son of God. Furthermore, as with *Jesus of Nazareth*, the whole "story line" builds from the introduction of the narrative of Mark right to its conclusion as the story of the Son of God, by his authority healing and casting out devils, declared as Son of God at his transfiguration, prophesying his death, being put to death for blasphemous claims, and rising from the dead to vindicate his status as Son of God.

In the second half of the nineteenth century, Heinrich Holtzmann (1832-1910) used Mark's Gospel, as the basis of a Liberal Protestant interpretation of Jesus, since that Gospel had no "supernatural" virgin birth or appearance of the risen Jesus to his disciples as in Matthew and Luke. Holtzmann claimed that Jesus wanted to found a kingdom of God in the ideal sense ("to wish to found a theocracy in the midst of the Roman Empire would have been the fantasy of a fanatic").[21]

So Jesus was a good guy who had great ideals of justice, but who was put to death by a narrow minded establishment.

How far Mark's Gospel actually is from this reductionist presentation! The actual story in Mark is of the Son of God defeating the spiritual powers of evil, as testified by God the Father at the baptism, and transfiguration, first by his miracles and then by his death and resurrection. It is a saving history.

The Pope therefore, in Jesus of Nazareth, is giving us similarly to Mark a sequential history of the adult life of Jesus up to the transfiguration, in order to show that he acts as God the Son bringing about salvation in history. And the historicity of the story of Jesus so told is essential to its meaning, and above all to its power to inspire persons to faith, hope, and love.

The Pope states "Today it is fashionable to regard Jesus as one of the great religious founders who were granted a profound experience of God".[22] On the contrary, the Pope says:

> Standing in marked contrast to the opinion of the people is the "recognition" of the disciples, which expresses itself in acknowledgement, in confession.[23]

For the Pope, this confession reaches a dramatic climax when Jesus walks on the water:

> The disciples in the boat fall down before Jesus, in an expression at once of terror and adoration, and they confess: "Truly you are the Son of God" [Matthew 14:22-33]. These and other experiences, found throughout the Gospels, lay a clear foundation for Peter's confession as reported in Matthew 16:16. In various ways, the disciples were repeatedly able to sense in Jesus the presence of the living God himself.[24]

For the Pope, this appearance of Jesus walking on the water is a theophany, manifesting himself as God Incarnate. For the Pope, that revelation of God, Jesus himself, is the meaning of the life of the historical Jesus.

Bultmann's flight from history and from revelation

In taking this stance, of seeing the life of the historical Jesus as the life of God Incarnate calling for a faith response, the Pope is contradicting two hundred years of Gospel scholarship, particularly as expressed in its most developed form in the hermeneutics of Rudolf Bultmann.

Bultmann began his prestigious career at the beginning of the twentieth century. He was looking back on a century where German criticism of the Gospels had thrown Christian faith entirely into question. Historical Jesus scholarship had now reached the point with William Wrede (1859-1906)[25] of even doubting whether Jesus believed himself to be the Messiah at all. Since, for Bultmann, we did not know any more whether Jesus considered himself to be the Messiah, then we cannot know his personality at all. However, for Bultmann, that did not matter too much, since, he argued:

> However good the reasons for being interested in the personalities of significant historical figures, Plato or Jesus, Dante or Luther, Napoleon or Goethe, it still remains true that this interest does not touch that which such men had at heart; for *their* interest was not in their personality but in their *work*.[26]

Now for the Pope and for those of us who likewise believe that the life of Jesus was nothing other than the manifestation of God Incarnate, to be interested in Jesus' *work* would not be necessarily a reductionist position. If we believed, with the writer of the Fourth Gospel, that Jesus miracles were the work, manifesting that he was, like his Father, creating healing by divine power. After healing the sick man at the Pool of Bethesda, Jesus is reprimanded by his adversaries for healing on the Sabbath.

> John 5:17 His answer to them was, 'My Father still goes on working, and I am at work, too.' John 5:18 But that only made the Jews even more intent on killing him, because not only was he breaking the Sabbath, but he spoke of God as his own Father and so made himself God's equal.

But Bultmann does not mean by "work", the creative divine work of Jesus demonstrating by his miracles that he was truly the revelation of the Father. He means rather, "In the case of those who like Jesus have worked through the medium of *word*, what they purposed can be reproduced only as a group of sayings, of ideas-as *teachings*."[27]

Having dismissed the miracles as legend, having dismissed the high Christology of the Gospels as Hellenistic speculation, for Bultmann, we are reduced just to knowing what Jesus taught as a religious leader of the first century AD. And that, as Bultmann goes on to say, is itself not an easy task, since we have to get behind the tradition to the real historical teaching, and to its situation in time which addresses us.[28]

At this point, we are introduced in one of Bultmann's early works, *Jesus and the Word*, to a foretaste of his existentialism. For Bultmann, the teaching of Jesus is not seen by him as the sayings of a wise man to be prudently followed, but as a summons to be answered:

> Therefore, when I speak of the teaching or thought of Jesus, I base the discussion on no underlying conception of a universally valid system of thought which through this study can be made enlightening to all. Rather the ideas are understood in the light of the concrete situation of a man living in time; as his interpretation of his own existence in the midst of change, uncertainty, decision; as the expression of a possibility of comprehending this life; as the effort to gain clear insight into the contingencies and necessities of his own existence.[29]

No one would disagree that the teaching of Jesus is a radical challenge to us as human beings in our situation of change. But what does the teaching of Jesus bring to us from God as a direction finder towards the right kind of change? It is here that Bultmann presents us with a view of revelation which is difficult to comprehend completely, but which certainly is not compatible with traditional Christian faith:

> Thus what the New Testament understands by revelation can only become clear when these two series of statements are both maintained and related to each other: (1) life is

revealed, Christ is revealed; (2) the word of proclamation and faith are revealed. The first series makes clear that revelation is not illumination or the communication of knowledge, but rather an occurrence, while the second series makes just as clear that this revelation-occurrence cannot be a cosmic process which takes place outside of us and of which the word would merely bring a report (so that it would be nothing other than a myth). Thus revelation must be an occurrence that directly concerns *us,* that takes place in us ourselves; and the word, the fact of its being proclaimed must itself belong to the occurrence.[30]

Thus for Bultmann, Christian faith does not consist of doctrines or moral precepts. In his radical form of Lutheranism, faith seems to have as its object simply faith. If Christian faith confessed with Paul, Jesus as *Kurios,* Lord [Philippians 2:11], then this must be myth. If commandments are presented which must be obeyed [1 Timothy 1:8-11], then these cannot be universally valid systems of thought, but only occurrences in our situation of change. Most of all for our purpose, objective historical events such as the miracles, the life and teaching, the death and resurrection of Jesus, cannot be a valid revelation because this for Bultmann is part of "a cosmic process which takes place outside of us and of which the word would merely bring a report (so that it would be nothing other than a myth)". For Bultmann, therefore, *there can be no revelation in history, but only in our subjective experience.*

History and experience

It is in this view of revelation that we discover the most profound difference between Bultmann's theology and that of the Pope's. In *Truth and Tolerance; Christian Belief and World Religions,* (German edition 2003), Joseph Cardinal Ratzinger stated regarding revelation:

Certainly, what touches us there effects an experience in us, but experience as the result of an event, not of reaching deeper into ourselves. This is exactly what is meant by the concept of revelation: something not ours, not to be found in what we have, comes to me and takes me out of myself, above myself, creates something new. That also determines the historical nature of Christianity, which is based on events and not on becoming aware of the depths of one's own inner self, what is called "illumination".[31]

No one can seriously doubt that this consciousness of a saving event, the event of Christ, is the whole tenor not only of the Gospels but of the rest of the New Testament. What is surprising is that Bultmann seems to be able to hold an opinion, as a distinguished exegete, which is at first sight at least contrary to all that the New Testament teaches. The Acts, indeed all the New Testament literature, knows from the beginning that Jesus, who was crucified by wicked men, has risen from the dead and is now seated at the right hand of God. The sources of Christian faith know of no other Christian beginning. Jesus Christ was not first and foremost a teacher, as Liberal Christianity wants him to be, but rather the risen and exalted Son of God who summons Israel near and far to repentance, baptism, and a new life of Christian communion (cf. Acts 2:36, 3:11-16, 4:26-31). The teaching of Christ became more and more important because of whom the early Christians considered him to be, namely, the exalted Son of God; rather than the other way round, that because the early Christians revered the teaching of Jesus, more and more Hellenistic categories came to be applied to him. Bultmann has to deconstruct the whole of the New Testament evidence in order to attempt to sustain his claim that the early church's interest was not in the personality of Jesus but in his work.

How then can Gospel scholarship still continue with such an opinion? It is precisely because, as we have seen already, historical Jesus scholarship still maintains the *starting point* of the post-Enlightenment position that the incarnation and the miraculous life of Jesus were added on to a "natural" Jesus by a credulous early Christian community. The Pope, on the contrary, in *Jesus of Nazareth,* begins from the opposite starting-point: "I believe that this Jesus – the Jesus of the Gospels – is a historically plausible and convincing figure".[32]

41

But can the Pope's starting point be validated from the viewpoint of historical criticism? Certainly, Dominic Crossan would think it could not. "For a believing Christian both the life of the Word of God and the text of the Word of God are alike a graded process of historical reconstruction, be it red, pink, grey, black or A,B,C,D. If you cannot believe in something produced by reconstruction, you may have nothing left to believe in."[33]

But reconstruction, in Crossan's terms involving prior deconstruction, consists of rejecting some evidence in favour of other evidence in the Gospels. Crossan rejects all evidence which is contrary to his thesis, that Jesus was a Mediterranean peasant leading an unsuccessful peasants' revolt. The Pope's methodology is on the other hand to reject none of the Gospel evidence *a priori*. He treats the Gospels as substantially historical, believing that such a starting point will be verified by his being able to present a coherent and credible life of Jesus from such a positive beginning. Again, can such a position be justified?

The "historical-critical method"

We live in a world where the scientific method has had enormous success. It is based upon empirical observation, leading to the formulation of physical laws which are then verified in constant practice. From time to time, science itself challenges its own most fundamental presuppositions, as with the New Physics and Einstein's Theory of Relativity. But in general, modern scientific history tells us that such challenges result eventually in accepted new formulas which then become fruitful in practical effect, such as the destructive or creative use of nuclear energy.

Since the eighteenth century, Christian biblical scholarship has attempted to find a method of studying the scriptures in such a "scientific" way. But it has never found universally agreed methods, particularly regarding the study of the four Gospels, in order to discover the "historical Jesus".

Albert Schweitzer, with his comprehensive and masterly

grasp of nineteenth century German critical scholarship, saw the problem right at the beginning of the twentieth century:

> From these materials (i.e. from the four Gospels) we can only get a Life of Jesus with yawning gaps. How are these gaps to be filled? At the worst with phrases, at the best with historical imagination. There is really no other means of arriving at the order and inner connexion of the facts of the life of Jesus than the making and testing of hypotheses.[34]

The Fourth evangelist himself, as we have seen, would have had no problem with admitting that his *Life of Jesus*, the Gospel of John, had such "yawning gaps" [John 21:25]. The question rather is what selection of supposed facts derived from the four Gospels we propose as our hypothesis in order to construct (or, if we choose with Crossan *et al* to deconstruct) our understanding of the meaning and significance of the life of Jesus of Nazareth.

We have already seen Mark presenting us with his selection. Written in 64 AD or even earlier, only one generation after the death and resurrection of Jesus himself, no one can deny that Mark *could* have been sourced by eyewitnesses of the actual life of Jesus. His interpretation of the data which he had to hand was that Jesus was recognised by the demons he threw out of people's souls as Son of God, made what were seen as blasphemous claims by his contemporaries, was condemned to death, and his tomb found empty by astonished women. Mark clearly believed that this Son of God had risen from the dead [Mark 16:1-8].[35] Mark proposes to us the hypothesis which he claims to have verified by historical fact; that this Jesus of Nazareth was none other than God become man for our salvation.

This interpretation was closed in advance to Rudolf Bultmann and the German critical school. That school was heavily influenced by the philosophy of Emmanuel Kant.[36] In Kant's philosophy, all scientific knowledge proceeds from a synthesis made by the mind without proven reference to the world. Therefore, all apparent knowledge of God can be only "the recognition of all our duties as divine commands".[37]

This philosophy, rejecting both the spiritual value of miracle and objective knowledge about God, was a decisive principle of twentieth century critical exegesis, only finding its synthesis in the theology of Rudolf Bultmann.

David Friedrich Strauss, in his penetrating analysis of the Christology of post-Reformation Europe, demonstrates to us how for Kant, the incarnation must in consequence itself be reinterpreted in such a subjectivist way:

> According to Kant also, it ought not to be a condition of salvation to believe that there was once a man who by his holiness and merit gave satisfaction for himself and for all others; for of this the reason tells us nothing; but it is the duty of men universally to elevate themselves to the ideal of moral perfection deposited in the reason, and to obtain moral strength by the contemplation of this ideal. Such moral faith alone man is bound to exercise, *and not historical faith*. (Italics mine).[38]

The Pope would have seen such a philosophy as totally incompatible with Catholic theology. It is said that, as Prefect for the Congregation for the Doctrine of the Faith, he had weekly personal meetings with his predecessor Pope John Paul II. He co-operated closely with the Pope on the writing of key documents. One such document, which has the clear stamp of Ratzinger's mind as well as that of John Paul II, was the encyclical *Fides et Ratio* ("Faith and Reason"), widely acclaimed, even by those who rejected its philosophy, as a major philosophical work of the twentieth century. The following paragraph radically counters the philosophy of Kant and his many followers, clearly asserting the ability of the human mind to obtain objective truth about itself and about its Creator:

> The second aspect of Christian philosophy is objective, in the sense that it concerns content. Revelation clearly proposes certain truths which might never have been discovered by reason unaided, although they are not of themselves inaccessible to reason. Among these truths is the notion of a free and personal God who is the Creator of the world, a truth which has been so crucial for the

development of philosophical thinking, especially the philosophy of being.[39]

Fides et Ratio here only develops a theme already taken up in the Second Vatican Council's document *Gaudium et Spes* ("Joy and Hope"), at which Ecumenical Council, we have already seen,[40] Ratzinger was already present as a *peritus*:

> 15. Man judges rightly that by his intellect he surpasses the material universe, for he shares in the light of the divine mind. By relentlessly employing his talents through the ages he has indeed made progress in the practical sciences and in technology and the liberal arts. In our times he has won superlative victories, especially in his probing of the material world and in subjecting it to himself. Still he has always searched for more penetrating truths, and finds them. For his intelligence is not confined to observable data alone, but can with genuine certitude attain to reality itself as knowable, though in consequence of sin that certitude is partly obscured and weakened.[41]

Being capable of knowing objective reality, and the existence of God by reason, as defined by the First Vatican Council,[42] the human being is able to recognise the truth of divine revelation, especially by miracles and signs which are intelligible to everyone, reason in this case working with faith.[43]

But is the presence of faith legitimate in a "scientific" investigation? This remains an unanswered question in modern Gospel scholarship. The Pope proceeds to answer that question affirmatively.

NOTES – CHAPTER TWO

1 JN, 228.
2 JN, 238-286.
3 JN, 235.
4 BMG, Chapter 3, 39-61.
5 QHJ, 2.
6 Cf. BMG, Chapter 6, 113-133.
7 JN, 219.

8 Second German Edition 1931, HST. For my critique of Bultmann's form-critical methodology, cf. BMG,53-58, which is itself based upon Benoit's devastating analysis in his article *Réflexions sur La Formgeschichtliche Methode,* in ET 25-61.

9 E.g. regarding the baptism of Jesus, Bultmann says, "Without disputing the historicity of Jesus' baptism by John, the story as we have it must be classified as legend. The miraculous moment is essential to it and its edifying purpose is clear." HST, *247. For a discussion of this text and Bultmann's interpretation of it, cf. BMG, 56.

10 E.g. Bultmann dismisses Peter's Confession in Mark 8:27-30 saying that the passage is to be "characterized as legend" where Peter says to Jesus in response to a question as to who Jesus is, [Mark 8:29] "You are the Messiah." HST, 257*-8*. For a discussion of this text and Bultmann's interpretation of it, cf. BMG, 56.

11 "And so there is no document extant that can be said to be the source of Mark", Trocme, Mark, 11.

12 HST, *369.

13 NTHIP, 270.

14 Moule, 1977, 37.

15 Green, Ed., 1977. BMG, 39.27, 29-30.

16 It is my opinion that, whatever solution one arrives at to resolve "The Synoptic Problem", it is most reasonable to agree with Bultmann at least to this extent, that Mark was the first of the three Gospel writers to put the sayings and deeds of Jesus into the narrative framework we call a "Gospel", at about 64 AD, or perhaps earlier. Even if we hold with the early tradition that Matthew was first, Matthew's Gospel could have existed originally as a collection of Jesus' teachings which Matthew used in a later edition to fit into the framework provided by Mark. "The apostle Matthew may, however, have been at the start of the gospel tradition if he gathered the sayings of Jesus together in a collection like Q". NJBC, 42:2, 630. For a discussion of the Synoptic Problem, cf. NJBC, 40, 587-595.

17 BMG, 140.

18 "Son of God", *huiou theou,* is absent from some MSS, but inferior to those which include it, e.g. B,D, L,W. Cf. Taylor, Mark, 152.

19 Vincent Taylor, Mark, 493, argues convincingly that the historical Jesus understood the Messiah as more than the Son of David. "The point therefore to be considered is whether the claim that Jesus is more than the Son of David must necessarily be assigned to the community, and not to Jesus himself. The allusive character of the saying favours the view that it is an original utterance; it half conceals and half reveals the 'Messianic Secret'. It suggests, but does not state the claim, that Jesus is supernatural in dignity and origin and that His Sonship is no mere matter of human descent. It is difficult to think that the doctrinal beliefs of a community could be expressed in this allusive manner. The intention in a doctrinal statement is that it

should be understood, whereas the purpose of the saying is to challenge thought and decision. This is the very idiom of Jesus Himself, as His message to the Baptist shows (Luke 7:22f.) But, demonstrably, it is not the tone or the method of primitive Christianity. In the earliest preaching and teaching there is nothing tentative, tantalizing, or allusive. The conviction that Jesus is the Son of God exalted in His right hand rings out as with the tones of a bell in such passages as Acts 2:34-6, 5:31, 10:42f., Romans 1:3ff, etc. The one speaker to whom Mark 12:35-37 can be credibly assigned is Jesus himself".

20 NJB, Mark, 15g, 1685: "For the Roman officer, this admission would not have its Christian content, but Mark clearly sees in it an acknow-ledgement that Jesus was more than a man."

21 NTHIP, 151-2. So also Dungan, 1999, 327: "Holtzmann's book (*Die Synoptischen Evangelien: Ihr Ursprung und geshichlichen Character*, 1863), with a few exceptions, was greeted as a masterpiece, not only because it seemed to proceed with such caution and deft mastery of the best of modernist Protestant Gospel scholarship, but also because it appeared to give a solid answer to the doubts raised by Strauss about the historical Jesus."

22 JN, 293.

23 *Ibid.*

24 JN, 301-2. Cf. My own treatment of the miracle of the Walking on the Water, defending its historical authenticity, in BMG, Chapter 12, *Jesus Walked on the Water,* 211-232.

25 BMG, 49-50, QHJ, 332, For Trocme's critique of Wrede, cf. TROC, 123-4.

26 Bultmann, 1934, 15.

27 *Ibid.*

28 Bultmann, 1934, 16-17.

29 Bultmann, 1934, 16.

30 EF, 91-2.

31 Ratzinger, 2004, 88-9.

32 JN, xxii.

33 Crossan, 1991, 426.

34 QHJ, 7.

35 Even if we discount, with the majority of scholars, Mark 16:9-20 as a later addition to the Gospel, cf. Above, 21, n. 26, the undoubted text of the Gospel proposes such faith in the resurrection, Mark 16:[5] "On entering the tomb they saw a young man in a white robe seated on the right-hand side, and they were struck with amazement. [6]But he said to them, 'There is no need to be so amazed. You are looking for Jesus of Nazareth, who was crucified: he has risen, he is not here. See, here is the place where they laid him'."

36 "M. Waldstein has shown, by a careful analysis, that Bultmann's theory of epistemology was entirely determined by the neo-Kantian philosophy of Marburg." Ratzinger, 2004, 134.

37 ODCC 773. "The moral law had no purpose beyond itself. There was no place for mystical experience, no need for a personal redeemer and not place (as in traditional Christianity) for the historical as such. Kant once expressed the view that as a man advanced in moral perception he found the practice of prayer increasingly unprofitable. Miracles, if they ever happened, could have no religious significance."

38 LJCE, 773-4.

39 Encyclical Letter *Fides et Ratio,* Pope John Paul II, to the Bishops of the Catholic Church on the Relationship between Faith and Reason. 15 September 1988, para.76. http://www.vatican.va/holy_father/john_paul_ii/encyclicals/documents/hf_jp-ii_enc_15101998_fides-et-ratio_en.html

40 Cf. Above, 14.

41 *Gaudium et Spes,* Pastoral Constitution on the Church in the Modern World, December 7th, 1965, para.15 http://www.vatican.va/archive/hist_councils/ii_vatican_council/documents/vat-ii_cons_19651207_gaudium-et-spes_en.html

42 Tanner, II, 810*, *On Revelation,* 2.1. http://www.piar.hu/councils/ecum20.htm#Chapter%201%20On%20God%20the%20creator%20of%20all%20things

43 *Ibid.,* Chapter 3 On Faith, No. 4.

CHAPTER THREE

BUILDING NEW FOUNDATIONS

- The Pope asserts his presupposition: "I believe that this Jesus – the Jesus of the Gospels – is a historically plausible and convincing figure".[1]
- We suggest that Newman's concept of "antecedent probability" would justify such a presupposition, with "conditional faith", rather than the scepticism which leads unnecessarily to deconstruction. Newman would argue that if God were to come to earth to save us, one might legitimately expect him to assume a human nature.
- In verifying this presupposition, the Pope fully acknowledges the limitations of historical criticism. But the Pope contends that, with such a prior act of faith, the unity of God's plan of salvation is perceived, and he maintains that this faith is based upon reason.
- We would go even further and suggest that the Pope in using this method is not even going beyond the bounds of legitimate historical Jesus research, provided that we abandon the anti-incarnational and anti-miraculous presuppositions of so much historical Jesus research. After all we argue, the verification of any historical event as fact is no more than an act of faith in the veracity of the human witnesses of that event.

Who has to prove what?

In *Jesus of Nazareth,* as we have seen, the Pope begins with the presupposition "that this Jesus – the Jesus of the Gospels – is a historically plausible and convincing figure".[2] But is such a presupposition valid? Has the Pope to be proved wrong in his starting point, or does he have to prove that the Jesus of the Gospels is a plausible and convincing figure before he can begin the investigation to write his *Life of Jesus.*

In his massive three-volume study, *A Marginal Jew,*[3] John P. Meier clearly sees the importance of this question. "This criterion (that of presumption) brings us squarely into the debate about where the 'burden of proof' lies: on the side of the critic who denies historicity or on the side of the critic who affirms it?"[4] Meier insists on the former. "However, common sense and the rules of logical argument seem to be on the side of critics like Willi Marxsen and Ben Meyer, who state the obvious: the burden of proof is simply on anyone who tries to prove anything."[5]

I have adopted this starting point in my book *Bad, Mad or God?* I have begun by not even presuming that Jesus of Nazareth existed, and attempted to find convincing proof that witnesses external to the Gospels and hostile to Christianity such as Tacitus accepted without question that Jesus existed.

I then worked through the criteria of historicity developed in what is called the New Quest,[6] to confirm the so-called *Critical Minimum* of facts generally accepted by historical scholarship as to what the historical Jesus said and did.[7] I verified those basic facts about Jesus agreed by most historical Jesus scholarship: that Jesus was baptised by John the Baptist, that he was reputed to be a miracle worker, that he became unpopular with the Jewish authorities, that he went up to Jerusalem to celebrate the Passover, and was condemned to death by crucifixion.[8]

At that point, critical scholarship usually comes to a dead stop. Any further conclusions of historical Jesus research are seen as the "Christ of faith" rather than of "the historical Jesus". I then outlined the three questions[9] which still remain after the Critical Minimum has been established:

• **Question One: How did the first Christians come to believe that Jesus was the divine Son of God?** Surely, there must have been something in the life of Jesus which led them to this belief? The resurrection itself would not have been sufficient. As the Pope says himself in *Jesus of Nazareth*, "Unless there had been something extraordinary in what happened, unless the person and the words of Jesus radically surpassed the hopes and expectations of the time, there is no reason to explain why he was crucified or why he made such an impact".[10]

• **Question Two: Why was Jesus put to death?** The Gospels say that it was because Jesus was seen as a blasphemer.[11] But historical Jesus scholarship generally will not accept this motive, because that would imply that the Gospels are correct when they claim that Jesus claimed to be the divine Son of God. Critical scholarship has never found another agreed reason for his crucifixion.

• **Question Three: How did the disciples turn from being frightened men at the death of Jesus to being his fearless apostles?** The Gospels tell us that that is because the women found his tomb empty on that first Easter morning, and that Jesus appeared bodily to his disciples as risen from the dead. But that is yet another "supernatural fact" which modern scholarship cannot accept. It has hardly produced a more convincing solution than that of the man who launched the Quest of the Historical Jesus, Reimarus. He said that the disciples were too comfortable with the clerical life they were leading when Jesus was preaching in Galilee to return to their humble fishing nets; so they invented the story of the resurrection, having stolen the body.[12]

Reimarus was hardly voicing a new theory, that the first Christians had stolen the body of Jesus and invented the story of his resurrection. Eighteen centuries before, the Gospel of Matthew recounts that this was the explanation given by the hostile authorities at the time of the death and burial of Jesus, to explain the disappearance of his body:

> 28:11Now while they [the disciples] were on their way, some of the guards went off into the city to tell the chief priests all that had happened. 12These held a meeting with the elders and, after some discussion, handed a considerable sum of money to the soldiers 13with these instructions, 'This is what you must say, "His disciples came during the night and stole him away while we were asleep." 14And should the governor come to hear of this, we undertake to put things right with him ourselves and to see that you do not get into trouble.' 15So they took the money and carried out their instructions, and to this day that is the story among the Jews.

Now of course, sceptics such as Reimarus would have dismissed the above account as pure early Christian propaganda, without historical basis. But, as I say in *Bad, Mad or God?*, on the other hand "It is certainly credible that this was the story told to counter the Christian account of the Resurrection. The critical view that it was an apologetic fiction is purely gratuitous."[13] A discussion of this story in Matthew only indicates immediately a confrontation between two apparently equally undemonstrated views; that the Gospel story might be faith-wish on the part of the early Christians, or that the body of Jesus really disappeared, because he had risen bodily from the dead. Can we begin to resolve this impasse?

A faith hypothesis?

Albert Schweitzer admits that historical Jesus scholarship from the beginning excluded the possibility that Jesus was truly God become Man, that he performed miracles which proved his divinity, and that Jesus could have appeared bodily to his disciples giving them the final demonstration that he was truly their divine Saviour:

> This dogma had to be shattered before men could once more go out in quest of the historical Jesus, before they could even grasp the thought of his existence. That the historic Jesus is something different from the Jesus Christ of the doctrine of the Two Natures seems to us now self-evident.[14]

But what if we shed this anti-incarnational presupposition to which Schweitzer fully admits as the dominating sentiment of nineteenth-century German criticism, carried over into the twentieth century by Rudolf Bultmann under the guise of existentialism? Schweitzer has already admitted, as we have seen, that there are no totally agreed criteria of historical critical scholarship to solve this question of Jesus. We have already quoted him as stating categorically "There is really no other means of arriving at the order and inner connection of the facts of the life of Jesus than the making and testing of hypotheses."[15]

What, then, if we take the stance opposite to the Historical Jesus Quest, and begin like the Pope with the hypothesis that the Gospels might be substantially reliable, including their "supernatural" dimension? They portray a man who was born of a woman called Mary who had not had intercourse with any man[16] who when he arrived at adulthood claimed to be the divine Son of God, who performed miracles such as raising the dead, who was accused of blasphemy by the religious authorities of his day and put to death as a common criminal for such apparently blasphemous statements; whose tomb was found empty three days after his crucifixion, and who, the Gospels claim, appeared bodily to his disciples promising them the gift of his Spirit until the end of time. What if we accepted conditionally this amazing happening as a starting point of our investigation?

With Roch Kereszty, we might call this an act of "conditional faith". Kereszty commends this concept of the philosopher Paul Ricoeur, and insists that this is necessary for any fruitful historical investigation.[17] Such conditional faith is particularly appropriate since as I have already outlined in my previous book,[18] every judgment as to what actually happened in history is of necessity an act of faith, what we might call an act of *historical faith*. We might put it into a formula:

X tells me that Y really happened. I believe X.

Such an act of historical faith is necessary whether we are verifying the fact of the Battle of Hastings with its thousands of witnesses, or the death of one's grandmother certified by the registry office. There is no acceptance of any event which has not been personally witnessed by ourselves without an act of faith in the witness or witnesses who testify to the facticity of that event. Thus any process of the verification of any historical event must of necessity begin with an hypothesis which is itself an act of either conditional faith or conditional doubt.

With such a starting point, of conditional faith, we could conditionally accept that it is at least possible that an entirely unique individual called Jesus of Nazareth arrived on the historical scene. We might then begin the process of finding out how we might test this hypothesis, attempting to establish historical criteria to possibly verify that this man was the one whom the Gospels claim him to be, the divine Saviour of the human race.

Coherence and antecedent probability

In claiming "that this Jesus – the Jesus of the Gospels – is a historically plausible and convincing figure"[19] the Pope is in fact not commencing with a criterion outside the generally accepted canons of modern historical investigation into the life of Jesus.

The New Quest would accept as a principle of authenticating the sayings of Jesus, *The Criterion of Coherence*. A saying of Jesus in the Gospels is likely to be historically authentic, historical Jesus scholarship allows, if it coheres with other sayings and deeds of Jesus. Meier presumes that this criterion will be used only when other criteria (which we will discuss later) have been established.[20] Edward Schillebeeckx sees, however, a legitimate extension of this criterion in forming "a total and historical picture of Jesus"[21] giving rise to what Schillebeeckx calls "sub-criteria".

I would maintain that at least at first sight it would therefore be quite legitimate for an historical Jesus researcher to begin, as does the Pope in *Jesus of Nazareth*, with the hypothesis "let us assume that the Gospels do present Jesus as an historically plausible and convincing figure". It would be then up to the Pope to verify this hypothesis in presenting that *Life of Jesus* showing that Jesus is in fact an historically plausible and convincing figure.

However, the logician Michael Huemer in his article *Probability and Coherence Justification*[22] cautions us from too easily using the coherence theory without "antecedent probability". In *The Structure of Empirical Knowledge*, Huemer takes Laurence BonJour to task, who had argued that coherence, among a set of empirical beliefs, can provide justification for those beliefs, in the sense of rendering them likely to be true. Huemer argues that coherence cannot provide any justification for our beliefs in the manner BonJour suggests *unless* some form of foundational justification is assumed. For Huemer, the argument that BonJour gives in favour of the thesis that coherence provides a kind of justification succeeds if and only if some beliefs have (at least weak) foundational justification. He uses the probability calculus to show that this central argument for coherentism is mistaken: the agreement of the witnesses' reports raises the probability that they are true only if an individual report has some degree of initial credibility.[23]

This exercise in mathematical logic would seem to justify Meier's caution regarding coherence as a criterion of credibility regarding the validation of sayings and deeds of the historical Jesus. The Pope, in order to justify his statement that the Jesus of the Gospels is "a plausible and convincing figure", would have to provide some antecedent foundational credibility. To put it simply, if three witnesses agree on a certain truth affirmation, that agreement has little value unless it can be initially justified as at least probably true.

Newman's *Grammar*: An historical apologetic

This kind of antecedent probability argument we find in John Henry Newman's *An Essay in Aid of A Grammar of Assent*. Eventually published on 15 March 1870,[24] the *Grammar* was the end of a long process of reflection on Newman's part. The central issue for Newman was the answer to the problem raised by the Enlightenment, perhaps for us expressed most ably by the philosopher-playwright Gotthold Ephraim Lessing (1729-81), who threw out the Enlightenment challenge to Christianity thus: "The Christian traditions must be explained by the inner truth of Christianity, and no written traditions can give it that inner truth, if it does not itself possess it".[25] On the other hand, Lessing had rendered

Christian faith as incapable of defending its inner truth by his holding the position that "the accidental truths of history can never become the proof of necessary truths of reason."[26]

On the one hand, Newman, as a convert to Catholicism of twenty years, was convinced that his newfound communion opened the door for him to certainty regarding the historical fact of revelation. He wrote in a letter, January 1868: "Can a man be as sure to himself of the fact that Christ once was on earth and was God, as that my friend is alive and is a second self to me? Catholics say that a man can; that... he can apprehend the Object of faith, as men in general apprehend objects of sight".[27]

On the other hand, Newman was fully aware of Lessing's objection, that an historical revelation could not be demonstrated adequately by syllogistic logic. That was the accustomed methodology of scholastic theology, most notably exemplified in the Five Ways of Thomas Aquinas demonstrating the existence of God. Such proofs depend upon necessary inference, such as demonstrating God's existence from the fact that everything is moved by something else to a necessary First Unmoved Mover.[28]

Newman realised that such a method of reasoning was inadequate in validating a revelation from God in history, *which always could have been otherwise.* God could have chosen another way of acting than that of sending his only begotten Son to save us. Or, preachers remind us from time to time, God could have decided simply not to forgive us our sins. Historical reasoning, as Newman outlines in the *Grammar*, uses more varied and complex methods than those of syllogistic reasoning:

> It is by the strength, variety, or multiplicity of premises, which are only probable, not by invincible syllogisms, – by objections overcome, by adverse theories neutralised, by difficulties gradually clearing up, by exceptions proving the rule, by unlooked-for correlations found with received truths, by suspense and delay in the process issuing in triumphant reactions – by all these ways, and many others, it is that the practised and experienced mind is able to

make a sure divination that a conclusion is inevitable, of which his lines of reasoning do not actually put him in possession. This is what is meant by a proposition being "as good as proved," a conclusion as undeniable "as if it were proved", and by the reasons for it "amounting to a proof" for a proof is the limit of converging probabilities.[29]

In considering, therefore, the historical evidence for the truth of the Christian faith, in his final chapter of the *Grammar of Assent*, named *Revealed Religion*,[30] Newman argues that it is antecedently probable that, if God were to provide salvation for the whole human race, he would send his Son to become man, to live and to die and to rise again to bring us into communion with himself.

> I think, then, that the circumstances under which a professed revelation comes to us, may be such as to impress both our reason and our imagination with a sense of its truth, even though no appeal be made to strictly miraculous intervention – in saying which I do not mean of course to imply that those circumstances, when traced back to their first origins, are not the outcome of such interventions, but that the miraculous intervention addresses us at this day in the guise of those circumstances; that is, of coincidences, which are indications, to the illative sense of those who believe in a Moral Governor, of His Immediate Presence, especially to those who in addition hold with me the strong antecedent probability that, in His mercy, He will thus supernaturally present Himself to our apprehension.[31]

This reasonable expectation of divine revelation, for Newman, would provide, in Michael Huemer's terms, that "foundational justification", that "initial credibility" which raises the historical picture of Jesus of Nazareth which the Pope insists he finds coherent in the Four Gospels to the level of certainty worthy of what Newman calls "real assent".

Surely, Newman would have agreed with Pope Benedict XVI that historical reasoning has limitations:

> We have to keep in mind the limit of all efforts to know the past: We can never go beyond the domain of hypothesis, because we simply cannot bring the past into the present. To be sure, some hypotheses enjoy a high degree of certainty, but overall we need to remain conscious of the limit of our certainties – indeed, the history of modern exegesis makes this limit perfectly evident.[32]

Modern scholars researching the historical Jesus would most certainly agree. Recently, J.G. Dunn has expressed severe reservations about criteria to which we have already referred, such as the criterion of coherence as a principle of the authentication of sayings of the historical Jesus:

> Few, however, are wholly satisfied with these criteria. If the criterion of dissimilarity is applied consistently, and only that material is added which coheres with the limited findings of the first trawl through the Jesus tradition, then the historical Jesus who emerges is bound to be a strange creature, with anything which links him to the religion of his people or to the teaching of his followers automatically ruled out of court, 'a unique Jesus in a vacuum'.[33]

Dunn's criticisms are similar to those expressed by Timothy Luke Johnson, who calls the criteria "slippery and subjective".[34] How then does the Pope consider that he can go beyond mere hypothesis to the certainty which he expresses in his Foreword to *Jesus of Nazareth*? Admitting all the complexities related to the modern study of the Gospels, the Pope still confidently affirms, "yet I wanted to try to portray the Jesus of the Gospels as the real 'historical Jesus' in the strict sense of the word".[35]

I would suggest that Newman's concept of antecedent probability, as also expressed by the modern mathematical logician Michael Huemer, could illuminate the Pope's methodology in *Jesus of Nazareth*. Newman's "coincidences", as he explains in the *Grammar*, are not sufficient in themselves to generate certainty that this or that is a divine revelation. But, as he further elucidates, taken in conjunction with faith in God not as only a deistic prime mover, but as the active Director of his own world, such coincidences may be elevated to a certain judgement of credibility if they are a fulfilment of the expectation generated by our consciousness of the antecedent probability that God will act to save us, *and that he will consequently give us the means of knowing when such a stupendous event has occurred.*

The Pope's Hermeneutic

If we keep these principles in mind, then it is easy to understand the Pope's starting-point in investigating the life of *Jesus of Nazareth*.

Firstly, the Pope wishes to transcend the bounds of historical criticism by using the principle enunciated in paragraph 12 of Vatican II's Dogmatic Constitution on Divine Revelation *Dei Verbum* ("The Word of God"), of the "unity of scripture", and reinforced by recent American biblical scholarship in developing the concept of "canonical exegesis":

> If you want to understand the Scripture in the spirit in which it is written, you have to attend to the content and to the unity of Scripture as a whole. The Council goes on to stress the need for taking account of the living tradition of the whole Church and of the analogy of faith (the intrinsic correspondences within the faith).[36]

This means for the Pope that we cannot understand the history of Jesus of Nazareth unless we immerse ourselves in the whole process of revelation:

> This process is certainly not linear, and it is often dramatic, but when you watch it unfold in light of Jesus Christ, you can see it moving in a single overall direction; you

can see that the Old and New Testaments belong together. This Christological hermeneutic, which sees Jesus Christ as the key to the whole and learns from him how to understand the Bible as a unity, presupposes a prior act of faith. It cannot be the conclusion of a purely historical method. But this act of faith is based upon reason – historical reason – and so makes it possible to see the internal unity of Scripture. By the same token, it enables us to understand anew the individual elements that have shaped it, without robbing them of their historical originality.[37]

That is why the Pope, after his initial *Foreword* briefly outlining his principles of interpretation,[38] and before he begins his *Life of Jesus of Nazareth* with Jesus' baptism,[39] begins with *Introduction: An Initial Reflection on the Mystery of Jesus.*[40]

These eight pages have a great significance for the Pope's argument. Before introducing the historical adult Jesus himself, the Pope outlines the *Old Testament expectation* of the Messiah to come. He focuses on Moses, who was a very special prophet in the history of salvation prior to the coming of Christ. He quotes Deuteronomy 34:10; "And there has not arisen a prophet since in Israel like Moses", we read, "whom the Lord knew face to face".[41] Moses spoke with the Lord face to face, "as a man speaks to his friend (cf. Exodus 33:11)."[42] This same Moses asked to see the glory of God. God replied saying "You shall see my back; but my face shall not be seen" [Exodus 33:23].[43]

For the Pope, this gives meaning to the promise of Deuteronomy 18:15, to the effect that "The Lord will raise up for you a prophet like me from among you... him you shall heed".[44] This new prophet will not simply see the Lord's back. He will have "a real, immediate vision of the face of God, and thus the ability to speak entirely from seeing, not just from looking at God's back. This naturally entails the further expectation that the new Moses will be the mediator of a greater covenant than the one that Moses was able to bring down from Sinai (cf. Hebrews 9:11-24)."[45]

The Pope continues:

> This is the context in which we need to read the conclusion of the prologue to John's Gospel: "No one has ever seen God; it is the only Son, who is nearest to the Father's heart, who has made him known" (John 1:18). It is in Jesus that the promise of the new prophet is fulfilled. What was true of Moses only in fragmentary form has now been fully realised in the person of Jesus. He lives before the face of God, not just a friend, but as a Son; he lives in the most intimate unity with the Father.[46]

Such a form of introduction to a study of the historical Jesus would be worlds away from what is customary in the past two hundred years of the Quest. But we return to Schweitzer's well formulated principle: "There is really no other means of arriving at the order and inner connection of the facts of the life of Jesus than the making and testing of hypotheses."[47] Why could such an Old Testament expectation not be such an hypothesis, to be tested by examining the actual life of the historical Jesus, as the Pope proceeds to do in *Jesus of Nazareth*?

I would wish to argue that the Pope is in this case not even going outside the limits of legitimate historical research. If the authentication of an historical event, as I have argued in *Bad, Mad or God?*[48] is nothing other than searching for criteria to make credible what has purported to be what actually happened in the past, why could not such criteria include that of a religious expectation fulfilled?

I have used a similar argument in my most recent work *Born of a Virgin: Proving the Miracle from the Gospels*. I have attempted first to argue, using the methods of historical criticism, that the accounts of the annunciation of the virginal conception of Mary to Joseph in Matthew's Gospel [Matthew 1:18-25] and to Mary in Luke's account [Luke 1:26-38] represent the earliest tradition we can trace back to source.[49] I have then argued that Matthew and Luke intended their accounts to be historical, to the extent at least that Mary gave birth to Jesus without intercourse with Joseph or with any male.[50]

I have finally submitted, however, that these accounts are

ultimately credible because they make sense of a much greater miracle than the virgin birth of Jesus, namely the incarnation itself.[51] In Newman's terms, the miracle of the virgin birth of Jesus is validated, having successfully passed the strenuous tests of historical criticism, because it is a fulfilment of the antecedent probability that God would wish to save us by his own Son becoming flesh for our salvation, that God who is not limited in his operations to secondary causes.

In terms of the First Vatican Council, it is part of the verification of divine revelation, a process which includes both faith and reason. Having asserted that we cannot accept God's revelation without the Holy Spirit's gift of faith, the Fathers of the Council go on to say:

> Nevertheless, in order that the submission of our faith should be in accordance with reason, it was God's will that there should be linked to the internal assistance of the Holy Spirit outward indications of his revelation, that is to say divine facts (*facta divina*), and first and foremost miracles and prophecies, which clearly demonstrating as they do the omnipotence and infinite knowledge of God, are the most certain signs of revelation and are suited to the understanding of all.[52]

NOTES – CHAPTER THREE

1 JN, xxii.
2 JN, xxii.
3 MJ1, MJ2, MJ3.
4 MJ1, 183.
5 *Ibid.*
6 BMG, 60. Robinson, J.M. *A New Quest of the Historical Jesus.* London, SCM, 1959.
7 BMG, 114-118.
8 BMG, 118-121.
9 BMG, 121-123.
10 JN, xxii.
11 Cf. BMG, Chapter 8, *You Have Heard the Blasphemy,* 134-150.
12 QHJ, 21. To verify substantially the Gospel accounts of the

resurrection, cf. O'Collins, G. 1973., 1987, Wright, N.T. 2003, BMG, Chapter 16, *The Resurrection: An Historical Event.*, 296-327.

13 BMG, 300.

14 QHJ, 3-4.

15 QHJ, 7.

16 This is the theme of my new book *Born of a Virgin: Proving the Miracle from the Gospels.* London, St. Pauls Publishing, 2007.

17 "If the above observations are valid, then no historian can interpret the available data about Jesus of Nazareth without at least a conditional faith in him, an affinity that enables the historian to appropriate the world of Jesus. Moreover-some background from other sources aside-the only way to the world of Jesus leads through the world of his eyewitnesses and the disciples of the witnesses, embodied in the writings of the New Testament. Thus, one cannot hope to understand "who Jesus was and what he intended" unless one gives conditional credence to the New Testament testimonies and attempts to reach the "real Jesus" through a critical but truly sympathetic examination of these testimonies", Kereszty, *Communio* 598-9.

18 BMG, 83-85.

19 JN, xxii.

20 MJ1, 176. BMG, 116.

21 Schillebeeckx, 96. BMG, 116.

22 From *Southern Journal of Philosophy* 35 (1997): 463-72.

23 "So where did BonJour's reasoning go wrong? After all, isn't it true that the concurrence of the witnesses' testimony constitutes a surprising coincidence, which requires some explanation? Well, surprising it may be, but the problem is just that under the assumption that the witnesses each have zero independent credibility, the hypothesis that the story they give is the truth is *not* an explanation of the coincidence. If there is no antecedent presumption that the witnesses are more likely to report the true value of x than to report any other value, the hypothesis that $x = 2$ is no sort of explanation of the fact of coincidence, since it would not render it any more likely that the witnesses would report that $x = 2$ (i.e., $P(A\&B|X)$ is no greater than $P(A\&B|\neg X)$. You might just as well propose the hypothesis that X is *false* as an explanation of why both witnesses agree that X – for that would make it just as likely that they would both assert X". http://home.sprynet.com/-owl1/bonjour.htm

24 GA, 11.

25 QHJ, 16.

26 ODCC, 817.

27 GA, 10. Nicholas Lash's perceptive Introduction to the *Grammar*, gives the reference in his footnote 45 to the letter as *Letters & Diaries* vol. 24, 12, cf. *Grammar*, pp.62, 95-96.

28 Everything therefore which is moved, must be moved by something else. If therefore that by which it is moved is itself moved, then it

follows that that which acts as the mover is also itself moved by something else; and that again by something else. But here we cannot proceed to infinity; because in this case there would be no first mover, and, in consequence, neither would there be anything else moving, because secondary movements do not move unless moved by a primary mover, just as a stick does not move unless it is moved by a moving hand. Therefore it is necessary to proceed to some Prime Mover, which is itself not moved by anything; and this everyone understands as God. Aquinas, *Summa Theologiae*, I., q.2, a.3.

29 GA, 254.
30 GA, 318-379.
31 GA, 333.
32 JN, xvii.
33 Dunn, 2003, 82. Dunn quotes Schillebeeckx, 1974, 94.
34 Johnson, 1997, 129; "We can observe in Meier's careful consideration of individual sayings, or specific actions, just how slippery and subjective the so-called criteria for historicity really are".
35 JN, xxii.
36 JN, xviii.
37 JN, xix.
38 JN, xi-xxiv.
39 JN, Chapter One, 9-24.
40 JN, 1-8.
41 JN, 3.
42 JN, 4.
43 JN, 5.
44 JN, 3.
45 JN, 5-6.
46 JN, 6.
47 QHJ, 7.
48 This is the theme of the entire chapter 4 of BMG, *Did It Really Happen?*, 83-102.
49 BV, Chapter Four, *Born of a Virgin: The Earliest Tradition.* 55-69
50 BV, Chapter Six, *The Birth Narratives; History, Midrash or Myth?* 93-133.
51 BV, 199.
52 Tanner, II, *807, Vatican I, Dogmatic Constitution on the Catholic Faith, Chapter III, *de Fide.* Cf. BMG, 18.

CHAPTER FOUR

ST JOHN'S GOSPEL: EYE-WITNESS SOURCE?

- In this context, the Pope sees the Gospel of John as crucial, since the whole agenda of the Fourth Gospel from start to finish is to present Jesus as the Word become flesh, to stimulate faith in Jesus as the only begotten Son of God.
- In contrast with much Johannine scholarship, the Pope sees the Fourth Gospel as fundamentally factual, since it is based upon the eye-witness testimony of "the beloved disciple", John the Son of Zebedee.
- In particular, the Pope affirms that Jesus' declaration of himself as identifiable with the JHWH revealed to Moses and the prophets ("Before Abraham was, I am" [John 8:58] is rooted in the historical Jesus' consciousness of his own being and mission. We give grounds for the historical authenticity of the absolute "I am" sayings in John and Jesus' assertion in John 10:32 that he and the Father are one.
- None of this would deny the creativity of the Fourth Evangelist in constructing the speeches and dialogues of Jesus in his own style and language. Nor would we deny that the Fourth Evangelist betrays a limitation in his Life of Jesus in restricting the selection of his material to focus entirely on the question of faith in Jesus' divinity. But John's history is in no way incompatible with that of the Synoptic evangelists, but only makes explicit what is implied in them, namely that Jesus claimed himself to be God during his lifetime on earth.

That you may believe

This is the explicit argument of the entire Fourth Gospel. The writer makes clear his intention at what many exegetes consider to be the original ending of the Gospel of John, with Chapter 21 added subsequently. (We shall be looking fully at this question later in this book.) His purpose is, as he states, at the close of Chapter 20:

> [30]There were many other signs that Jesus worked in the sight of the disciples, but they are not recorded in this book. [31]These are recorded so that you may believe that

Jesus is the Christ, the Son of God, and that believing this you may have life through his name.

This singleness of purpose of the writer of the Fourth Gospel is as evident throughout his Gospel in his selection of events to describe and interpret, as much if not more than we have seen regarding Mark's more punchy account:

- The Prologue, 1:1-18. The evangelist proclaims Jesus as truly the Word become flesh, the revealer ("exegete", 1:18) of the Father.
- John the Baptist declares that he himself is not the Christ. Rather, the one on whom the Spirit descends at his baptism, Jesus, is truly the Chosen One of God [1:34].
- At the first miracle recorded in the Gospel, the turning of water into wine, we are told by the evangelist that Jesus thereby showed his glory, and his disciples believed in him [2:11].
- At the Pool of Bethesda, curing the man paralysed for thirty-eight years, Jesus states, to the scandal of his onlookers, that he works and his Father works on the Sabbath. The Jews (or "Judeans")[1], wish to put him to death because he called God his Father and so made himself God's equal [5:18].
- In Chapter 6, after the miracles of the Multiplication of the Loaves [6:1-15] and of the Walking on the Water [6:16-21], Jesus reveals himself as the Bread of Life, and promises, to the amazement of his hearers, that they must eat his flesh and drink his blood in order to have eternal life [6:53].
- In Chapter 7, Jesus goes up for his third and final visit to Jerusalem. He declares himself to be the Light of the World [8:12], and explicitly claims divinity by saying "Before Abraham was, I Am" [8:58]. His hearers wish to stone him for blasphemy.
- After having been cured by Jesus, the man blind from his birth said, "'Lord, I believe,' and worshipped him" [9:38]. Jesus calls himself the Good Shepherd [10:11], forming his own flock of those like the man born blind who know him and follow him.

- Jesus is challenged by the Jews to say whether he is the Christ, but Jesus responds by saying "the Father and I are one" [10:30], thus provoking his hearers to take up stones to stone him for blasphemy.
- In the last of his seven miracles recorded in John, Jesus summons the dead Lazarus alive from his tomb [11:43], and prophecies his own death [12:23], to reveal the glory of God, which the heavenly voice confirms [John 12:28].
- At his trial, those who accused Jesus gave as their reason for handing him over to Pilate for the death penalty: "We have a Law, and according to the Law he ought to be put to death, because he has claimed to be Son of God" [19:7].
- As we have quoted above, having recounted the appearances of the risen Jesus to his disciples, the evangelist states as the whole purpose of his narrative: "These are recorded so that you may believe that Jesus is the Christ, the Son of God, and that believing this you may have life through his name" [20:31].

This central theme of the Fourth Evangelist, of demonstrating that Jesus is the divine Son of God (not just a human Messiah), is equally evident in his selection of events from the life of Jesus, and his interpretation of those events.

Gone is the strongly ethical message of John the Baptist, so evident in the Synoptic accounts. 'Repent, for the kingdom of Heaven is close at hand' [Matthew 3:2, cf. Luke 3:3]. There is no demand, as in Luke 3:10-14, for mercy towards the poor, those who have two tunics giving one to those who have none, for justice from the tax collectors, for the soldiers not to bully and intimidate. Rather, the entire narrative about John the Baptist is taken up with the question as to who Jesus is.

Similarly, the accounts of the miracles in John emphasise their Christological meaning rather than their healing effects. The healing of the man at the pool of Bethesda is followed by the claim of Jesus to be working on the Sabbath as his Father is working, thus causing his hearers to think that he is blaspheming, since Jesus was making himself equal to God

[5:18]. Likewise, the healing of the man born blind [9:1-7] is followed by a long dialogue between the cured man and the authorities about who the man was who had cured him, culminating in the man's excommunication [9:34], followed again by the man believing in Jesus and worshipping him [9:38].

But the clearest indication of the evangelist's intent is in the fact that the narrative itself appears totally unbalanced in terms of it being a *Life of Jesus*. The Galilean ministry is confined to the first six chapters of the Fourth Gospel, and even there it is punctuated by two visits to Jerusalem in Chapters 2 and 5. Two-thirds of the entire Gospel, Chapters 7-21, takes place in a time scale of scarcely two months, from the final visit of Jesus to Jerusalem for the Feast of Tabernacles [7:2] until his death and resurrection. Here are Schweitzer's "yawning gaps" in the life of Jesus with a vengeance!

John shares with the Synoptics the same amount of narrative content relating the passion and death of Jesus [18-19, cf. Matthew 26-27, Mark 14-15, Luke 22-23], followed by diverse accounts of the resurrection. What is distinctive in the Fourth Gospel is the long core section, Chapters 7-12, culminating in the raising of Lazarus [11:43], which all takes place in Jerusalem during Jesus' final visit. The narrative has no other subject matter than the question as to the identity of Jesus, his claims to divinity [8:58, 10:30] and followed by his inevitable arrest in Chapter 18.

In contrast, Mark has only three chapters [11-13] recounting from the final entry into Jerusalem, until Jesus' Last Supper and Arrest. Matthew has a longer narrative [21-26] expanding Mark and parallel to his version of events, but following a much longer account of the birth and public ministry of Jesus [1-20]. Luke [19:28-21:38] returns to Mark's brevity in his account from the Entry up to the beginning of the Passion Narrative proper [22-23]. But the Synoptics in no way closely parallel John's focus on the last weeks of Jesus' early life, precisely because their intention is not explicitly to narrate the conflict during Jesus' life concerning his divine claims.

John's Gospel: A source for the *Life of Jesus*?

None of this diversity of John from the other three Gospels would necessarily threaten the historicity of the Johannine Gospel. Some trot out the mantra "The Gospels are not biographies of Jesus", without telling us what a biography is. But all biographies must select material, and many leave "yawning gaps" just as Schweitzer finds in the Gospel narratives when judged as material for a Life of Jesus. Such "yawning gaps" appear because the events left out of the biographer's account are not considered by him or her as relevant to the purpose of the narrative.

In *Bad, Mad or God?* I made reference to a book I read on holiday *The Assassination of Marilyn Monroe*.[2] This fascinating account of the mysterious death of the iconic sex symbol of the post-war era contains little about the film star's early life, and indeed little detail about her illustrious career. It focuses on whether her death was suicide, an accident, or even murder by the Kennedy clan.

None of the Four Gospels have a title in the text itself, only added later by church tradition. It would not be totally far-fetched if the title were given to the Fourth Gospel *The Assassination and Rising of the Son of God*, with Chapters 1-6 seen as an introduction, Chapters 7-12 as the inevitable preparation for the unjust death of Jesus in his teaching during the final weeks of his life in Jerusalem, Chapters 17-18 as his arrest and crucifixion, and 20-21 as the account of his victorious resurrection.

In terms of historical biography, that would be a perfectly legitimate agenda. It would completely justify the disproportionate amount of space given in John's account to the final preaching of Jesus in Jerusalem; particularly since Luke 19:47 recognises that "he taught in the Temple every day". And, as we have seen, all three Synoptic Gospels do devote significant space to that final Jerusalem visit. John only expands that content.

This disproportion in the Johannine narrative devoted to the last days of Jesus in the Jerusalem temple environment would be even more authenticated, for the Pope in *Jesus of*

Nazareth, if we accept that Zebedee, the father of the disciple John traditionally identified as the author of the Fourth Gospel, was not just a simple fisherman, but was also a priest. The Pope quotes the speculative but to him credible view of Henri Cazelles:

> It is thus quite possible that Zebedee is a priest, but that at the same time he has his property in Galilee, while the fishing business on the lake helps him make ends meet. He probably has a kind of pied-à-terre in or near the Jerusalem neighbourhood where the Essenes lived.[3]

This makes full sense of the assertion in the text of John's Gospel that the "other disciple", again traditionally identified as the author of the Gospel, was as the son of a priest "known to the high priest" [18:16] and so would have naturally concentrated on those events situated in the Jerusalem temple.

Thus in *Jesus of Nazareth*, the Pope concludes his resolution of *The Johannine Question* with the assertion that the Fourth Gospel is an authentic source for the life of Jesus:

> With these observations, we have already taken a decisive step toward answering the question of the historical credibility of the Fourth Gospel. This Gospel ultimately goes back to an eyewitness, and even the actual redaction of the text was substantially the work of one of his closest followers within the living circle of his disciples.[4]

But those researching into the historical Jesus almost unanimously do not accept the Fourth Gospel as a significant source for the life of Jesus. We must now attempt to discover why.

Dunn's critique

We may take as typical of the view of perhaps a large proportion of Johannine scholars that of J.G. Dunn, a distinguished New Testament scholar, with more recently a massive first volume on the Historical Jesus, *Jesus Remembered.*[5]

Dunn expresses his judgement on the historicity of the

70

Fourth Gospel in four closely argued pages in *Christology in the Making – An Inquiry into the Origins of the Doctrine of the Incarnation.*[6] In this book, Dunn wishes to demonstrate how the Christian doctrine of the Incarnation that Jesus was truly God became Man, originated in the earliest years of the Christian faith, as evidenced in the four canonical Gospels and in the rest of the New Testament.

Dunn's conclusion of his careful examination of the evidence is that *"We cannot claim that Jesus believed himself to be the incarnate Son of God; but we can claim that the teaching to that effect as it came to expression in the later first-century Christian thought was, in the light of the whole Christ-event, an appropriate reflection on and elaboration of Jesus' own sense of sonship and eschatological mission."*[7]

In order to come to this negative conclusion, Dunn has to reject the evidence of the Fourth Gospel, which for him is, at least at first sight, plain that Jesus did have consciousness of himself as the pre-existent Son of God:

> Certainly John's answer seems clear enough. A regular feature of Jesus' discourses in the Fourth Gospel is precisely his talk of God as his Father and of himself as God's Son – he calls God 'Father', more than 100 times and himself 'Son' 22 or 23 times. For the first time we find one of the key words of the later creeds used of Jesus – (only-begotten) – not only in the prologue but in one of Jesus' discourses [John 1:14,18, 3:16,18]. Linked with the Father-Son theme is the regularly-expressed conviction of his own *pre-existence* – of a prior existence in heaven with the Father [6:62, 8:38, 10:36, 17:5], of his descent from heaven [3:13, 6:33, 38, 41ff, 50f, 58], of his coming from God [3:31, 8:42, (13:3), 16:27f, 17:8] into the world [3:19, 9:39, 10:36, 12:46, 16:28, 18:37]. The climax is probably reached in the most powerful of the 'I am' sayings, where Jesus' claim to pre-existence achieves its most absolute expression – 'Before Abraham was, I am' [8:58].[8]

Dunn then goes on to give three main reasons why he concludes that this emphasis in John upon Jesus as fully conscious of his own divinity is "presenting us with developed rather than original tradition".[9]

1. John's style, of long discourses and dialogues which are so different from the Synoptic style of collections of short pericopes. "The best explanation still remains that the Johannine discourses are meditations or sermons on individual sayings or episodes from Jesus' life, but elaborated in the language and theology of subsequent Christian reflection".[10]

2. John has Jesus expressing his relationship with God the Father, as his Son, much more frequently: "Mark 3, Q 4, special Luke 4, special Matthew 31, and John 100 times"[11]. The only clear parallel with the Synoptics is the one statement of Jesus that many call the "stray Johannine logion", "Everything has been entrusted to me by my Father; and no one knows the Father except the Son and those to whom the Son chooses to reveal him." [Matthew 11:27, Luke 10:22]. "On this evidence", claims Dunn, "it is scarcely possible to dispute that here we have straightforward evidence of a burgeoning tradition, of a manner of speaking about Jesus and his relation with God which became very popular in the last decades of the first century".[12]

3. This applies for Dunn especially to affirmations in John regarding Jesus' pre-existence. "It is scarcely credible that a saying like John 8:58, or the other 'I am' sayings ('the bread of life', 'the light of the world', etc.) were part of the original Jesus-tradition... The most obvious explanation once again is that in a relatively insignificant element of the earlier tradition John has found the inspiration to fashion an invaluable formula for expressing Christianity's claims about Christ."[13]

Response to Dunn

There can be no question here that Dunn is expressing what has become a commonplace opinion among biblical scholars.

The Pope acknowledges this fact, with regret, quoting with disapproval the exegete Ingo Broer:

> The Gospel of John thus stands before us as a *literary* work that bears witness to faith and is intended to strengthen faith, and not as a historical account.[14]

The Pope comments:

> What faith does it "testify" to if it has left history behind? How does it strengthen faith if it presents itself as an historical testimony – and does so quite emphatically – but then does not report history? I think that we are dealing here with a false concept of the historical, as well as with a false concept of faith and of the Paraclete. A faith that discards history in this manner really turns into "Gnosticism". It leaves flesh, incarnation – just what true history is – behind.[15]

On the contrary, the Pope affirms:

> What the Gospel is really claiming is that it has correctly rendered the substance of the discourses, of Jesus' self attestation in the great Jerusalem disputes, so that the readers really do encounter the decisive content of this message and therein, the authentic figure of Jesus.[16]

The above issues will be an important part of our investigation subsequent to this introduction. But even at this point, we can point to a *non sequitur*. Johannine scholarship in fact is plagued by *non sequiturs*. It simply does not follow that, because the Gospel of John is written in the style of the evangelist that it must be a later fictional development of the Synoptic tradition.

The Pope's view is echoed in Schnackenburg's three-volume commentary on John. Schackenburg freely admits that the long discourses of Jesus in John are not usually the *ipsissima verba* (the "actual words") of the historical Jesus, although they may well contain such actual sayings memorised by the evangelist.[17] But in general, Schnackenburg freely admits that the discourses of Jesus in John are what we would call reported speech rather than quotations. Yet, Schackenburg insists: "The deep faith of the writer moved him to clothe the thoughts and words of Jesus in their present dress, but his intention was to let the earthly Jesus speak and express his own thoughts".[18]

In this connection, the *Instruction of the Pontifical Biblical Commission Concerning the Historical Truth of the Gospels*, 21 April 1964, makes a commonsense statement about the non-necessity of having the *ipsissima verba* of Jesus in order for their correspondence with facticity to be verified:

> For the truth of the story is not at all affected by the fact that the Evangelists relate the words and deeds of the Lord in a different order, and express His sayings not literally but differently, while preserving (their) sense. For, as St Augustine says, 'It is quite probable that each Evangelist in narrating a saying believed it to have been his duty to recount what he had to in that order in which it pleased God to suggest it to his memory – in those things at least in which the order, whether it be this or that, detracts in nothing from the truth and authority of the Gospel. [19]

We have already seen that the disproportion in the Johannine Gospel narrative devoted to the last days of Jesus in Jerusalem is no bar necessarily to it being a substantially historical account of at least one aspect of the life of Jesus. Nor, then is Dunn's objection that the speeches of Jesus are in the style of the evangelist any barrier necessarily to what John says as being a reliable reporting of what Jesus actually said.

Jesus and the Father

Similarly, Dunn's second difficulty, namely the *relative frequency* of John's expression of Jesus' relationship with his Father, and its exclusive quality, in the Synoptic tradition, is not necessarily a difficulty regarding the historicity of the Fourth Gospel. If there had been no text from the Synoptic Gospels which spoke of such a relationship, then at least we would have an argument from silence. The *argumentum ex silentio* is always dubious, although at least it has some weight. But what force has an argument from *infrequency of mention*?[20]

We may even agree with Dunn "that here we have straightforward evidence of a burgeoning tradition, of a manner of speaking about Jesus and his relation with God which became very popular in the last decades of the first century".[21]

But could that burgeoning tradition not have its roots in what the historical Jesus actually said about himself? We quote those startling words of Jesus again, from the translation used by Dunn:

> Everything has been entrusted to me by my Father; and no one knows the Son except the Father, just as no one knows the Father except the Son and those to whom the Son chooses to reveal him. [Matthew 11:27]

As for its authenticity as a genuine saying of the historical Jesus, the only reason of substance to leave it out of the sayings of the historical Jesus is that its Christology is too high, which is itself a circular argument.[22] Indeed, the principle of multiple attestation,[23] that the saying is in two different contexts, in the Synoptic tradition and in John, would at least give one reason for its authenticity.

If we then assume the hypothesis, contrary to Dunn, and with the Pope, that the writer of the Fourth Gospel was an eye-witness who was concerned in his Gospel to write history, then more than one explanation is immediately at hand for the *infrequency of mention* of the Synoptic "stray Johannine logion".

Firstly, biblical scholars speak of "pluralism" within the New Testament. It is quite possible that the early Christians were *embarrassed* by the full divinity of Christ, particularly within the Jewish branch of early Christianity. In the process of the selection[24] of the tradition, the Synoptics simply do not wish to overstate the incarnation. But nothing for that reason prevents the germ idea of the incarnation being there in the earliest tradition, and derived from the historical Jesus.[25] In such a case, the infrequency of mention of the relationship of Jesus with his Father in the Synoptic tradition would be an

75

argument for rather than against its authenticity. In spite of the embarrassment of the Synoptic evangelists concerning the high Christology of Matthew 11:27, it was still included precisely because it was a genuine saying of Jesus.

Another possibility is that the Fourth Gospel represents the more intimate teaching of Jesus to his disciples. This is the view of Dreyfus, who answers this question[26] of the infrequency of mention of the unique relationship of Jesus to the Father by proposing that Jesus disclosed his divinity not to all his disciples, but to an intimate group of them, e.g. as he showed his transfiguration only to Peter, James and John [Mark 5:37]. To the crowd, Matthew 12:34 tells us, Jesus would speak only in parables; but we are also told, Jesus gave the interpretation of his parables to his disciples secretly, as Mark 4:11 tells us: He (Jesus) told them, 'To you is granted the secret of the kingdom of God, but to those who are outside everything comes in parables'.

We may concede the point that, in his selection of the speeches of Jesus by John in his own literary style, material may have been included which was taught by Jesus exclusively to his disciples, but set in the Fourth Gospel in the context of a public declaration by the Lord.

But the Fourth Gospel also insists that Jesus spoke about his divinity not only to the disciples, but also to the crowds. From Chapter 7 onwards, when Jesus goes up to Jerusalem for his final and tragic visit, Jesus dialogues with the "crowd" (*ochlos*, 7:20), and with the Pharisees and other Jewish groups [7:45] right up to Chapter 12 [cf. 12:9, *ochlos*], immediately before the Last Supper followed by his arrest. The Synoptic Gospels, in restricting Jesus' teaching to that of the parables, sets that teaching in the context of the Galilean public ministry. But John, on the contrary, puts the final declaration of Jesus publicly to his own people in the Temple shortly before he was arrested. There it was the time not for parables, but for plain speaking, even if this led to his death.

He said "I AM"

Dunn's third objection is the most serious. He claims that "It is scarcely credible that a saying like John 8:58, or the other 'I am' sayings ('the bread of life', 'the light of the world', etc.) were part of the original Jesus-tradition... The most obvious explanation once again is that in a relatively insignificant element of the earlier tradition John has found the inspiration to fashion an invaluable formula for expressing Christianity's claims about Christ".[27]

We must admit first of all with Dunn that the "I am" (Greek *egó eimi*) statements attributed to Jesus in John are a unique statement of Jesus' self-identity, even as compared with the highest Christology of the Synoptics. Even Matthew 11:27, the "stray Johannine logion", of Jesus knowing the Father and the Father knowing the Son, does not necessarily imply the faith of Christians as expressed in the fourth-century Creed of Nicea that Jesus is "God from God, light from light, true God from true God, begotten not made, of one being (Greek *homóousios*) with the Father". A special relationship does not in essence necessarily mean that Jesus is ontologically one with God his Father. Arius, the Alexandrian priest so vigorously opposed by the orthodox Athanasius, would have accepted such a special relationship between Jesus and God, but not that Jesus was himself truly God.[28]

The key texts in John are where "I am" occurs on the lips of Jesus without a predicate – as distinct from I am with a predicate, for example: "I am the bread of life" [6:48], "I am the good shepherd" [10:11]:

8:24: "Unless you come to believe that I AM, you will surely die in your sins"

8:28: "When you lift up the Son of Man, then you will realise that I AM"

8:58: "Before Abraham even came into existence, I AM."

13:19: "When it does happen, you may believe that I AM."

Various authors attempt to weaken the force of these statements of Jesus in John, claiming that Jesus in the absolute "I am" affirmations is not claiming his full divinity as expressed in the Catholic Creeds. I discuss these views in *Bad, Mad or God?*[29] But for a fuller discussion, I referred in my book to the strangely neglected monograph of David Mark Ball, *I am in John's Gospel: Literary Function, Background and Theological Implications.*[30]

Ball convincingly argues that, to understand the background of the absolute I am sayings, the parallels are not extra-biblical, as some have argued. Ball is unconvinced by these extra-biblical parallels.[31] He counters by referring to scholars who see the background to the *I am* sayings in John rather in Judaism contemporary with Jesus and the writing of the Fourth Gospel. He cites Dodd's *Interpretation of the Fourth Gospel,* where Dodd links *ani hu* ("I am He" Isaiah 43:10), translated in the LXX and in John as *egó eimi,* with Rabbinic expression of the divine Name.[32] Stauffer agrees with Dodd, and links Isaiah 40-55 with the Dead Sea Sect, in, for example, the *Manual of Discipline* which states in 8:13 f, "They are to be kept apart and to go into the wilderness to prepare the way of the HUAHA there..." [cf. Isaiah 40:3]. HUAHA is therefore the Dead Sea Sect's reference to the divine name. "Presumably this is made up of the HUAH (HE) and A (signifying Elohim, God)."[33]

Ball is even more convincing when he sets the "I am" sayings in their literary context in the Gospel of John of Peter's confession of faith, "You are the Holy One of God". 6:69b for Ball forms a kind of dramatic inclusion with "I am, fear not" *ego eimi mé phobeisthe* 6:20b, spoken by Jesus to his terrified disciples while walking on the water, and "I am the bread of life", *egó eimi ho artos tés zóés,* 6:35. Peter responds to give Jesus the acknowledgement in faith that his wonderful deeds of Walking on the Water and Feeding the Five Thousand have revealed Jesus as truly I AM.

A similar meaning becomes clear if we look, with Ball, at Chapter 8, the dramatic dialogue in Jerusalem between Jesus and "the Jews". We see first a similar inclusion. *egó eimi* in 8:12, where Jesus says that he is the Light of the World, and

8:58, where he says, "Before Abraham was, I am". Ball claims that "the striking similarities between John 8 and Isaiah 42-43 suggest that the narrator expected the understanding reader to have a knowledge of the same"[34] that is to Isaiah's use of *ani hu*, the statement of the divine name which Jesus applies to himself, and thus incurs not surprisingly the reaction from his unbelieving audience that he is blaspheming. Even more significant for Brown is John 8:28, which looks back to Isaiah 43:10. JHWH says that He has chosen his servant Israel "that you may know and believe me and understand that *egó eimi*."[35] Thus Jesus, clearly for Ball, claims to be nothing less than the JHWH of the scriptures.

The final clinching of the argument surely comes towards the climax of the final Jerusalem Temple dialogues in John 10:30, where he declares that "I and the Father are one". As I argue in *Bad, Mad or God?*[36] the background is the famous shema `yisra'él, yhwh ʿlóhéynu yhwh 'echad*. The NRSV translates [Deuteronomy 6:4]: "Hear, O Israel: The LORD is our God, the LORD alone". But the older RSV translates, as usual, more literally, "Hear, O Israel: The LORD our God is one LORD". That could also be translated, "Hear O Israel. YHWH is our God. YHWH is One". The latter seems to be the best translation.[37] It seems to be a highly ontological statement, that YHWH is one.

What does it mean when Jesus says that he and the Father are one? Is there not a clear implication that Jesus is joining the Father as *yhwh ehad*, sharing in the oneness of YHWH? This would be a form of idolatry, and so certainly blasphemous. If Jesus' hearers take it that way, and want to stone him, we could hardly blame them. If Jesus wanted to avoid such an implication, surely he should have been much more careful in his language. Again, he is using a highly Semitic form of stating his identity.

Exegetically, surely, Ball has argued his case. The *I am* sayings can only be interpreted as Jesus claiming full divinity, both by their meaning in terms of the Old Testament statements about JHWH, and in terms of their literary context. But – and this is the key question – did the historical Jesus say all this, or was this the fictional affirmation of the faith of the "Johannine Community"?

The historical Jesus said "I AM"

It is surely at this point that we arrive at the most profound disagreement between the Pope's interpretation of the history of Jesus of Nazareth and the hypotheses of modern scholarship. The Pope, in his introduction to the Fourth Gospel picture of Jesus, focuses on the biblical concept of "remembering", as with the disciples remembering after the resurrection the text "Fear not, daughter of Zion; behold, your king is coming, sitting on an ass's colt" [Zechariah 9:9], and now seeing its reference to the Palm Sunday entry of Jesus into Jerusalem [John 12:16].[38] The Pope relates this concept of "remembering" to Jesus' affirmation of his self-identity as the divine Son of God:

> This means that the Gospel of John, because it is a "pneumatic Gospel", does not simply transmit a stenographic transcript of Jesus' words and ways; it escorts us, in virtue of understanding-through-remembering, beyond the external into the depth of words and events that come from God and lead back to him. As such, the Gospel is "remembering", which means that it is faithful to what really happened and is not a "Jesus poem", not a violation of the historical events. Rather, it truly shows us who Jesus not only was, but is; who can always say "Before Abraham was, *I am*" [John 8:58]. It shows us the real Jesus, and we can confidently make use of it as a source of information about him.[39]

I interpret the Pope's words here in this way. The discourses of Jesus in John are constructs of the evangelist, in his language and in his style. But within those discourses, there is genuine historical information about Jesus, which the disciples "remembered" after the resurrection and gave new emphasis. This is true most of all concerning the affirmations of Jesus concerning his self-identity.

Scholars in general do not accept that the historical Jesus said, as he does in John 8:58, "Before Abraham was, I am". Rather, this is interpreted as the credal affirmation of the "Johannine Community", a branch of the primitive church especially influenced by high Christology which it attributed to John the Son of Zebedee. This developed its doctrine particularly in reaction to Judaism, itself struggling to renew its identity after the destruction of the Jerusalem Temple in 70 AD. As Dunn says, "the relationship between Christianity and Judaism reflected in the Fourth Gospel is most clearly that of the eighties and nineties when the breach between synagogue and church, between Jesus' 'disciples' and 'the Jews' had become final (cf. especially John 9:22, 12:42)".[40]

The key text concerns the reaction of the Jews when the man is born blind. His terrified parents were frightened even to admit their son had been healed because of the threat of excommunication: "His (the man born blind's) parents said this because they were afraid of the Jews; for the Jews had already agreed that anyone who confessed Jesus to be the Messiah would be put out of the synagogue." [John 9:22]

The general critical opinion is that this is not credibly a situation which applied during the life of the historical Jesus. During his life, it is generally thought, the followers of Jesus were not excommunicated. Rather, Jewish Christians were excommunicated only after AD 70. But firstly, the Benediction referred to which excommunicates Christians from Judaism was by no means certainly aimed at Christians who believed that Jesus was God. J.A.T. Robinson first argues that the wording of the Benediction referred to by Brown dating from the Second Century excommunicating Christians was expressly intended "against Hebrew Christians of an extreme Judaizing kind, for whom the fourth gospel would have been anathema".[41] Secondly, Robinson argues that the idea of Christians being excommunicated is expressed in other words in the New Testament much earlier than a late John, (e.g. Acts 13:45-50, 1 Thessalonians 2:14).[42]

We must admit that John 9:22 is the only reference in the four Gospels explicitly stating that followers of Jesus were subject to excommunication during his lifetime. But again, this is a question of the credibility of the Gospel picture of Jesus in general. If we adopt the critical opinion that the historical Jesus made no claims to divinity, then it is hardly possible that his followers would have been excommunicated.

81

But if, as John tells us, Jesus did claim divinity explicitly, most clearly during his last days in Jerusalem, then it is most credible that his followers would have been excommunicated.

In *Bad, Mad or God?*[43] I argued that indeed there seems no reason, apart from dogmatic prejudice against the historical Jesus having a high Christology himself, why "I and the Father are One" and the absolute *I am* sayings should not go back to the historical Jesus, *together with the reaction of the hearers of Jesus that he was committing blasphemy by saying those words.* I argued that the very principles of the authentication of Jesus' sayings elaborated after the New Quest of the sixties verified these sayings:

1. **Double Discontinuity**, i.e., *A saying in the Gospels by Jesus is likely to be authentic if it could not have been derived from Judaism at the time of Jesus or from the early Church after him.*[44] This, considered to be one of the most valuable of all the criteria authenticating the sayings of the historical Jesus, surely applies to the *I am* sayings and to "I and the Father are One". Those sayings attributed to Jesus by John are doubly discontinuous both with Judaism and with the early church formulations. No Jewish prophet ever claimed to be divine himself (those sayings are discontinuous with Judaism): and the early church, in formulating its doctrines about Christ, never used that very Semitic expression *I am* (discontinuous with the faith formulations of the primitive church). Indeed, we might doubt whether the Greek speaking and thinking Gentile Christians of the first three centuries, after they had lost the majority of converts from Judaism, even understood those references.

2. **Coherence**. *A saying of Jesus in the Gospels is likely to be historically authentic if it coheres with other sayings and deeds of Jesus.* The absolute *I am* sayings also satisfy the criterion of Coherence. Jesus was accused of blasphemy for saying "Before Abraham was, I am" and "I and the Father are one" [John 8:58, John 10:31]. This is coherent with Jesus being accused of blasphemy since it gives a

more than sufficient reason why he was accused. As I have argued above,[45] critical scholarship has never given any convincing reason why Jesus was arrested and crucified; but the four Gospels are clear. Jesus was arrested and crucified because his contemporaries thought he had blasphemed.[46] Thus if we accept the four Gospels as historically reliable, against the general critical view, then John's Gospel provides us with the climax of the tragic drama of Jesus' conflict with his own fellow Jews who could not understand him and his message. Finally, in the Jerusalem Temple courtyard, Jesus makes his explicit claims to be truly God become Man, and his opponents attempt to stone him for blasphemy. And this tragic climax to the drama is not the fiction of the Johannine Community, a besieged and paranoid Christian group separating itself from Judaism by becoming more and more extreme in its exalted view of Christ.[47] Rather, as the Fourth Gospel tells us, it actually happened in the life of the historical Jesus.

3. **Sufficient Reason.** *A saying in the Gospels is likely to be from the historical Jesus if it explains what would otherwise be inexplicable.*[48] The *I am* sayings in John also satisfy the Criterion of Sufficient Reason, because they link in with what is in the Synoptic Gospels only hinted at implicitly, namely the ontological relationship of Jesus with his Father God. They make explicit what is only implicit in the Synoptic Gospel statements about the status of Jesus.

Implicit to explicit

Dunn, in my opinion, has not adequately presented how high the Christology of the Synoptic Gospels in fact is, as compared with the Fourth Gospel. For instance, Dunn does not discuss, as we have, the question of the unanimity of the four Gospels in their testimony that Jesus was handed over to Pilate having been condemned for blasphemy by the

Sanhedrin. This is crucial because, as we have seen, if Jesus was actually handed over to Pilate for blasphemy, then it raises the question as to whether Jesus' claims were historically much higher than that of being a prophet, even an "eschatological prophet".

Stephen T. Davis, while, with so many rejecting the Fourth Gospel as a source for the divine self-consciousness of Jesus, is on the contrary quite clear that, from the evidence of the Synoptic Gospels, the historical Jesus claimed to be God, but "implicitly". Davis notes in particular that, in the Synoptic presentation of the teaching of Jesus, he "spoke with 'authority', not citing sources or precedents of famous rabbis".[49]

Davis here would be in agreement with J.A.T. Robinson, in his provocative study *The Priority of John* in putting the *ego eimi* absolute statements on the lips of Jesus, John is only making explicit what was implicit in the Synoptic view.[50] That becomes even clearer when, as we did earlier, we trace Mark's Gospel Outline,[51] from the beginning when Jesus is declared to be the Son of God by the divine voice at his baptism in the Jordan river by John, right to his condemnation by the high priest at the Sanhedrin for blasphemy and the women running away with fright when they discover the tomb of Jesus empty.

We would willingly agree with Bultmann when he said, as we quoted earlier,[52] that the whole story of Mark, as chronologically the first Gospel in the general critical view, presents a *theos anér*, a divine man. Our disagreement with Bultmann would be in seeing this *theos anér* as a fundamentally Hellenistic concept, created by the burgeoning faith of the primitive Gentile Christian community. Rather, together with the Pope in *Jesus of Nazareth*, we would proceed from the hypothesis that Mark is presenting fact, a Jewish prophet who was manifestly more than a prophet by the astounding things that he said and did, testified by the earliest apostolic witnesses and put eventually into Gospel form by the four evangelists.

John's Christology is in this case not at all contrary to that presented in the Synoptics. Rather, Davis argues that the historical Jesus implicitly claimed to be God, and this provides good grounds for the early Christians worshipping Him,[53] for which worship, as Dreyfus argues,[54] we have good first- or at least early second-century evidence.

Now if John is only making explicit what is already implicit in the historical portrait of the other evangelists, then why must we consider his explicitation a result of the reflection of the Johannine School upon the tradition rather than an explicitation by the historical Jesus himself during the course of his life on earth? Rather, again according to the principles of the New Quest, the I *am* absolute sayings in the Fourth Gospel and the climactic statement of Jesus that he and the Father are One are rather authenticated on the principle of Sufficient Reason, by making explicit what was only implicit, making understandable what would otherwise be not understood.

The meaning of the implicit statements in the Synoptic Gospels which seem to infer that Jesus is the divine Son of God are made explicit by Jesus identifying himself with the JHWH who spoke to Moses on the holy mountain. The timing too is right. Jesus will die anyway. That had already been decided by his enemies. If Jesus was truly God become Man, why would he not say so just before his crucifixion, even if his own disciples could not understand it at the time? The Holy Spirit would jog their "memory" (in the Johannine sense of "memory" expounded by the Pope as we have seen above) after Jesus had risen from the dead.

The Synoptic Gospels do not contain this historical information because they use the chapters before the arrest and crucifixion of Jesus to collect together groups of sayings of Jesus, no doubt spoken at various times during his public ministry, which they considered apt to record as taking place either on the journey to Jerusalem, or after his solemn entry into the Holy City. Indeed, the Synoptic evangelists appear to give little historical information regarding the whole period of the beginning of Jesus' final journey to Jerusalem and his entry.[55] Certainly, the historical information they contain does not in any way seriously contradict the long Johannine account from Jesus' entry into Jerusalem for the Feast in Chapter 7, until the beginning of the Last Supper in Chapter 13.

Rather, John's account of those last days in Jerusalem appears explicitly as an essentially historical narrative, taking of course into account the inclusion of Jesus' speeches and dialogues which we freely admit are Johannine constructs. But the movement of the narrative, while compellingly dramatic, gives every impression of being the record of an historical event, the tragedy of the inexorable path which Jesus took in those final days in Jerusalem towards his arrest and crucifixion:

- Jesus goes up to Jerusalem privately for the Feast of Tabernacles, and suddenly appears in the Temple declaring himself to be a Teacher come from God. He accuses his hearers of not keeping the Law of Moses, which causes an angry reaction [7:1-24].
- Jesus' enemies are planning his arrest [7:30]. But Jesus continues to provoke his hearers by insisting that he has truly come from God and that from him flow rivers of living water [7:38]. This causes dispute among his hearers, and the chief priests and Pharisees register their alarm and incredulity at the police reporting that "There has never been anyone who spoke like him" [7:46].
- Chapter 8 is a long dialogue between Jesus and his hearers which becomes ever more acrimonious as Jesus makes his famous statement "before Abraham was, I am" [8:58], leading to his opponents taking up stones to stone him for blasphemy [8:59]; but Jesus "hid himself and left the Temple".
- In 9:1-7, Jesus cures the man born blind, and as a result the man tells the Jews that surely Jesus must come from God. This causes the anger of the authorities, and they excommunicate the poor man [8:34]; but he meets Jesus and says "Lord, I believe, and worshipped him" [9:38].
- In Chapter 10, Jesus claims to be the "Good Shepherd" [10:14], obviously implying that the man born blind now cured has been let into the fold, whereas those who do not believe in Jesus, as he has already said, are living in darkness [9:39-41].
- At the Feast of the Dedication, Jesus finally makes clear

his claim. He and his heavenly Father are one [John 10:30]. He is the Son of God [John 10:36]. They want to arrest him then, but Jesus eludes them and flees across the Jordan [11:40].

• The final straw was the raising of Lazarus from the dead, which increased significantly support for Jesus. "From that day onwards they determined to kill him" [11:53].[56]

A reader of these chapters of the Gospel has the same dark sense of gloom and inevitable tragedy which is expressed dramatically as for instance in Shakespeare's *Othello*, that tale of jealousy and hate leading to murder. It is not surprising, therefore, that a mounting chorus of scholars who do not accept the substantial historicity of the narrative in the last decade of the twentieth century blamed the "Johannine Community" for being anti-Semitic.[57] This community, it argued, having been cast out of the synagogue after the Fall of Jerusalem and the decrees of Jamnia, vented their fury on those who stayed in orthodox Judaism by vilifying "the Jews" for putting Jesus to death by constructive hostility as expressed in John 7–12. This fiction, for those scholars, was the beginning of long centuries of the Christian persecution of Jews. For Casey, for instance, the conclusion follows that the Gospel of John should be struck out of the Christian canon of scripture.[58]

On the contrary, I have argued in *Bad, Mad or God?*, that if we accept my submission is correct, that Jesus did make divine claims implicitly in the Synoptic Gospels and explicitly in John, then the kind of tense and hostile dialogues which we find in those chapters of the Fourth Gospel describing Jesus' last days in Jerusalem make complete historical sense; and that, far from being anti-Semitic, reflect a conflict between one Jew's understanding of his being and mission and his equally Jewish opponents. As I state in *Bad, Mad or God?*:

We have argued to the historical authenticity of Mark 14:57–65. In the Marcan version of the trial of Jesus, the high priest asks Jesus whether he is the Christ, the Son of the living God. Jesus replies "I am; and 'you will see the Son of Man seated at the right hand of the Power,' and

87

'coming with the clouds of heaven.'" It is this which the high priest sees as blasphemous. All condemn him as worthy of death.

But why did the high priest ask him that particular question? Mark himself indicates that, right at the beginning of Jesus' public ministry, he offended his Jewish hearers by saying to the paralytic let down through the roof "Your sins are forgiven you" [Mark 2:5]. As we have seen,[59] throughout the Gospel of Mark, there is cast the shadow of Jesus' impending death. But we would have to say that Mark does not give us a clear lead-up to Jesus' arrest. Surely, if Jesus were to be indicted for blasphemy, there would have to have been some kind of climax whereby Jesus' enemies in high places came to realise that the only solution would be to arrest him.

This is precisely the information given us by John, in Chapters 7-10.[60]

A most enlightening comment on the relationship between John and the Synoptics was made by T.E. Pollard in his lecture *St. John's Contribution to the Picture of the Historical Jesus* at Knox Theological Hall, Dunedin, in 1964, which seems to me to express the matter perfectly:

> On Collingwood's definition of the real task of the historian, it could well be argued that John is a better historian than the Synoptists. John portrays Jesus as the one who at every point is conscious of his Messianic function as Son of God, whose every action, thought and word are governed by this consciousness. There is no need to interpret this portrait as an invention by John or a falsification of what Jesus really was. Rather it is an attempt to portray Jesus as he was, in his earthly life, in and for himself. It is not that this Jesus of St John is any less human than the Jesus of the Synoptics; it is rather that John penetrates with deeper insight into the inner springs of the personality of Jesus. Nor was John's portrait a more highly developed theological interpretation; rather because of his deeper insight he makes explicit what is implicit, and, for the most part, veiled in the Synoptics.[61]

If, then, Pollard (and indeed the Pope) is right, and the Fourth Gospel is a true history of Jesus emphasising whatever in that history is relevant to the declaration of his own being and identity, then we come at last to the question as to who wrote the Fourth Gospel. History cannot itself be written by insight, even by divine revelation. It can only be written by those who were eye-witnesses of an historical event, or by those who had at least access to eye-witness testimony. So who, then, *did* write the Fourth Gospel? Who was John?

NOTES – CHAPTER FOUR

1   For my discussion of this issue, cf. BMG, 274-279.
2   Donald H. Wolfe, *The Assassination of Marilyn Monroe.* London, Little, Brown and Company, 1998.
3   Cazelles, H. *Johannes. Ein Sohn des Zebedäus. 'Priester und Apostel.* Communio 31(2002), 479-84, quoted in JN, 224-5.
4   JN, 227.
5   Dunn, 2003.
6   Dunn, 1980, 29-32.
7   Dunn, 1980, 254.
8   Dunn, 1980, 29.
9   Dunn, 1980, 30.
10 *Ibid.*
11 *Ibid.*
12 *Ibid.*
13 Dunn, 1980, 31.
14 Broer, I. 1998, 197, quoted in JN, 228.
15 JN, 228.
16 JN, 229.
17 Even the *Jesus Seminar* agreed that we do not need to have the *ipsissima verba* of Jesus in order for the speeches of Jesus reported in the four Gospels to be substantially what Jesus said, or even would have said, cf. FG, 36, BMG, 172-175.
18 Schnackenburg, I, 24.
19 BI, 395, No. 930.
20 M. Casey would also deny its authenticity because it does not occur frequently enough. "If the historical Jesus had used this key term extensively as John says he did, the faithful Christians who transmitted the synoptic tradition would have transmitted it extensively." Casey, 1991, 25. But this is surely another *non sequitur.* Bultmann HST 166* only says that Matthew 11:17 seems "at first sight" to be a

Hellenistic formulation, for him an extraordinarily cautious remark. Viviano says of *I praise you Father*, "This is a typical Jewish blessing formula, but with Jesus' intimate *Abba*-Father address added (5 times in three verses". NJBC, **42**:75, 653.

21 *Ibid.*

22 Casey, 1991, 25. Bultmann HST 166* only says that Matthew 11:17 seems "at first sight" to be a Hellenistic formulation, for him an extraordinarily cautious remark. Viviano says of *I praise you Father*, "This is a typical Jewish blessing formula, but with Jesus' intimate *Abba*-Father address added (5 times in three verses". NJBC, **42**:75, 653.

23 BMG, 115-6.

24 Cf. DV 19, which speaks of the process of synthesis, selection and explication in the formation of the Gospel tradition.

25 As in particular we have demonstrated in BMG, Chapter 8, *You have Heard the Blasphemy*, 134-153.

26 "*Si Jésus avait enseigné sa pre-existence et sa divinité aussi clairement que saint Jean le dit, pourquoi les autres évangelistes n'en ont rien dit?*" Dreyfus, 1984, 71.

27 Dreyfus, 1984, 31.

28 ODCC, 83. One point of clarification in this discussion will be useful here. Dunn, *Ibid., 30,* and also Theissen/Merz, HJCG, 96, speak of John's Gospel proclaiming the "pre-existence" of Jesus. The notion of "pre-existence" can be confusing, since in the Jewish worldview of the time of Jesus, as expressed in the Synoptic tradition, it was thought that Elijah, certainly not a divine being in the Jewish tradition, or indeed John the Baptist or one of the prophets [cf. Luke 9:7-8] would return for the great and terrible day of the Lord. [Malachi 4:5]. Elijah was now waiting in heaven somewhere, ready to descend in his chariot, where he had ascended assumed into heaven in the sight of his prophetic son and successor Elisha [2 Kings 2:12]. The Synoptics do therefore know about pre-existence. The real problem is not first and foremost that of pre-existence. Rather, it is the orthodox Christian view of a person being both God in the full sense and Man in the full sense, as he seems to be presented in the Fourth Gospel.

29 BMG, 240-247.

30 JSNTS, 124, Sheffield Academic Press, 1996.

31 IAM, 30.

32 Dodd, IFG, 94-5.

33 Stauffer, 1960, 145.

34 IAM 93.

35 Blomberg, 2001, 149, accepts the view of Motyer, 1997, 209, who "plausibly concludes that John 8:58 'would not be heard as a claim to *be God*. It *would* be heard as a claim to be a divine agent, anointed with the name and powers of God, and (in this case) active in the genesis of Abraham'". But this ignores the context of the four absolute

I AM sayings; as Brown says, "Jesus is presented as speaking in the same manner in which Yahweh speaks in Deutero-Isaiah". Brown, I, 537.

36 BMG, 247-249.

37 The Revised Version, 2nd. M. translates Deuteronomy 6:4 that way. It certainly is grammatically and syntactically possible. S.R. Driver, *A Critical and Exegetical Commentary on Deuteronomy*, Edinburgh, T. and T. Clark, 1902, put this as one of four possible translations, 89, n.30, (a). "J. is our God, J. alone." (b). "J. is our God, J. is one." (c). "J. is our God, J. alone." (d). "J. our God is one J." But Driver favours (d). "J. our God is one J." which is materially the same as "J. is our God, J. is one", which seems to me to read more easily.

38 JN, 232.

39 JN, 234-5.

40 Dunn, 1980, 30.

41 Robinson, 1976, 273.

42 Robinson, 1976, 273-4.

43 BMG, 261-2.

44 Cf. BMG, 115.

45 BMG, 122.

46 BMG, Chapter 8, 134-153.

47 This fictionalisation of the "Johannine Community" led scholars towards the end of the twentieth century to accuse the Gospel of John of being anti-Semitic. E.g. Kysar in Kysar, R. *Anti-Semitism and the Gospel of John.* In Evans, A.E., and Hagner, D.A., ed. *Anti-Semitism and Early Christianity. Issues of Polemic and Faith.* Minneapolis, Fortress Press, 1993, 113-127. My response is in BMG, 268. "If, as Kysar argues, "the Jews" are a fictional group in the Gospel story who exist there to support the flagging faith of the Johannine community, the Johannine community itself becomes a prototype, even *the* prototype, of two thousand years of anti-Semitism. But, if, as we shall now demonstrate, "the Jews" in the Fourth Gospel are defined in terms of the rôle they played as a group limited in the place and time of the historical Jesus, then the author of the Fourth Gospel can in no way be accused of anti-Semitism. Rather, the Fourth Gospel described a situation of conflict *within Judaism itself,* and a situation of conflict which existed before, even if only just before, Christianity was born. Once again, the Fourth evangelist is telling us about the historical Jesus, and in this case a vitally important set of facts about the opposition to him during his own day, from his own people".

48 BMG, 116. On BMG, 262, I gave as the third criteria applying to the *I am* absolute sayings of Jesus that of Multiple Attestation, namely that *A saying of Jesus in the Gospels is likely to be historically authentic if it is attested in more than one independent literary source (e.g. Mark, Q, Paul, John), and/or in more than one literary form or genre.* BMG, 115. While I would continue to contend that the *I am* absolute sayings in

John, and the statement of Jesus that he and the Father are one, fulfil the first two criteria I listed, that of Double Discontinuity and of Coherence as discussed above, I now admit that it is less certain to attribute Multiple Attestation to those sayings. I would partially agree with Dunn here that "Again it is possible to see a Synoptic-type root for the weighty 'I am' sayings – Mark 6:50, 13:6, 14:62.; but again the indications are clear and strong that the weightier Johannine sayings are a *development from* the earlier tradition at best tangential to the earlier tradition" 1980, 30-31. Rather than a development, I would argue that the Johannine absolute *I am* sayings make explicit what is implicit in the Synoptic *I am* sayings. I would also argue that Jesus himself was making explicit in the Jerusalem dialogues recorded in John 7-12 what was only implicit in his saying to the frightened disciples, while walking on the water, "I am: do not be afraid", and to the high priest at his trial "I am: and you will see the Son of Man…" Thus the Johannine *I am* sayings, I would now maintain, rather *explain what would otherwise be inexplicable*, namely fulfil the criterion of Sufficient Reason rather than of Multiple Attestation.

49 Davis, *et al*, ed., 2002, 241.

50 PJ, 388-389. So also Oscar Cullmann: "Might we not have a special kind of teaching here? It would not be secret, or systematically withheld from the majority of disciples, but it would have been more intimate teaching which not all the disciples knew (and which they may have barely understood). The author of the Gospel of John may have developed it *freely*, in the way that we know, but still keeping Jesus' teaching as a foundation." Cullmann, 1976, 82.

51 Above, 35-36.

52 HST, *369.

53 "The prevalence and centrality of the worship of Jesus in early Christianity from an early date has frequently been underestimated…" Davis *et al*, ed., 2002, 234.

54 Dreyfus, 1984, 18. 234.

55 Cf. above, 68, "In contrast, Mark…" for the Synoptic Gospel texts concerned.

56 Blomberg, 174, 2001, argues convincingly against those critics who claim that the resurrection of Lazarus could not have been "the climactic catalyst for the plot that will eventuate in Christ's death" 9c.53). Blomberg argues that the disciples could have been privy to the debates in the Sanhedrin which condemned Jesus through "leaks", and that both John and the Synoptics know of multiple, previous plots to kill Christ (Mark 3:6\\: Luke 4:28-29; John 5:18, 10:31-33), so why should these later references be viewed as mutually exclusive?"

57 Bieringer *et al*, ed., entitle their recent symposium 2001, *Anti-Judaism and the Fourth Gospel*. This acknowledges the difficulty of using the term "anti-Semitic" of a work, the Fourth Gospel, which recent scholarship has so affirmed is itself fundamentally Jewish.

58 Casey, 1996, 229. "Our major conclusion follows ineluctably. The fourth Gospel is profoundly untrue. It consists to a large extent of inaccurate stories and words wrongly attributed to people. It is anti-Jewish, and as Holy Scripture it has been used to legitimate outbreaks of Christian anti-Semitism. A cultural defence is therefore inadequate. This is a serious problem for Christian churches which have it among their most sacred texts".

59 BMG, 141.

60 BMG, 271.

61 PJ, 363. Pollard's lecture St John's Contribution to the Picture of the Historical Jesus appeared in Forum 16.6, August 1964, 2-9.

CHAPTER FIVE

WHO WROTE THE FOURTH GOSPEL?
THE *STATUS QUAESTIONIS*

- Much recent Johannine scholarship works from the presupposition that the Fourth Gospel in its final form was not written by an eye-witness of the events recorded. Scholars work from the presumption that, by the end of the first century AD, when the Gospel was finally written, the Gospel reflects the faith of the "Johannine Community" rather than what the historical Jesus actually said and did.
- I submit that this presupposition has never been proven, but arises from historical scepticism concerning the content of the Fourth Gospel narrative.
- However, such scepticism is not justified, as the Pope affirms in *Jesus of Nazareth,* and as we have demonstrated in the preceding introduction. The Gospel of John contains vital historical information concerning the declaration of the historical Jesus regarding his own identity and earthly mission.
- Thus it is appropriate for us to re-examine the evidence for the authorship of the Fourth Gospel by John the Son of Zebedee.

The Pope's position on the authorship of the Fourth Gospel is not a simple identification of the authorship of that Gospel with John the Son of Zebedee, one of the Twelve Apostles called by Christ and among those disciples the three closest to Jesus, namely Peter, James and John, who were invited by the Lord to go with him to the Mount of Transfiguration [Matthew 17:1 \\]. This, as we shall soon discuss, is Church tradition.

Rather, the Pope accepts the conclusions of Peter Stuhlmacher,[1] who identifies the author of the Gospel of John rather with "John the Presbyter", or "John the Elder", a second "John" referred to by the fourth-century Church historian Eusebius of Caesarea as close to the Apostles.[2] Of course, we will have to consider this view of the authorship of John in more detail in the second part of this book.

According to the classification of W. Sanday, who at the beginning of the twentieth century went from Oxford to the Union Theological Seminary,[3] New York to deliver lectures on The Criticism of the Fourth Gospel, the Pope has not adopted a "conservative opinion" regarding the authorship of the Fourth Gospel, which he categorised as one who held that John the Son of Zebedee was actually the author, but a "mediating theory".

I have argued in *Bad, Mad or God?* that the positions adopted regarding who wrote the Fourth Gospel are still as varied as when Sanday went to New York in 1904. I argued that there are still authors who adopt any one of four positions regarding the authorship of the Gospel of John:

1. Conservative opinion. This was represented in Sanday's day by writers such as Westcott (1880) and many continental authors, who maintained that the author of the Fourth Gospel was John the Son of Zebedee. Carson (1991) and J.A.T. Robinson (1985) would espouse such a "conservative position".

2. Mediating theories which held that another disciple was the author, e.g. John the Elder. The Pope quotes Martin Hengel (1989) in his support for this view.

3. Partition Theories, Wendt (1886). These proposed that the author was John plus a Redactor. Many modern exegetes hold redaction theories, as we shall see later in discussing in more detail the various redaction theories on offer. But those who seriously consider an apostolic author at the beginning of the editorial process of writing the Gospel, rather than 4 below, are often uncertain as to who this originating apostolic author in fact was, e.g. Moloney (1998).

4. Uncompromising Rejection. These denied eye witness and apostolic authorship, e.g. Jülicher (1904). This is the view of Rudolf Bultmann (1941) and of many authors who follow him.

5. Perhaps we may add a fifth category to Sanday's, those who are simply uncertain as to who the author was, who consider that the evidence is not persuasive either for or against traditional authorship. We would place Moloney (1998) in that category, and Pheme Perkins (1989).[4]

Historicity and authorship

So far in this book, we have discussed the historicity of the Fourth Gospel account of the life of Jesus without any serious discussion as to who was the author of this Gospel. Obviously, we must now get down to such a consideration. But, as we have seen, the Pope's position is not that authorship is in itself of overriding importance. To him, what really matters regarding the Fourth Gospel is whether whoever wrote it was concerned to write in any sense fact rather than fiction.

In adopting what Sanday called a "mediating theory" regarding the authorship of the Fourth Gospel, the Pope sees this as no threat to its historicity. This is because he identifies the enigmatic "beloved disciple" mentioned in the text of the Gospel with John the Son of Zebedee. This "beloved disciple", known personally by John the Presbyter, for the Pope is the guarantee of the historical worth of the Fourth Gospel:

> The Gospel traces its origins to an eyewitness, and it is clear that this eyewitness is none other than the disciple who, as we have been told, was standing under the Cross and was the disciple whom Jesus loved (cf. John 19:26). This disciple is once again named as the author of the Gospel in John 21:24. In addition, we meet this figure in John 13:23, 20:2-10, and 21:7 and probably in John 1:35 and 18:15-16 as well.[5]

The importance for the Pope in identifying the beloved disciple as the Son of Zebedee is the implication that the Fourth Gospel is based upon apostolic eye-witness testimony. The Pope claims that "it is quite possible to see Zebedee's son John as the bystander who solemnly asserts his claim to be an eyewitness (cf. John 19:35)…"[6] To support this position, the Pope says "Now, the French exegete Henri Cazelles, drawing on studies by J. Colson, J. Winandy, and M.-E. Boismard has shown in a sociological study of the Temple priesthood before its destruction ("Johannes") that such identification is actually quite possible".[7] John's father, Zebedee, the Pope argues, was not just a "simple fisherman", but a member of the educated priestly class.

From the beginning of modern Johannine research, the question of authorship has been inextricably connected with the issue of the historicity of John.

At the beginning of the nineteenth century, when Gospel criticism was fully under way, scholars were initially in favour of the historicity of the Fourth Gospel. Bretschneider, the famous General Superintendent at Gotha (1776-1848) had listed a collection of *loci* in the Gospels where John seems to be historically unreliable compared with the Synoptics. But the great Friedrich Schleiermacher had thrown his full weight behind the Fourth Gospel as the most reliable because it contained fewer miracles than the other three Gospels; and Bretschneider declared himself convinced by the arguments of the prestigious Berlin professor.[8]

It was David Friedrich Strauss, who shattered the Christian world in Germany with his *Das Leben Jesu Bearbeitet* ("The Life of Jesus Critically Examined"), First Edition 1835,[9] the authorship of the Fourth Gospel was irrelevant. Even if John the Apostle had written it, it still for Strauss would have been myth. It was the *intention* of the writer of the Fourth Gospel which made his work the most mythical of all four Gospels.

John is clearest of all about the divinity of Christ, the constant theme of the whole Gospel narrative. The smaller number of miracles for Strauss means nothing. In the evangelist's intention, these miracles are given a much more loaded meaning than in the Synoptics. From the very first miracle at Cana of Galilee, the turning of water into wine, where according to John Jesus "manifested his glory; and his disciples believed in him" [John 2:11], "it is entirely in the spirit of the fourth gospel, to place in relief the exaltation of Jesus as the divine logos".[10]

For Strauss, the incarnation itself was philosophically impossible. As a radical Hegelian, he could not accept that a human individual could be the divine Son of God and remain so for all eternity. This is consistent with the Hegelian view that only the Absolute Idea survives the historical process of thesis, antithesis, and synthesis. Strauss demythologises the incarnation by turning the God-man into the ideal of humanity.[11]

Scepticism of the authorship of the Fourth Gospel thus began with philosophical scepticism about its historicity. For Strauss, the Fourth Gospel just did not present a credible picture of the historical Jesus. Jesus could not have seen himself as the divine logos. Thus, by the end of the nineteenth century, and the beginning of the twentieth, critical scholarship had come to reject authorship by John the Son of Zebedee. If the Fourth Gospel was so far in spirit from the worldview of Jesus of Nazareth himself, it was hardly likely that one of Jesus' own disciples could have written it. The argument went that way round.

Rudolf Bultmann, beginning his prestigious career at the beginning of the twentieth century, was heir to this tradition of historical scepticism. As we have seen already, he shared the view that the historical Jesus, as far as we can know his teaching, was a Jewish rabbi whom the Hellenistic Christian community elevated to a being of divine status. Thus, for him, the traditional ascription of authorship to John the Son of Zebedee was not even worthy of consideration. The German original Edition of Bultmann's Commentary on John, Göttingen, Vandenhoeck and Ruprecht, 1941, has no introduction, but simply begins on page 1 with commentary on 1:1-18, *Der Prolog*. The English Edition of Bultmann's Commentary on John, as we shall consider later, has a summary, indeed we might say dismissive, Introduction written for Bultmann by Walter Schmithals, presumably with the author's complete approval.[12]

The Johannine community

In the second half of the twentieth century, the terms of the debate about authorship of the Fourth Gospel did not change much as compared with Sanday's classification of the four different views, which we have seen above; except perhaps with a number of scholars being more agnostic about any position to be adopted.[13] Certainly, not everyone dotted the 'i's and crossed the 't's with all of Bultmann's negative conclusions either as to authorship or as to historicity.

What did become standard practice was that more and more the methodology of studying the Gospels began from the position that the Fourth Gospel did not tell the story of the historical Jesus, but rather reflected the high Christology of the so-called "Johannine Community". This went together with redaction theories, or "stage" theories of composition, because with each successive redaction or stage in the formation of the Gospel of John, the Christology went higher, and the historicity went progressively lower.

Therefore, by the end of the first century, when the Fourth Gospel was reaching its final shape, the Johannine Community, a church of Jewish Christians seeing itself as the successors of the Apostle John, was faced by a new more organised and stronger Rabbinic Judaism after the Destruction of Jerusalem by the Roman armies in 70 AD. The Johannine Community itself became more defensive in reaction, and emphasised those points of disagreement with their Jewish past, such as Jesus being the Messiah, being driven even further, to present Christ as the Logos, the Word become flesh, and to attribute to Jesus the I AM statements referring to JHWH in the Old Testament. This high Christology did not at all reflect the statements of the historical Jesus about himself, who, as was generally thought by the scholars, only saw himself to be the unique agent in the process of establishing God's kingship over men.[14]

Naturally, this would render most of what the Pope outlines in his book *Jesus of Nazareth* as being the life of the historical Jesus rather to being an expression of the "Christ of faith". This would be verified both in those texts of the Synoptic narratives which as we have seen promote a much higher Christology than of Jesus being merely an "eschatological prophet", and most of all in the Fourth Gospel where Jesus explicitly states his full divine identity.

Thus, particularly from the studies of J.L. Martyn onwards, who first published *History and Theology in the Fourth Gospel*, 1968, scholars perused the Fourth Gospel not to find the words and deeds of the historical Jesus, but rather what Raymond E. Brown described as "The Community of the beloved disciple: The Loves, Lives and Hates of an individual church in New Testament times".[15] Thus, for instance, the dialogue of Jesus with the Samaritan woman in John, Chapter 4, becomes in this methodology not the account of an incident in the life of the historical Jesus, but a description of the hypothetical relationship between the Samaritan sect and the Johannine Christians.[16]

To this extent, Bultmann still reigns in Johannine studies, through the "Johannine community". Scholars work on the assumption that St John's Gospel does not give us the history of Jesus, but only glimpses into the faith and life of the primitive Christian community. If John's Gospel does give us any history, for so many modern scholars, it can only be described as historical scraps, in the first stages of redaction, namely that the disciples of Jesus were formerly disciples of John the Baptist [John 1:35]; that Jesus only goes up to Jerusalem once in the Synoptic tradition cf. Matthew, Mark and Luke; [cf. Matthew 16:21] while in John, Jesus goes up to Jerusalem three times: [John 2:13, 5:1, 7:10]. Many scholars think that at least John is more likely to be correct.[17]

Timely indeed is the warning of J. Beutler in the important symposium *La Communauté Johannique et son Histoire* against "science fiction" regarding the reconstructed history and sociology of the Johannine Community.[18] Thomas Brodie's stricture, after quoting the various opinions as to the identity, ideas and history of the Johannine Community, that "given the diversity of views, it is clear that the actual process of reconstructing is extremely hazardous",[19] is likewise most relevant. Yet scholars still often work under the presumption that a long process of redaction has left the final text of the

Fourth Gospel without essential historical value, being rather only a reflection of the faith community which produced it.

We have argued that, on the contrary, with the Pope in *Jesus of Nazareth,* John's Gospel gives us a reliable history of Jesus from a particular perspective, namely the public life, miracles, teachings, arrest, death and resurrection of the divine Son of God. The speeches are a Johannine construct, but contain what Jesus actually said, in particular his divine claims.

This, we have claimed, is all credible historically. This must reopen the debate about the authorship of the Fourth Gospel. If the story is historically credible, then it follows that we must seriously raise the question: who was the eye-witness, or eye-witnesses who provided the sources for this history? If we can demonstrate that there are solid reasons for the Fourth Gospel to be based upon eye-witness testimony, then what we have attempted to demonstrate previously, the Gospel's historical coherence, can confirm that apostolic authorship.

In what follows, granted the popularity of hypotheses regarding the hypothetical "Johannine Community", we will have to examine redaction theories particularly carefully. We shall discover that the proofs alleged for redaction in John are generally flimsy, which means even more that the denial of the essential historicity of John on redactional basis is likewise without any solid foundation.

NOTES – CHAPTER FIVE

1   JN, 226.
2   JN, 225.
3   Sanday, 1905, 22-3.
4   NJBC, **61:12**, 946-7.
5   JN, 222.
6   JN, 225.
7   JN, 224.
8   QHJ, 85.
9   LJCE, xxiv-xxv.
10 LJCE, 526.

11 LJCE, 780. "Humanity is the union of two natures-God become man, the infinite manifesting itself in the finite, and the finite spirit remembering its infinitude; it is the child of the visible Mother and the invisible Father, Nature and Spirit... It is Humanity that dies, rises, and ascends to heaven, for from the negation of its phenomenal life there ever proceeds a higher spiritual life; from the suppression of its mortality as a personal, national and terrestrial spirit, arises its union with the infinite spirit of the heavens. By faith in this Christ, especially in his death and resurrection, man is justified before God; that is, by the kindling within him of the idea of Humanity, the individual man participates in the divinely human life of the species."

12 Bultmann, 3.

13 A typically cautious, judicious, and non-committal approach can be found in Mark Edwards' commentary on John, 2004, yet being a comprehensive and pleasing presentation of all the complex introductory questions involved, 1-14.

14 CBQ, 1967, 341.

15 Brown, 1979.

16 "There is real reason to doubt that historically during his ministry Jesus converted many Samaritans to his preaching; and the appearance of the story in John (like the story in Acts 8) may well represent the post-resurrectional history of the Christian movement." Brown, 1979, 39. However, both Blomberg, 2001, 104, and Schnackenburg, I, 420, see no reason whatever to doubt the historicity of the narrative.

17 Theissen and Merz insist that although the Gospel of John "is the most stylized on the basis of theological premisses... Nevertheless, the Gospel of John, which is independent of the Synoptics, is not worthless. At some usually quite emphatic places it hands down data which diverge from the Synoptics, and can go back to old traditions." HGCG, 36.

18 CJH, 28. "*Tous ces travaux ont leur poids, mais ils restent souvent très spéculatifs. A ce propos, une mise en garde contre la "science fiction" historique n'est certainement pas inopportune*".

19 Brodie, 1993, 20.

Part Two
The Evidence for Authorship

- Having shown that the Gospel is at least initially credible historically, I shall now attempt to show that, in ignoring the real possibility of the substantial historicity of the Fourth Gospel, scholars have abandoned the strong evidence from external sources, that is early church tradition, and the internal evidence, that is evidence from the text of the Gospel itself, that the Gospel is linked with an eye-witness source.
- This evidence, however, is not compelling without being combined with a demonstration of that historical credibility of the Gospel which we have already shown in Part One, and which the Pope affirms.

INTRODUCTION

I have already touched briefly on the question of the authorship of John in my book published in 2004, *Bad, Mad or God? Proving the Divinity of Christ from St. John's Gospel.*[1] All that I attempted to achieve in that brief consideration of the authorship of the Fourth Gospel was to establish at least that there was a *prima facie* case for there being at least some authentic material from the historical Jesus in John. I then went on to consider specifically the historicity of the miracles of Jesus in John, particularly the Multiplication of the Loaves and the Walking on the Water, together with the historicity of the I AM statements of Jesus as declarations by him of his divinity, and finally his resurrection in order to demonstrate the reasonableness of Christian faith in the incarnation.

In this part, my aim is rather to consider evidence for the authorship of the Fourth Gospel by John the Son of Zebedee, one of the Twelve disciples of Jesus, indeed one of the three intimate disciples Peter, James, and John, whom Jesus took with him up the Mountain of Transfiguration [Matthew 17:1-5\\].

The external evidence for the authorship of the Fourth Gospel, that is evidence from sources outside of the Gospel, and internal evidence, that is evidence from the text of the Gospel itself, have been examined in detail in many good commentaries, to which the reader may be referred, and to which I will be making constant reference in what follows.[2]

What I add to these already existing studies on John is an attempt to put all the evidence together cumulatively to build up the case for the traditional authorship.

To summarise, my conclusion will be that the Gospel of John was most probably written by John the Son of Zebedee, who used no identifiable literary sources. Any editorial work was most likely done by the evangelist himself or herself, or at least by a redactor imbued entirely with the ideas of the evangelist. There is no compelling evidence of redactional insertions with theological motivation (e.g. by conflicting ecclesiastical groups of the late first century with their own theological agendas). All seems to be the work of the evangelist, John the Son of Zebedee, even if he might have used a scribe.

None of these above arguments are incontrovertible. But the evidence builds up cumulatively in favour of traditional authorship. And I submit that at each stage of the argument the conclusion I have made is at the very least equally possible and most frequently much more likely than the alternatives proposed.

Finally, it is obvious that none of these arguments has the force to assert for the historicity of the Fourth Gospel if the literary *genre* is myth as Strauss claimed. Theoretically, even if the Gospel had been written by John the Apostle, he could have written myth. Such a position has never been taken seriously in critical scholarship. But this only shows the importance of our Part One, where we have demonstrated that it is reasonable to accept that in the Fourth Gospel we have an account which is essentially historical. These arguments must be joined with the arguments from external and internal evidence for apostolic authorship.

Does it matter?

Some would say that the question of the authorship of any particular Gospel is purely academic. But regarding the Fourth Gospel at least, it would surely add strength to that doctrine of the incarnation if its principal literary testimony, the Fourth Gospel, were demonstrably written by an apostolic eye-witness, or at least had apostolic eye-witness testimony behind it. In this connection, it might well be worth quoting an article written a century ago by a biblical scholar. The author, R.H. Strachan, is writing at the beginning of the twentieth century, when the critical approach to the Fourth Gospel was crossing over from Germany to England. He wishes to convince us that the question as to who the author of the Fourth Gospel was is not of purely academic interest. He summarises what seems to me to me a balanced view of the importance of the authorship of this particular Christian testimony:

> *Introduction* – It is important to remember that the Kingdom of Christ was in being before the Gospel records were written. They did not originate the institution, but are themselves the expression of it. Previous to the publication of the Johannine Gospel, which is the latest of the four, St Paul had completed his mission to the Gentiles; and in Ephesus, where the Gospel was written his doctrine had already an assured place in the Christian Church. It is therefore historically untrue to say that faith in the Divine Person and work of Jesus is destroyed if the authenticity of the Fourth Gospel cannot be proved. For the basis of our faith we must dig deeper than the results of critical investigation.

> The question, however, of the authorship of this Gospel is more than a merely academic one. It occupies a unique position. None of the other three claims to be written by the man whose name it bears, but the Fourth Gospel is issued with an explicit statement to that effect (21:24).

> Moreover, its contents are vitally connected with the individuality of the author. The very way in which his identity is studiously concealed shows that the writer is himself conscious that the Gospel contains a personal testimony, which he does not hesitate to present as objective and impersonal. We desire to know who it is that claims to be an eye-witness; who it is that narrates events and discourses of Jesus so distinct in character from the Synoptics, and yet meant to occupy a place alongside these without contradiction; who it is that has so boldly mingled historic fact and ideal conceptions, that has given to the Person of Christ a timeless cosmic significance, and has represented our Lord in His acts and in His words as Himself justifying that impression and those claims.

> If, as is certain, the work is influenced by developed theological conceptions, and reflects the contemporary

historical situation of the Christian Church, we desire *to* be certain that the writer was in a position not seriously to misrepresent the actual facts. This is no merely antiquarian question. There can be no doubt that the Gospel is intended to be read as the work of the Apostle, and it would seriously detract from its value, if, as extreme critics are more and more inclined to allow, that claim means only that it contains a nucleus of Johannine tradition. The same objection applies to all partition theories of the Gospel (e.g. Wendt's), and it is assumed in this article that their authors have failed to prove their case.

If, on the other hand, the writer was the beloved disciple, an eye-witness possessing a specially intimate knowledge of the mind and character of Jesus, we have an assurance that when, for example, he wrote the opening sentences of the Gospel, he felt himself in touch not merely with current theological thought, but with the historic fact of the consciousness of Jesus of Nazareth. So far from being a stumbling-block to the Johannine authorship, the Prologue even gains in value and significance with the acceptance of the traditional view. The striking juxta-position in the Prologue of the timeless Logos idea and the historical witness of the Baptist, to whom the conception was unfamiliar, and the frequent mention of the Baptist throughout the Gospel, even at times when the situation scarcely demands it (e.g. 10:40-42), are saved from abruptness only if the Writer is developing an impression made on him by his earliest teacher, who led him to Christ. His experience stretches in one continuous whole from that time to this when he begins to write.[3]

Strachan's words may appear naïve to one well versed in the complex literature on the Fourth Gospel. For instance is the author of 21:24 the author of the whole of the Gospel? Each of his statements is questioned by Johannine exegetes. But Strachan is presenting what is no doubt the result of a direct, albeit simple, reading of the Gospel of John. If we accept the basic historicity of the Fourth Gospel, as Strachan does, then that Gospel becomes an important testimony to the central

Christian doctrine of the Incarnation. And if it was written by an eye-witness, or even by a friend or disciple of an eye-witness, its historicity would seem at least at first sight to be confirmed.

Contrariwise, those who deny the historicity of the Fourth Gospel can proceed further to question the Incarnation on the grounds that the historical Jesus never claimed to be divine. As we outlined in *Bad, Mad or God?* [4] in the second half of the twentieth century, both in Britain with the symposium *The Myth of God Incarnate* [5] and in America with the *Jesus Seminar,* [6] a not inconsiderable number of radical Christian scholars explicitly rejected the doctrine of the Incarnation as past its sell-by date precisely on the grounds that the Fourth Gospel was a myth. [7] These have had a great influence on the Anglo-Saxon academic world.

This is only one more instance of the isolation of biblical studies from theological questions, a phenomenon which we shall briefly discuss in our General Conclusions. In reality, the following dismissive comment by Schmithals, who wrote the Introduction to Bultmann's Commentary on John for the English translation of the original German (the German Edition [8] has no introduction, but simply begins on page 1 with commentary on 1:1-18, *Der Prolog*) is now implicitly accepted without question by a large constituency of scholars:

> We are not in a position to say anything definite about the author or about the redactor. The Gospel does not name either person, and the superscription of the Gospel comes from a later time. From 21.24f (cp. 19.35*)* we gather that the redactor holds the author to be an eye-witness of the life of Jesus. He identifies him with the problematic figure of the beloved disciple, mentioned in 13.23, 19.26f, 20.2–10 (hardly in 18.15f), and in the redactional appendix 21.20-23 it is assumed that the disciple has died. But the Gospel itself does not mention this identification (see on 13.30).
>
> Later the beloved disciple was equated with John, the son of Zebedee and brother of James, a member of the circle of the Twelve, and it was claimed that he died in

advanced age in Ephesus. The first clear testimony to this tradition is offered by Irenaeus III, 1.2. But John the son of Zebedee must have been killed by the Jews very early, as Mark 10.39 shows, and as is indicated by several witnesses of the ancient Church. Moreover the Gospel itself makes no claim to have been written by an eye-witness. And in no way does it give occasion to presume that an eye-witness lies behind it, rather it completely contradicts such an assumption.

Now the much discussed testimony of Papias (in Eusebius, H.E. III, 39.3f.) refers not only to John the son of Zebedee but also to the Presbyter John, who may have written the Book of Revelation. Probably Irenaeus and the whole later tradition confused the Ephesian Presbyter with the son of Zebedee of the same name. Prior to Irenaeus, then, the Presbyter John could have been regarded as the author of the Fourth Gospel, and possibly this was already the view of the redactor of the Gospel. But this assumption, of course, is quite uncertain, and it is no longer possible to demonstrate the correctness of such an opinion. The author remains unknown to us. [9]

We will answer Schmithals point by point. The reader will note that he has used the kind of cumulative demonstration which we ourselves will use now in the opposite and positive direction in favour of apostolic authorship. We have already countered Schmithals *a priori* dismissive rejection of any possibility that the Gospel is based upon eye-witness testimony in our Part One. But now we will answer in much more detail Schmithals specific reference to the Gospel itself denying its own status as based upon eye-witness testimony. ("Moreover the Gospel itself makes no claim to have been written by an eye-witness. And in no way does it give occasion to presume that an eye-witness lies behind it, rather it completely contradicts such an assumption.") On the contrary, we will attempt in this book to show that the Gospel does in fact make a claim to be based upon eye-witness testimony, and that such a claim is credible.

CHAPTER SIX

THE DATE OF THE FOURTH GOSPEL

- **Our earliest manuscripts of the Fourth Gospel are demonstrably reliable relating to the original edition of the Fourth Gospel.**
- **The date of the Fourth Gospel agreed by all scholars, that is the end of the first century and the beginning of the second, is within the possible lifespan of eye-witnesses of the life, death and resurrection of Jesus.**

If our New Testament manuscripts are not reliable texts related to the first edition of the Gospels in the first century AD, then it would be fruitless to discuss any question of their dating either from external or internal sources.

In *Bad, Mad or God?* I have already shown that our New Testament manuscripts are such.[10] I can summarise my argument there as follows:

> Thus we have an interesting paradox. Because the Christian scribes made mistakes in their transmission of the text (unlike the Jewish Massoretic scribes who were meticulous copyists[11]), and thus produced families of texts based upon common scribal errors or glosses, we cannot go back to a single original later than the beginning of the second century AD. *And because the variations between those early manuscripts are generally speaking minute, we can be certain that the unknown original manuscript on which all depended did not differ significantly from the manuscripts we have before us.*[12]

In addition, we have a special piece of evidence regarding the Fourth Gospel. May I quote briefly again the summary of my argument in *Bad, Mad or God?*:

> "P[52], Papyrus Rylands Greek 457", is "a small piece of papyrus, 3.5 by 2.3 inches in size, with seven lines of writing on each side".[13] On one side is John 18:31-33,

and on the other side is John 18:37-38, the account of the trial of Jesus in the Fourth Gospel. C.H. Roberts, who first studied and published his results in *An Unpublished Fragment of the Fourth Gospel* (Manchester: the Manchester University Press, 1935) concluded that P[52] is to be dated between 94 and 127.[14] This dating is accepted without question in the demanding world of New Testament scholarship.[15]

Potential eye-witness testimony

The *terminus ante quem,* the fixing of the latest date for the writing of the Fourth Gospel, has been determined by the discovery of papyrus P[52] mentioned above. The fragment was discovered in Egypt, and as we have seen, cannot be dated later than 130 AD.

Thus it is clear that John's Gospel was circulating in Egypt in that period:

> The theory that John was composed in Egypt has had little support. If, as is generally supposed, it was composed in Asia Minor (or even Syria) we must allow time for it to have reached Egypt and to have passed into common circulation there. Moreover, the Bodmer Papyri reflect partially different textual traditions of the Gospel, that is, P[66] is closer to the text we later find in Codex Sinaiticus; P[75] is almost the same as the text of Codex Vaticanus. The development of such variation must have required time. To sum up, the positive arguments seem to point to 100-110 as the latest plausible date for the writing of the Gospel, with strong probability favouring the earlier limit of 100.[16]

Brown, if anything, errs on the side of caution here. Unanimity is not common where Fourth Gospel scholars are concerned; but, as to the upper limit of the date of the Gospel, such unanimity exists. Nineteenth century theories dating the Gospel to the end of the second century, together with emerging Gnosticism, have all been abandoned.[17] J.A.T.

Robinson graphically presents the consensus in his *Redating the New Testament*:

> With marginal variation at each end (and even Bultmann goes down as far as 80 for the first composition), the span 90-100 is agreed by Catholic and Protestant, by conservative and radical, by those who defend apostolic authorship and those who reject it, by those who believe that John used the synoptists and those who do not.[18]

We can therefore be safe at putting the upper limit, the *terminus ante quem*, at somewhere at the turn of the second century AD. But could the Fourth Gospel have been written even earlier? Robinson thinks so, and it is at least challenging to reflect briefly on his position, carefully, expertly, and painstakingly argued as it is.

There is a strong Christian tradition to the effect that the Apostle John, the Son of Zebedee, lived to a great age, in fact into the reign of the Emperor Trajan (98-117). Presuming that Jesus died about 30 AD, and that John then was a disciple of 20-30 years of age, then he could have lived to 110 AD, the date universally agreed as the *terminus ante quem* of the Fourth Gospel. His great age is testified to by Irenaeus, Bishop of Lyons who lived at the end of the second century, and is our main testimony to John apart from the evidence internal to the Gospel itself. Irenaeus also said that John wrote his Gospel after the other three.[19]

From this, both some elements of early Christian tradition and most modern scholars have taken Irenaeus to mean that John also wrote his Gospel when he was of a great age. But Robinson questions whether this was in fact the case; and whether there was a possibility that the Fourth Gospel was written much earlier, in fact before 70 AD when the Roman armies defeated the rebellious Jews, sacked the Temple, carried off many Jews into slavery, and turned Jerusalem effectively into a Roman camp.

Robinson produces many arguments to the effect that the writing of St John's Gospel reflects a period *before* the destruction of Jerusalem in 70 AD rather than *after* it. Not many scholars have accepted Robinson's view of an earlier possible date, although his reasoning is as always intriguing. But at least there is first of all an increasing consensus among the scholars that, even if the final edition of the Gospel is as late as the nearly unanimous scholarly opinion, at least parts of John go back to an early pre-Gospel tradition of the life and teaching of Jesus. This is since the epoch-making studies of C.H. Dodd in *The Historical Tradition in the Fourth Gospel.*[20]

Following Dodd, and in keeping with his own theory of the staged composition of the Fourth Gospel which we will be considering later, Brown dates "Stage 1 of the composition of the Gospel to the period between 40 and 60".[21] That is indeed early. But regarding the final edition of the Gospel, Brown gives the earliest date at around 80:

> There is a reasonably precise indication for the *terminus post quem* for the dating of John in the theme of excommunication from the synagogue which, as we saw in Part V; B, plays an important role in the Gospel. The problem does not seem to have been acute before 70; and the datable incidents like the formulation of the twelfth blessing in the *Shemoneh Esreh* and the use of formal excommunication at Jamnia belong to the period 80-90. This evidence makes unlikely a date before 80 for the final written composition of the Gospel, and indeed makes the 90s the probable era.[22]

But Robinson is highly sceptical of Brown's, and others', interpretation of John's reference to excommunication here. The text concerns the reaction to the Jews when the man is born blind. His terrified parents were frightened even to admit their son had been healed because of the threat of excommunication: "His [the man born blind's] parents said this because they were afraid of the Jews; for the Jews had already agreed that anyone who confessed Jesus to be the Messiah would be put out of the synagogue" [John 9:22].

The general critical opinion is that Jewish Christians were excommunicated after 70 AD. Thus the date of the final edition of John is fixed at its lower limit at this year. But Robinson is equally sceptical of this argument. He argues first

114

that the wording of the Benediction referred to by Brown was expressly intended "against Hebrew Christians of an extreme Judaizing kind, for whom the fourth gospel would have been anathema".[23] Secondly, Robinson argues that the idea of Christians being excommunicated is expressed in other words in the New Testament much earlier than a late John (e.g. Acts 13:45-50, 1 Thessalonians 2:14).[24]

It is not necessary now to go into Robinson's arguments in detail. What is important to emphasise at this stage is that there are arguments for an earlier date for John from a distinguished New Testament scholar. These arguments at least should enable us to date the Fourth Gospel from 60 AD at the earliest to 110 AD at the latest. Either end of this dating is within the lifetime of an eye-witness of the events of Jesus' life in the first thirty years of the first century AD, and well within the lifetime of second-hand witnesses, i.e. those who knew those who were eye-witnesses.

NOTES – INTRODUCTION AND CHAPTER SIX

1   BMG, 156-172.
2   Cf. below, 285-6, *Commentaries on St. John's Gospel.* I used extensively the more detailed commentaries, especially those by Barrett, Brown, Carson, and Schackenburg. These provide comprehensive introductions to the Gospel, examining the evidence fully, with varied but judicious conclusions.
3   DCG, 869-70.
4   BMG, 22-25.
5   MGI.
6   FG, 7. With reference to the Apostles Creed, the authors of *The Five Gospels* state "The figure in this creed is a mythical or heavenly figure, whose connection with the sage from Nazareth is limited to his suffering and death under Pontius Pilate". Of the seventy or so American scholars who in the *Jesus Seminar* decided both that the Fourth Gospel was devoid of substantial historical content, and that the doctrine of the Incarnation itself was a myth included, for instance, Robert Fortna, whose radical redaction theory we will consider later.
7   MGI, 4. John Hick, editor, states: "the later stages of that development (i.e. the early Christian development of the doctrine of the Incarnation) were greatly influenced by the evidence of the Fourth Gospel

understood in a straightforwardly historical way. How else could one interpret a Jesus who said 'Before Abraham was, I am' and 'I and my Father are one'? As I was still being taught in my confirmation class, such a Jesus must be either 'mad, bad or God'. But if the Fourth Gospel is understood in a less straightforwardly historical way (as on general critical grounds I believe it has to be) then its implications for doctrine may prove to be somewhat different from what they appeared to earlier ages to be."

8 Göttingen, Vandenhoeck and Ruprecht, 1941, 3.
9 Bultmann, 12.
10 BMG, 75-78.
11 Kenyon, 1939, 37-8.
12 BMG, 78.
13 Finegan, 1975, 85.
14 Finegan summarises Roberts' conclusions:"Palaeographically, the way individual letters are formed has been compared (Roberts, *op.cit.* pp.13-16) most closely with papyri of the end of the first or beginning of the second century, among them ones bearing dates corresponding to 94 AD and 127 AD. It is probable, therefore, that the present papyrus also belongs at the end of the first or beginning of the second century, at all events hardly later than 125 AD. Since the text is of the Gospel according to John, the papyrus is evidence that that Gospel was circulating in Egypt already at this date. As a copy of such date of a portion of a New Testament text, the papyrus is our presently earliest known fragment of any part of the New Testament". Finegan, 1975, 86.
15 BMG, 161-2.
16 Brown, I, LXXXIII.
17 Brown, I, LXXX11.
18 Robinson, 1976, 261.
19 Robinson, 1976, 257.
20 Dodd, 1965.
21 Brown, I, LXXXIV.
22 Brown, I, LXXXV.
23 Robinson, 1976, 273.
24 Robinson, 1976, 273-4.

CHAPTER SEVEN

INFLUENCES ON
THE FOURTH GOSPEL WRITER

- Influences upon which are alien to Christianity, such as Gnosticism and Greek philosophy, are not demonstrably present in the Fourth Gospel such as to make the author of that Gospel dependent upon those ideas.

- On the other hand, Semitic influences such as evidenced in Qumran, Jewish Apocalyptic and Rabbinic Judaism, are clearly present, showing that the Gospel is most credibly a Jewish document of the first century AD.

- The author of the Fourth Gospel is not dependent upon the Synoptic Gospels to the extent that Matthew, Mark and Luke are dependent one upon each other; although it is most likely that John knew any one, two, or all three of them.

- Contained within the narrative of the Fourth Gospel is an "historical tradition" (C.H. Dodd) of words and deeds of Jesus going back earlier than the composition of the Gospel itself.

- There is no clear evidence of significant influence by St Paul or his writings, even though the author clearly shares the same Christian faith.

We first have to ask how important were external influences on the genesis of the Fourth Gospel, or indeed of Christianity in general. It is no argument against the truth of Christianity that it used patterns of thought originally alien to itself, in particular Hellenistic ideas. That is particularly important if we remember that the scholars date the Fourth Gospel towards the end of the first century AD. We would expect that any new movement would engage in a fruitful dialogue with other forms of thought. The writer of the Fourth Gospel, whoever he or she was, would have had decades in which to develop, using all the intellectual tools to hand. The extent to which the new movement was able to assimilate ideas originally alien to itself would be a sign of its strength, not of its weakness.

On the other hand, it would be decisive against Christianity if we discovered that there was nothing distinctive about its doctrines, but that they were merely a copy of the religious and philosophical movements of the time. Nor would the Johannine picture of Jesus of Nazareth then be credible, since all point out the essentially Jewish character of the Jesus of the Synoptic tradition.

In the fourth and fifth centuries, the Christian theological genius Augustine of Hippo (354-430),[1] was well aware of the parallels between Christian ideas and the philosophy current in his own day, and yet also the distinctiveness of Christian teaching. C.H. Dodd began his *The Interpretation of the Fourth Gospel* with a quotation from St Augustine who, in a passage of the *Confessions* (vii. 9), writes:

Thou didst procure for me through a certain person – some books of the Platonists translated from Greek into Latin. There I read – not in so many words, but in substance, supported by many arguments of various kinds – that in the beginning was the Word, and the Word was with God, and the Word was God. The same was in the beginning with God. By him were all things made, and without him was not anything made. That which was made in him was life, and the life was the light of men. And the light shineth in darkness and the darkness comprehended it not. And that the soul of man, though it bear witness of the light, is not itself the light; but the Word of God, being God, is the true light that lighteth every man that cometh into the world. And that he was in the world and the world was made by him, and the world knew him not. But that he came unto his own and his own received him not, but as many as received him to them gave he power to become sons of God, even to them that believe on his name, I did not read there. Again I read there that God the Word was born not of the flesh nor of blood, nor of the will of man, nor of the will of the flesh, but of God. But that the Word was made flesh and dwelt among us I did not read there.[2]

Augustine recognises striking similarities of terminology and of ideas between the Fourth Gospel and Greek philosophy. But at the same time, Augustine saw the difference between Greek philosophy and John, namely that only in John does *the Word become flesh* [John 1:14]. This essential difference which Augustine perceived eventually led him back to Catholic Christianity and out of the Gnostic Manichaean heresy[3] to which he was attached for some time. Incidentally, this difference was apparently as clearly perceived by scholars at the time when Westcott wrote his classic Commentary in its original edition in 1880: "It is admitted on all hands that this central affirmation, 'The Word became flesh', which underlies all he wrote, is absolutely new and unique'.[4]

Much more than the Synoptic Gospels, St John's Gospel, most of all in its Prologue [John 1:1-18], seems to breathe the air of the Hellenism which was essentially the culture of the whole of the Roman Empire. Furthermore, as more and more Gentiles were converted to the new Christian faith, it became increasingly necessary to express the Christian faith in Greek as well as Jewish terms. This process culminated in the great Christological Councils, defining the Church's Christology, in the fourth and fifth centuries. But it began with St Paul in the fifties and sixties AD.

The most serious question was thus raised by Augustine centuries ago. Can the idea that the divine *logos* became flesh, that is became human and lived among us as the divine glory [John 1:14] be found anywhere else in the philosophical and religious literature of the first century AD?

Plato?

Christianity spread phenomenally in the first and second centuries AD, when the most influential philosophy was that of **Plato** (427-347 BC).[5] As Dodd explains, "The theory of a world of eternal forms, of which phenomena are the shadows, reflections, or symbols, had found wide acceptance, and in one form or another it reappears in various types of religious philosophy in the Hellenistic world".[6] In his famous cave,

Plato sees the human being looking away from the light on to the wall of a cave. All he sees are flickering shadows caused by a reflection of the light behind him.

Dodd links the idea in John's Gospel of the "true light" [1:8b] i.e. the "genuine light" (*to phós to aléthinon*) with Platonism. The Logos is the eternal form of God, rather than simply a phenomenon or a shadow. If you like, the Logos is the light shining into the cave.

Stoicism?

Equally important was **Stoicism**, a school of philosophy founded at Athens by Zeno of Citium (335-263 BC). "The system may be described as a form of materialistic pantheism or monism in contrast to Platonic idealism on the one hand and Epicurean hedonism on the other."[7] Stoicism itself had a strong Logos doctrine. For the Stoic, the Logos was the World Reason, not transcendent and omnipotent as the Judaeo-Christian God, but the all-pervading rational principle of the universe. To live ethically consisted in living one's life in conformity with this Logos.

Clearly, John has affinities in terminology with Plato and Stoicism. But, as Augustine had already perceived, Plato could not foresee in his philosophy the Eternal Ideas becoming incarnate in a single human individual; nor could the Stoic see the eternal Logos being fully expressed in a human individual. Any educated Greek would have been acquainted with Platonism and Stoicism. After all, they had been in currency in the Greek world for centuries, transmitted in the Middle East originally by Alexander the Great when he conquered the known world in 333 BC. But no one would suggest, or has suggested, that the fundamental ideas of the Fourth Gospel took their origin from Greek philosophy. The differences are too great.

John may have used Platonic and Stoic ideas in his Gospel in order to express his faith in Jesus of Nazareth as the *logos*. But he did not receive his central idea about Christ as the *logos* become flesh from Plato nor from the Stoa. The case is entirely similar regarding Philo of Alexandria.

Philo?

Philo of Alexandria (c.20 BC–c.59 AD)was a Jewish thinker and exegete[8] who belonged to a wealthy priestly family in Alexandria, Egypt. During the last two centuries BC Alexandria became a Jewish colony of great importance. Apparently more Jews lived there than in their own land. It was at Alexandria that the translation from Hebrew into Greek of the Old Testament at least began, called the Septuagint (LXX),[9] it was to become the Christian Old Testament. Alexandria was an important meeting point for Old Testament ideas and Greek philosophy.

Little is known about Philo, except that in 39 AD he took part in a delegation to Rome to plead the Jewish cause. But his extant writings are voluminous. He used the allegorical method of interpretation of the Old Testament, seeing the events of the Old Testament as archetypes. In this way, he paved the way for the Christian Alexandrian interpretation of the Old Testament. Philo used the expression Logos. But, as Dodd says, "In spite of all personification, Philo is not thinking of a personal guide and companion. The Logos is the world of Ideas. Knowledge of God comes by the unseen archetypes".[10] Dodd was convinced that Philo was significant for Johannine thought.[11] As far as I can see, there would not be much of a problem if he were, particularly since we are dealing with a first century Jewish thinker. Why should not John have been influenced by Philo, particularly if Philo helped the evangelist understand the nature of Christ more profoundly?

Brown puts it more soberly. "Personally, we believe that the evidence points rather toward a common background shared by both Philo and John. Perhaps Braun, *Jean Théol,* II, p.298, has phrased it best: if Philo had never existed, the Fourth Gospel would most probably not have been any different from what it is."[12] In other words, there is no solid evidence that John, contemporary with Philo, ever used him. But if he did, the central incarnational idea of Christianity is in any case not found in Philo's thinking, and we must look for another source of the Christian doctrine of the Word become flesh.

Gnostic movements?

A more serious challenge apparently came from what some scholars have suggested, and have even thought they have demonstrated, namely that the central ideas of the Fourth Gospel originated in Greek philosophical and religious movements in the early Christian centuries. These scholars would insist that the Fourth Gospel had imported an alien idea into the Christian community towards the close of the first century AD, as part of its evolution. This idea was induced through the Hermetic literature, Philo, Gnosticism, and the Mandaean Gnostic sect. The conclusion, if such a theory was accepted, would be that the essential ideas in the Gospels, and in particular in the Gospel of John, about Christianity do not derive at all from the historical Jesus, but from some other religious movement. We should therefore not call ourselves "Christians", but Gnostics. But the evidence for these movements changing Christianity essentially is thin. Let us take each in turn.

The Hermetic literature?

In Egypt, in the second and third centuries AD, a body of Greek literature grew up attributed to a Hermes Trismegistus, a legendary sage of ancient Egypt believed to have been deified as the god Thoth (=Hermes).[13] As Dodd explains, the Hermetic religion was its own combination of Platonic and Stoic philosophy, which philosophical cocktail "was one of the fore-runners of neo-Platonism".[14]

Most of the Hermetic writings are later than that of the Fourth Gospel. But some scholars have suggested that their "hypothetical early stages are used to explain the thought of the fourth evangelist". A better explanation might be that in the similarities the two literatures share (e.g. vocabulary like "light", "life", "word") they are both dependent on a theological terminology more ancient than either of them; namely, the terminology that sprang from the combination of Oriental speculation on Wisdom and Greek abstract thought. Such a combination is already exemplified in the pre-Christian period in the deuterocanonical Book of Wisdom".[15] This emphasises the importance of the knowledge which the author of the Fourth Gospel has of the late Wisdom literature of the Bible. But it says little of any real evidence for the influence of the Hermetic literature on the Fourth Gospel.[16]

The Gospel of Thomas?

Gnosticism was a bewildering complex of "new age" philosophies and practices, which mainly flowered in the early Christian era in the Roman Empire. The basis of Gnosticism was that, by a prescribed system, the initiate could attain to true "knowledge" (*gnôsis*). Gnosticism was dualistic, to the extent that it recommended escape from the world of matter, which was essentially evil. Escape was either by extreme asceticism, or extreme hedonism. Gnosticism was linked to Platonism, to the extent that Plato's world of ideas led to an elevation of the spiritual at the expense of the material.

In 1947, at Chenoboskion in Egypt, there was the important discovery of a group of Gnostic documents in Coptic.[17] One of the Gnostic Gospels, *The Gospel of Truth*, and another *The Gospel of Thomas*, have been compared with St John's Gospel. *The Gospel of Truth* is developed Gnosticism, but *The Gospel of Thomas* is more primitive. Yet, as Brown says, "there is still a considerable distance between John and *Thomas*, for characteristically Johannine terms are used in *Thomas* in a manner quite different from Johannine usage".[18]

The Odes of Solomon?

In similar vein, Schnackenburg[19] makes a detailed comparison between the Gospel of John and the *Odes of Solomon*, which are also linked with second-century AD Egyptian Gnosticism. Ode 11,6, for instance says "And speaking waters touched my lips from the fountain of the Lord plenteously; and I drank and was inebriated with the living water that doth not die; and my inebriation was not one without knowledge". This is reminiscent of John's dialogue with the Samaritan woman at the well:

> Jesus said to her, "Everyone who drinks of this water will be thirsty again, but those who drink of the water that I will give them will never be thirsty. The water that I will give will become in them a spring of water gushing up to eternal life." [John 4:13-14]

But again, Schnackenburg insists, expressions are used which depart from the Johannine usage; there is no personal relationship with the spiritual life given by Jesus, as in John; and regarding dependence, it is much less likely for Schnackenburg that John depends on the Odes of Solomon; "the dependence is rather the other way round".[20]

The dependence of the Gnostic literature on the Christian is even more likely granted the dates of the two sources. There is no sure evidence of pre-Christian Gnosticism. All the hard evidence we have about Gnosticism post-dates Christian sources, and comes from the middle of the second century onwards. Regarding the *Gospel of Thomas*, Meier quotes Ménard as saying that "The Greek original [of the Gospel of Thomas]... has always been dated about AD 140, and there are so far no reasons to modify that conclusion". He places the Coptic version at the end of the second century.[21] This means that the presumption must be that the Christian sources inspired Gnosticism rather than the other way round. An examination of the Mandaean material leads to an ever firmer conclusion in that direction.

The Mandaeans?

The Mandaean religion is practised at the present day in a small community resident in Iraq. Their sacred writings are written in a dialect of Aramaic. None of the manuscripts is older than the sixteenth century. Palaeography cannot trace them back earlier than 700 AD, the early Islamic period. As

Dodd immediately says in his detailed consideration of the Mandaean hypothesis:[22] "For any history of the Mandaeans and their beliefs before 700 we are dependent solely on inference and speculation".[23] Speculation there indeed has been, by considerable scholars such as M. Lidzbarski, R. Reitzenstein, and R. Bultmann.

The Mandaeans were a Gnostic sect. Dodd calls their writings a "farrago", without any consistency of thought. "But in its main intention it is based upon a dualism not unlike that of the Manichees".[24] The soul in the world is a prisoner, tormented by the powers of evil. That soul might win through by the due performances of the Mandaean ritual, "combined with the communication of a myth which declares that the powers of light have already overcome the powers of darkness".[25]

As Dodd describes it, the redeemer myth of the Mandaeans is bizarre and difficult to comprehend.

> He says, "I am God, the Son of God, whom my father has sent here." He declares to you, "I am the first Messenger, I am Hibil-Ziwa, who am come from on high." But confess him not, for he is not Hibil-Ziwa. Hibil-Ziwa is not clothed with fire. Hibil-Ziwa does not reveal himself in that age. On the contrary, Enosh-Uthra comes and betakes himself to Jerusalem, clothed with a garment of water – clouds. He walks in bodily form, yet he is clothed with no bodily garment. There is no fiery wrath in him. He goes and comes in the years of Paltus (Pilate), the king of the world. Enosh-Uthra comes into the world with the might of the high King of Light. He heals the sick, makes the blind to see, cleanses the lepers, lifts up the crippled who crawl upon the ground, so that they can walk, makes the deaf and dumb to speak, and raises the dead. He wins believers among the Jews, and shows them: There is life and there is death, there is darkness and there is light, there is error and there is truth. He converts the Jews to the name of the high King of Light.[26]

In effect, for the Mandaeans, there is a Christ and an anti-Christ. Hibil Ziwa is in the end overcome by the true Christ Enosh-Uthra. Another strand of the Mandaean documents tells of the birth of Johana (=John the Baptist), and of Jesus Christ coming to receive baptism from John in humility. But then this Jesus "perverts the speech of Johana, alters the baptism in Jordan, perverts the words of the truth, and preaches blasphemy and deceit in the world".[27]

The theory of Lidzbarski, Reitzenstein, and Bultmann is that Mandaeanism goes back in a primitive form to the first century AD, and that a group of Nazoreans [cf. Matthew 2:23] or proto-Mandaeans were the original followers of the Baptist. These three scholars claim that Christianity grew out of the Baptist sect, and in the end rebelled against it. Evidence for this is thought to be found in Acts 19:1-7, where a group of the followers of the Baptist are told the more perfect way of Christ and are baptised. This conceals, it is maintained, an underlying Baptist group which was really the Nazarean sect, and which eventually Christianity supplanted.

Bultmann claimed that the Redeemer myth, expressed in the Gospel of John, originated in the Mandaean redeemer. To argue this, Dodd explains, he "sets out a formidable list of parallels".[28] But Dodd argues that in no case is there any evidence that John's Gospel is dependent on the Mandaean documents; and reminds us that our manuscript evidence for John goes back to the fourth century (not to mention the fragment P[52] to be dated 150) whereas for the Mandaean we have extant manuscripts only of the sixteenth century!

The Pope understandably characterises Bultmann's certainty that "its (the Mandaean sources) *greater age* remain firmly established" as "breathtaking".[29] Schnackenburg perhaps gives us the clue why Bultmann lent his heavyweight authority behind this fantastic theory. There remains the most difficult problem which Bultmann posed at the start: is not the basic Johannine concept of the heavenly envoy, the revealer, who as revealer brings redemption, fully intelligible only in the light of the Gnostic "myth of the redeemer", and is not this myth impressively displayed by the Mandaean texts?[30]

We are back to the fundamental Bultmann problem. If

the historical Jesus is no longer the source of the ideas of the Fourth Gospel, then the "history of religion" school must search elsewhere – perhaps anywhere – to find its source, however hypothetical a source that might be.

But we do not need to seek in Gnosticism for any "redeemer myth". If, as we have demonstrated *Bad, Mad or God?*,[31] Jesus himself claimed to be the transcendent Messiah (cf. Psalm 110), then there is a whole strand of thought in the Old Testament by means of which the early Christians, and more than likely Jesus himself, links this Messiah to suffering for Israel, not least the Servant Songs in Isaiah. Cf. Isaiah 53:7-8, Acts 8:28-33, where the Ethiopian eunuch has that passage in Isaiah interpreted for him by Philip the deacon.[32]

To summarise, therefore, we have no clear evidence that the Fourth Gospel was influenced at its main source by alien streams of thinking such as Gnosticism, the Hermetic Literature, or Mandaeanism. On the contrary, all the evidence suggests that it is more likely that the Fourth Gospel influenced other religions such as Gnosticism or Mandaeanism. As for Plato, Philo, and Stoicism, there is no reason why the early Christian writers, and particularly the writer of the Fourth Gospel, should not have been influenced by them. But these philosophical currencies in no way can explain the distinctive ideas in the Fourth Gospel itself.

Positively, therefore, we are beginning to gain an impression of a writer who is highly cultured. He (we will assume at least for the moment that the author is male) is fully knowledgeable of Greek philosophical ideas current at the close of the first century AD, but not so as to embrace fully any of them. Rather, as a man of letters, the writer uses those philosophical ideas to put over a most distinctive and novel idea of his own, as we saw immediately when we quoted Augustine of Hippo, that the *logos* became flesh.

That impression grows still further when we consider Jewish influences on the writer of the Fourth Gospel. He is a cultured *literatus*, knowledgeable of Gentile philosophical and religious ideas, but above all he is a Jew of the first Christian era.

John's Gospel, a Jewish document of the first century AD – Qumran

We have already referred to the view that the ideas in the Fourth Gospel about Jesus as the eternal Son of God, the Logos, had their origin in Greek thinking rather than Jewish Christianity. This, as we have seen, was the general view in New Testament criticism during the first half of the twentieth century. Since the Second World War, however, this situation has changed, to the extent that, while acknowledging parallels with Greek contemporary thought, Raymond Brown, perhaps the foremost Catholic New Testament exegete in the last quarter of the twentieth century, in his 1966 Anchor Bible Commentary, reflects a growing scholarly emphasis upon the Jewishness of John:

> It is no accident that Jesus is called a rabbi more frequently in John than in any other Gospel. Moreover, in John the thought of Jesus is expressed in a peculiar theological vocabulary that we now know to have been used by an important Jewish heterodox group in Palestine.[33]

Brown is referring to the Qumran sect, whose scrolls were discovered on the shores of the Dead Sea in 1947. At first, the media made sensationalist statements about the threat to Christianity which this discovery made. But now, a more sober assessment has reversed that judgement. The differences between Qumran and Christianity are indeed much greater than the similarities. On the other hand, parallels are significant. Ideas which in the nineteenth century were said to prove the Hellenistic origin of John's ideas, such as his contrast between darkness and light [1:4-5,9], Jesus as the truth [14:6], and the Spirit of Truth [14:17,26], are present in the documents of the first century AD in Judea and are thoroughly Semitic.

Furthermore, we are sure that the ideas in Qumran pre-date the Gospel of John. This contrasts strongly with what we have seen regarding Gnosticism, for which we only have positive evidence after the first century AD. The Qumran monastery was destroyed in 68 AD, and existed for a century and a half before it.[34] So it is at least possible that Qumran has influenced St John's Gospel, or more likely shared a common influence, for instance in its dualism opposing light and darkness, good and evil. Brown sums up "What can be said is that for *some* features of Johannine thought and vocabulary the Qumran literature offers a closer parallel than any other contemporary or earlier non-Christian literature either in Judaism or in the Hellenistic world. And, in fact, for such features Qumran offers a better parallel than even the later, post-Johannine Mandean or Hermetic writings".[35]

Brown still concludes that "In our judgement the parallels are not close enough to suggest a direct literary dependence of John upon the Qumran literature, but they do suggest Johannine familiarity with the type of thought exhibited in the scrolls. (We must allow the possibility that this thought and vocabulary were not the exclusive property of the Qumran Essenes)".[36] Brown here refers to a Jewish heretical movement which flourished in Judaism called the Essene movement, well known to scholars before the discovery of the Scrolls, and with whom the Qumran sect has been identified. The Essenes were a pious sect which originated in the second century BC and disappeared from view in the second century AD.[37]

Is it possible that John the Baptist, and indeed Jesus himself, were influenced by the Qumran Essenes? This is certainly a more fascinating and plausible influence than a Greek Gnosticism we only know from the second century. After all, the Qumran monastery was on the shores of the Dead Sea during the first century AD, by the Judean desert where John the Baptist was preaching [Matthew 3:1]. We know also that Jesus followed John into the desert, and was baptised by him [Matthew 3:13 \\]. There are significant differences between Qumran and John. Qumran has no idea of the message of repentance addressed to the whole world, central to John's proclamation, nor of the healing miracles as a sign of the coming kingdom, central to Jesus' original message. But perhaps their thought worlds were even closer than that admitted by Brown, due to a geographical contact in the Judean desert of the first century.

129

A recent book by Paula Fredriksen, *Jesus of Nazareth King of the Jews: A Jewish Life and the Emergence of Christianity*, does not flinch from seeing the radical implications for Johannine study which the discovery of the Qumran scrolls demands, implications which Fourth Gospel scholarship has yet fully to draw out:

> Before the Scrolls' recovery for example, many scholars regarded the Gospel of John as presenting a very Hellenized fundamentally non-Jewish image of Jesus. They consequently discounted this Gospel as both late and intrinsically non-historical, and they favoured the synoptic tradition (Matthew, Mark and Luke) when in search of the Jesus of history. The discovery of the Scrolls – whose place, date, and completely Jewish context is very secure – undermined this view of the Fourth Gospel. For the Scrolls like John speak the language of Children of Light and Children of Darkness; they too, envisage struggle between the two realms. One need not posit then, as earlier scholars did, that such language and thinking point to a late or non-Jewish origin for John's Gospel. The Scrolls incontrovertibly show that early first century Jewish Jews spoke and thought in similar ways. And an earlier Jewish context of composition for John's Gospel then reopens the question of its historical value for reconstructing Jesus' life.[38]

It is precisely the purpose of this book to take Johannine scholarship forward as a result of discoveries such as at Qumran, as Fredriksen wishes, and, as does the Pope in *Jesus of Nazareth*, to reopen the question of the historical value of the Fourth Gospel for reconstructing Jesus' life.

Apocalyptic literature?

Another fascinating line of enquiry is the link between the Fourth Gospel and late Jewish apocalyptic, especially late Jewish non-biblical works, such as the (Ethiopic) Enoch (300 BC), the Book of Jubilees (second century) and the Assumption of Moses.[39] This literature in particular used the Book of Daniel, written in the second century BC during the Maccabaean period, claiming heavenly revelations from ancient patriarchs like Enoch and Moses. The Fourth Gospel has almost certainly a reference to Daniel 7:14 in John 5:25-27: "Very truly, I tell you, the hour is coming, and is now here, when the dead will hear the voice of the Son of God, and those who hear will live. For just as the Father has life in himself, so he has granted the Son also to have life in himself; and he has given him authority to execute judgment, because he is the Son of Man".

Barrett[40] thinks indeed that this is the case:

> As I watched in the night visions, I saw one like a human being coming with the clouds of heaven. And he came to the Ancient One and was presented before him. To him was given dominion and glory and kingship that all peoples, nations, and languages should serve him. His dominion is an everlasting dominion that shall not pass away, and his kingship is one that shall never be destroyed.

In Daniel, the one coming is "like a son of man" (*k͑ bar ͑nash*), in Greek Daniel *hós `uios anthrópou*, similar to John "because he is the Son of Man" (*hoti huios anthrópou estin*). Also the one like the human being, like the son of man, is "given dominion and glory and kingship". We have examined the use of the exalted "Son of Man" in *Bad, Mad or God?*, by Jesus himself, and demonstrated their authenticity, as a means of expressing his self-identity.[41] Clearly, apocalyptic was an important theological *genre* in Judaism of the first century AD.

Now we come on to those strains of influence which are certainly to be found in the Fourth Gospel. These are all that we would expect from an author who is writing a formative Christian Gospel in the second half of the first century AD and who is writing about events which happened in the Roman province of Syria between 27 and 33 AD.

Rabbinic Judaism?

Rabbinic Judaism is that huge and important body of ideas which was crystallised after the Fall of Jerusalem in 70 AD and the Council of Jamnia, thought to have taken place about 100 AD.[42] There is no doubt that the formation of what we know now as Rabbinic Judaism was influenced by the growth of Christianity, and which the post-Jamnia movement saw as a kind of counter-Reformation, a return to the roots of Judaism in response to the Christian movement. As a result, a large body of literature, called in general the Talmud (teaching) emerged. These teachings are Rabbinic commentary on the Old Testament.[43]

Now, the difficulty in assessing where the influence of these writings on St John's Gospel is concerned is that we often do not know how late or how early a particular teaching of Rabbinic Judaism is.[44] No doubt much of the Talmud is early, and pre-dates the beginning of the Christian era. But the Talmudic documents we possess today are very much later, well into the Christian era, after the fifth century AD. It is therefore quite possible that the Fourth Gospel, in its references to the Judaism current in the time of Jesus, is actually speaking about teaching, laws and customs which no longer applied after Jesus' own time.

One thing is clear; the author of the Fourth Gospel knew Rabbinic Judaism, and no doubt Rabbinic Judaism influenced his thought. The Fourth Gospel is aware not only of the Old Testament, but also of the Rabbinic interpretation of it. The Rabbis of Jesus' time interpreted the Old Testament according to their living tradition, which, according to the Synoptic Gospels, Jesus respected, "The scribes and the Pharisees sit on Moses' seat" [Matthew 23:2]; even if he disagreed sometimes with their conclusions [e.g. Mark 2:25].

C.H. Dodd brings out strongly the influence of Rabbinic Judaism on the thought of the Fourth Gospel. For instance, in John 7:22-24, Jesus defends his practice of healing on the Sabbath by saying that circumcision was allowed on the Sabbath. Dodd quotes more than one Jewish authority to the effect that "circumcision repels the Sabbath commandment".[45]

The author of the Fourth Gospel seems here to be well acquainted with the Rabbinic interpretation of the Sabbath law.[46]

Furthermore, the idea of the pre-existence of the Logos in John is paralleled with the idea of the pre-existence of the Torah in Judaism. "Seven things were created before the world was created; the Torah, Repentance, Paradise, Gehenna, the Throne of Glory, the Sanctuary, and the Name of the Messiah."[47] Again, we do not know when Rabbinic Judaism introduced these speculations about the Torah. Was it possibly influenced by Christianity? What is important, however, is that Judaism saw no problem in teaching the pre-existence of the Torah, just as the Fourth Gospel taught the pre-existence of Jesus as the Logos, and linked Jesus with the idea of the Torah, claiming that he himself claimed to be the Way [John 14:6] (the *halakah*, the moral interpretation of the Law). Here is evidence of an intra-Jewish debate, where the author of the Fourth Gospel is presenting very much a Jewish Jesus.

Likewise, there was Judaistic speculation about the Word of God, the *memra*. The Logos was the Son of God, just as the Torah was the daughter of God.[48] Westcott, well over a century ago, made the same connection as did Dodd much later:

> In the Targum of Onkelos on the Pentateuch, which is the oldest in date, the action of God is constantly though not consistently referred to as "His Word" (Memra, *mymr*, *mymr'*). Thus it is said that the Lord protected Noah by His word, when he entered the ark" (Genesis 7:16) that He "made a covenant between Abraham and His word" (Genesis 17:2); that the word of the Lord was with Ishmael in the wilderness (21:20)...[49]

Westcott was convinced that the Rabbinic tradition which almost personified the Word, as it did the Torah, was early: "They [the Targums] were most probably not committed to writing in the shape in which we now have them, till some time after the Christian era; but all evidence goes to shew that they embody the interpretations which had been orally current from a much earlier time".[50] Far from the Fourth Gospel idea of the Logos being fundamentally a Greek idea, therefore, we only have to search in the Rabbinic tradition for very clear echoes of its explicitation.

The author of the Fourth Gospel, according to C.H. Dodd, was likewise well acquainted with Jewish Messianic expectations. "The Messiah of the Jews is to be a descendant of David, He is to appear no one knows whence, He is to work signs and to reign as king, and He is to abide for ever"[51] [cf. John 7:27,42, 12:34,]. For evidence of this Jewish background, Dodd draws not only upon the Targums, but upon late Jewish apocalyptic, such as the Similitudes of Enoch.[52]

Finally, the author of the Fourth Gospel, Dodd demonstrates, knows about Jewish Rabbinic reflection upon the Name of God. In the Jewish tradition, the Name of God JHWH (revealed first to Moses, cf. Exodus 3:13-15) was more and more withdrawn from public use, until eventually it was never used in the public reading of scripture. The name ADONAI (My Lord) was substituted whenever JHWH appeared in the text of the Old Testament. This reverence for the divine name was linked in Rabbinic thought with the coming of the Messiah in the age to come: "In this age the prayer of the Israelites is not heard, because they do not know the *shem hammephorash* (i.e. the mysterious name); but in the age to come God will reveal it to them".[53] Dodd then argues that Jesus' own self-designation in John, I AM (*egó eimi*) "That you may know that *egó eimi* [John 8:28] is in reality a translation of the Hebrew *'ani hu'* the divine name, that you may know that *'ani hu'*, I AM" [Isaiah 43:10].

In John, therefore, Jesus is revealing himself precisely as the secret name of God. [54] Especially important as it is in *Jesus of Nazareth* as part of the Pope's whole argument, Jesus' own self-designation,[55] is rooted solidly in Rabbinic Judaism, of which the writer of the Fourth Gospel shows ample knowledge. These Jewish roots are well established, in contrast with much less convincing Hellenistic and Gnostic speculations which we have looked at above.

The Old Testament?

The author of the Gospel of John is steeped in the Old Testament, which he knows deeply. Barrett sums up, "It seems that John regularly used the LXX in making his Old Testament quotations, but that he was capable of going direct to the Hebrew, and on occasion did so".[56] This is clearly a contrast, for instance, with the Letter to the Hebrews, whose author consistently uses the Septuagint, or is very close to it.[57] John is also very simple and straightforward in his use of the Old Testament, not using the Alexandrian allegorical interpretation. Barrett says "John's profound thematic usage, founded as it is upon the figure of Jesus, is hard to parallel. John also uses Old Testament material extensively in the symbolic language which abounds in his gospel. This is seen most clearly in the extended allegories of the Shepherd [10:1-16] and the Vine [15:1-6]. Neither of these looks back to a single Old Testament passage, but each is full of Old Testament imagery."[58] John again then works exactly as one would expect a Jew living in Israel in the first century AD.

Dodd has more than anyone else demonstrated that the true background of the Prologue was the Wisdom literature of the Old Testament. This again obviates the necessity of going outside Christianity to Hellenistic inspiration. Dodd draws the parallels which are vitally important to understand not only the Prologue, but the entire Christology of the Fourth Gospel. So Dodd compares "**In the beginning was the Word**" [John 1:1] with "The Lord created me **in the beginning of his ways**" [Proverbs 8:30], and "all things came to be through him" [John 1:3], as with "Wisdom is the architect of all things" [Wisdom 7:22]. [59]

Clearly, the author of the Prologue of the Fourth Gospel is equating Wisdom (Greek *sophia*) with the Logos. He uses Word rather than Sophia in his Prologue precisely because he wishes to look back first and foremost, not to the Wisdom literature, but to the even more important Torah, the book of Genesis 1:1. We remember that Torah refers not first and foremost to the Law, but to the *teaching* of God, primarily for the Jew expressed in the first five books of Moses, but even more "the totality of God's self-revelation":[60]

> **In the beginning** when God created the heavens and the earth, the earth was a formless void and darkness covered the face of the deep, while a wind from God swept over the face of the waters. Then God said, "Let there be light"; and there was light. [Genesis 1:1-3]

I have marked in bold the words used both in Genesis 1:1-3, Proverbs 8:30 and John 1:1-3. "In the beginning" reminds us immediately of Genesis. "Light" as a theme links both Genesis and Wisdom with the Prologue. But the author's masterstroke is to turn the verb (God said) into a noun (in the beginning was the Word), thus personalising the Logos. The verb "said" (in Hebrew *dabar*) occurs eight times in Chapter 1 of Genesis.[61]

John has found his ideas, not in Greek speculation, but in the Wisdom literature of the Old Testament, and even more that Wisdom literature read in the light of the book of Genesis, the Torah. All the evidence is consonant with the author being a Jew living in the Roman Province of Syria during the first century AD.

To summarise: The author of the Fourth Gospel is well acquainted with the Judaism of the first century in Palestine itself; both in its "unorthodox form", Qumran and the Essenes, and in its more "orthodox" vein in Apocalyptic, in Rabbinic Judaism, the Old Testament, and in particular late Wisdom. But his intimate knowledge of these ideas again does not take away from the distinctiveness of his own teaching. He is a cultured Jew of the first century AD, writing what we call a Gospel (remembering that the title "Gospel" was an ecclesiastical addition), transmitting his faith in Jesus as truly the divine Son of God in order to give the world the eternal life offered by Jesus as the risen and ascended Lord. The origin of that unique message, we submit, cannot come from anywhere but from within Christianity itself, most plausibly from the historical Jesus.

Dependence on the Synoptic Gospels?

Did John know and use the Synoptic Gospels? It is at least *a priori* likely, or at least possible, that John knew of them, because those Gospels, it is generally assumed, were written earlier than, or at least published in their final form before, the Fourth Gospel. The most popular theory, as we have discussed earlier,[62] usually called the Two Document Hypothesis,[63] is that Mark was written first, c.64 AD,[64] then Matthew second (75-90),[65] and Luke third, both about (80-85).[66] Therefore, unless there was complete isolation between the various Christian communities, there is a fair chance that the author of the Fourth Gospel was at least acquainted in some way or other with one, with two, or indeed with all three of the other Gospels. And even if he were demonstrably an eye-witness, this would not prevent him using other accounts of the life and teaching of Jesus to help him write his own account.

However we answer the question as to the dependence of the Fourth Gospel on the Synoptics, all agree that the dependence of John on Matthew, Mark and Luke, is not as great as their dependence on each other. Clearly (and this was evident to the early Church Fathers[67] as well as to modern criticism) Matthew, Mark and Luke have *copied* each other in some way or other. Even if a scholar does not accept the most popular Two Document Hypothesis, but one of the other solutions to the Synoptic Problem, all assume a truly *literary relationship* between the three Synoptic Gospels.

But the Fourth Gospel is not related in such a way that anyone could possibly say with similar certainty that John *copied* Mark, Matthew or Luke, only that he might have *used* them in some way or other. To demonstrate this point, it is worth setting out in *synopsis*, i.e. "looking together", at the four accounts of the Cleansing of the Temple by Jesus:

Matthew 21:12-13	Mark 11:15-17	Luke 19:45-46	John 2:14-17
v.12 And Jesus went into the Temple, and cast out all those who were buying and selling in the Temple; and he turned over the tables of the money changers and the stools of those who sold pigeons	v.15b And (Jesus) went into the Temple, and going in he cast out those who were buying and selling in the Temple; and he turned over the tables of the money changers and the stools of those who sold pigeons v.16 and he did not allow anyone carrying anything through the Temple courtyards.	v.19 And Jesus went into the Temple and began to cast out the merchants	v.14 And (Jesus) found in the Temple those who were selling cattle, sheep and pigeons, and also the money changers sitting at their tables. v.15 And making a whip out of chords he drove all of them out of the Temple; and he overturned the tables of the money changers and scattered their coins. v.16 and to those who sold the pigeons he said, 'Take these out of here! Do not make my Father's house a market place!'
v.13 And he said to them, 'It is written, '**My house shall be called a house of prayer**, but you have made it a den of thieves'	v.17 and he taught them saying, 'Is it not written that **My House shall be called a house of prayer for all the nations? But you have made it into a den of thieves!**	v.46 And he said to them, 'It is written, **My house shall be a house of prayer**; but you have made it a den of thieves'	v.17 His disciples remembered that it was written, '**The zeal; of your house has consumed me**'.

The reader will immediately notice that Matthew, Mark and Luke are very similar in wording, with only the occasional variation (e.g. Mark's reference to Jesus stopping anyone carrying anything through the Temple courtyards). But then, regarding the Fourth Gospel, we find that the wording of John is very different. For example, the scripture quotation, 'the zeal of your house has consumed me' [Psalm 69:9], does not appear in the Synoptics; while the Synoptic proof text from the Old Testament appears in various forms, "My house shall be called a house of prayer, but you have made it a den of thieves." a conflation of two texts, Isaiah 56:7 and Jeremiah 7:11. Similarly, John refers to a whip of chords, not mentioned by the Synoptics: all four state that Jesus turned over the tables of the money-changers; but only John has Jesus addressing the pigeon sellers directly. It does not seem that John was copying Matthew, Mark, and Luke in their present form, even if he might have been influenced by their account in one way or another, or perhaps by a third account of the Cleansing of the Temple which we do not now have to hand.

Since Gardner-Smith's study in 1938, who noticed these literary differences throughout the Fourth Gospel, in comparison with the Synoptics, it has been less and less common for Johannine scholars to uphold the theory that John is based on any of the Synoptics.[68] But if John did not copy Matthew, Mark or Luke in a demonstrable literary way, then did he use any of these three Gospels in a more general sense? We may pose the question in the same way as does Dwight Moody Smith:

Theologically more important than the question of John's knowledge or use of the synoptic gospels is the question of how he stands in relation to the synoptic tradition. To what extent does he know it or assume knowledge of something like it? Hoskyns, pp.18-74, has compiled a striking array of evidence to support the thesis that John assumed a widespread knowledge of something like the synoptic tradition about Jesus.[69]

This is much more difficult, if not impossible, to verify. Is John truly relying on the Synoptics, or is he drawing upon a common tradition, oral or written, in some form now unknown to us? Even those who posit some relationship between the Synoptics and John make that relationship by no means easily testable.

For instance C.K. Barrett presents a list of parallels between John and Mark's Gospel, for example Mark 1:7//John 1:27.[70] But at the close of the examination of those parallels, Barrett says no more than, "It cannot be said that the data that have now been collected amount to proof that John knew and used as a source our second gospel, but they do seem sufficient to make plausible the view that John had read Mark, thought that it contained a suitable gospel outline, and often – perhaps involuntarily – echoed Mark's phrases when writing about the same events".[71] Some perhaps would not call that Johannine dependence on Mark at all, but only John *using* Mark.

Barrett's reference to the Gospel outline is most significant for our purposes. Matthew and Luke have an outline similar to Mark. It seems that all the four Gospels have a common outline of the ministry of Jesus from his baptism onwards. Barrett notes that we have here "quite a striking chain of very significant events"[72].

Below we reprint this outline from Barrett:[73]

Sequence of Events	Mark	John
a. The Work and Witness of the Baptist	1:4-8	1:19-36
b. Departure to Galilee	1:14 ff.	4:3
c. Feeding of the Multitude	6:34-44	6:1-13
d. Walking on the Lake	6:45-52	6:16-21
e. Peter's Confession	8:29	6:68 ff.
f. Departure to Jerusalem	9:30 ff.	7:10-14 10:1,32,46
g. The Entry	11:1-10	12:12-15
The Anointing[74]	14:3-9	12:1-8
h. The Last Supper, with predictions of betrayal and denial	14:17-26	13:1-17:26
i. The Arrest	14:43-52	18:1-11
j. The Passion and Resurrection	14:53-16:8	18:12-20:29

Barrett considers that the similarity in "the sequence of (c) and (d) is not readily explicable except on the hypothesis of literary relationship".[75]

But is the hypothesis of a literary relationship between John and Matthew, Mark, and Luke the only possibility? Is not a common tradition of *historical memory* at least possible? Those three events – Jesus feeding the multitude, then being seen by his disciples walking on the Sea of Galilee, and finally Peter's Confession of Faith – are quite memorable historical events *precisely in that sequence.* Is it incredible that Peter's confession should follow such prestigious miracles, and to some extent be both causally related to them, and remembered in that sequence? In *Bad, Mad or God?* we have strongly contested for the historicity in particular of the miracle of the Walking on the Water.[76] Sufficient to note here is that if those two miracles occurred factually in the experience of the astounded disciples, then the sequence of one miracle following the other would also not be difficult to remember, and the other events recorded in the above sequence.

We would make a similar response to Thomas L. Brodie, who in his fascinating study *The Quest for the Origin of John's Gospel* is convinced that John is dependent on Mark for its literary structure. For instance, Brodie presents very plausible parallels between Mark 8:22-26 and John 9:1-7,13,15.[77] These are accounts in both Gospels of the cure by Jesus of a blind man. Both Mark and John have Jesus spitting and anointing his eyes. Both have Jesus *sending* the man away. In Mark 8:26 Jesus sends the man back to his people, and in John 9:7 Jesus tells the man to wash in the pool of Siloam, which John tells us means "sent".

It is not impossible that Brodie is correct in one point of his analysis, namely that, in writing the Fourth Gospel, the evangelist had Mark's Gospel before him and was influenced by its literary structure, form, and content.

But how are the great variations in detail which we have already noted between the Synoptic and the Johannine accounts of the Cleansing of the Temple to be explained? The differences in the respective Marcan and Johannine accounts of the man born blind are equally striking. Are John's additions all the result of his vivid imagination, working on the Marcan account?[78] Contrary to Brodie, Brown finds the Fourth Gospel account of this miracle evidence of John's independent historical tradition:

> Actually, the similarities between the various Synoptic accounts and John's account are rather few... John is certainly not dependent on any single Synoptic account, nor is there any convincing evidence that John is dependent on any combination of detail from the various Synoptic scenes. The most striking and important features in John are not found in the Synoptic scenes, for example: *blind from birth; use of mud; healing through the water of Siloam; interrogation about the miracle; questioning of parents.* Of course, these strikingly different details are often the very points that serve the Johannine theological interests, and therefore one is hard put to prove scientifically that they were not invented for the sake of pedagogy. Some points that might be mentioned in favour of the primitive and authentic character of the Johannine story are the use of spittle, the brevity with which the miracle is narrated, the local information about the pool of Siloam, the acquaintance with the fine points of the Sabbath rules. In general, then, it seems that probability favours the theory that behind chapter ix lies a primitive story of healing preserved only in the Johannine tradition (so also Dodd, *Tradition,* pp.181-88). The evangelist with his sense of drama has seen in this story an almost ideal example of a sign that might be used to instruct his readers and strengthen them in their belief that Jesus is the Messiah (xx 31), and has elaborated the tale with that goal in mind.[79]

Brown acknowledges the difficulty of making historical judgements, an acknowledgement with which any post-critical study must concur. But prior even to the decision about the historicity of any given detail of the narrative, Brown sees the necessity of pinpointing an independent tradition in John not dependent for detail on the Synoptic Gospels. In this respect, Brown is following C.H. Dodd, who, after his important study published in 1953, *The Interpretation of the Fourth Gospel,* to which we have already made ample reference, wrote another epoch-making work on the Fourth Gospel. In 1963, he published *The Historical Tradition in the Fourth Gospel*.[80] As with *The Interpretation of the Fourth Gospel*, Dodd's second monograph challenged accepted positions in Johannine scholarship.

Dodd outlines the way he intends to demonstrate an "historical tradition" behind the Fourth Gospel. He begins with the question "Can we in any measure recover and describe a strain of tradition lying behind the Fourth Gospel, distinctive of it, and independent of other strains of tradition known to us?"[81] Dodd contrasts this with the other possibility, popular with criticism just before his own time, that John simply depends on the Synoptic Gospels. He then works out a careful methodology which he intends to apply throughout his book:

> The presumption, therefore, which lay behind much of the earlier criticism – that similarity of form and content between two documents points to the dependence of the later of these documents on the earlier – no longer holds good, since there is an alternative explanation of many such similarities, and one which corresponds to the conditions under which gospel writing began, so far as we can learn them: namely, the influence of a common tradition. To establish literary dependence something more is needed – some striking similarity in the use of words (especially if the words are somewhat unusual) extending over more than a phrase or two, or an unexpected and unexplained identity of sequence, or the like. It is evidence of this kind that has convinced most critics that the Synoptic evangelists made use of written sources in certain parts of their works, and it is the lack of such evidence in other parts, in spite of a general parallelism, that has led many rightly to limit the use of such sources more narrowly than was at one time custom-ary. In comparing, therefore, a given passage in the Fourth Gospel with a parallel passage in the older gospels, we have to inquire whether there are coincidences of language or content going beyond what might be reasonably expected in works having behind them the general

tradition of the early Church, and next whether any marked differences might be accounted for (supposing he were copying the Synoptics) by known mannerisms of the evangelist, or his known doctrinal tendencies. If not, then there is a *prima facie* case for treating the passage as independent of the Synoptics, and we have to ask whether it has characteristics, in form or substance, or possible indications of a *Sitz im Leben,* which would associate it with traditional material so far as this is known to us.[82]

Dodd's researches were complex; but he came to the firm conclusion that "The above argument has led to the conclusion that behind the Fourth Gospel lays an ancient tradition independent of the other gospels and meriting serious consideration as a contribution to our knowledge of the historical facts concerning Jesus Christ".[83] This tradition Dodd assumed to be oral.[84] "That any authentic information about Jesus must at first have been transmitted orally does not admit of doubt, and all recent work has tended to emphasise both the importance and the persistence of oral tradition".[85]

Dodd gives many examples of what he calls this "historical tradition", independent of the Synoptic tradition and available to and used by the author of the Fourth Gospel.[86] For example, "the pre-Johannine tradition had a full and detailed account of the Passion and the events immediately preceding it".[87] All these examples, for Dodd, are manifestly John drawing upon his historical tradition, which tradition goes back for him before 66 AD.[88]

For Dodd, this is not the end of the investigation, however. The question remains, how based upon fact is this material from the Fourth Gospel's own historical tradition? By "historical tradition", Dodd means no more that the tradition in question is a story or saying relating to Jesus:

> For unquestionably the tradition, in all its forms, *intends* to refer to an historical episode, closely dated *sub Pontio Pilato,* apart from which (this is the uniform application) there would have been no church to shape or hand down such a tradition. It is in this sense an historical tradition,

whatever degree of absolute historical or factual value may attach to various parts of it.[89]

For Dodd, therefore, to find an early Johannine "historical tradition" does not necessarily mean that we have found *an historically reliable Gospel account*. The task indeed looks daunting, perhaps never-ending. But perhaps Dodd himself has to be asked a further question. We need now to go back to his initial discussion of method. He has argued effectively that material distinct from the Synoptics has been drawn upon by John. But who says that it is an *oral tradition* to which the author of the Gospel taps in at source? What if the so-called *oral tradition* upon which the writer of the Fourth Gospel draws is his own eye-witness testimony?

Dodd has assumed that there is an oral tradition underlying the Gospel tradition, the Fourth as well as the other three. No doubt oral tradition underlies the Gospels in some shape or form.[90] But need it be the *community* which was the custodian of this oral tradition? Could not in some instances the oral tradition be nothing other than the evangelist himself or herself, writing from his or her own experience? Or at least could it not be a later editor working on eye-witness oral and/or written traditions which were to hand,[91] but which that later editor could to some extent at least verify factually from his or her own experience of the life and times of the historical Jesus?

Dodd discusses earlier the question of the authorship of the Fourth Gospel by John the Son of Zebedee.[92] He has great respect for the arguments for traditional authorship, but prefers at the end to remain agnostic. He adds, "But in fact the question of authorship is not as important for the problem of historicity as has been supposed".[93] Dodd says with that we could not immediately presume that the account in the Fourth Gospel is straight history even if we knew the name of its author. We would agree at least to the extent that in an apologetic, even if we were certain that the author was the apostle John, we would have to demonstrate that the author intended to write what was substantially historical fact, and that he had done so. This we have already attempted to do in our Part One.

We can also agree with Dodd, that even without discussing the question of the authorship of the Fourth Gospel, we can come to some positive conclusions regarding the origins of the Fourth Gospel. We have adopted the method at the beginning of this chapter of looking at the origin of the Fourth Gospel in a more generic way. We have asked, are the manuscripts reliable? How early is the work? Did the author use extraneous ideas to write what he claimed to be a Christian Gospel? Does he show knowledge of the Jewish milieu and tradition of the first century AD? What use did he make of the other Gospels?

Each of these questions has returned a positive answer for us. The Fourth Gospel is credible as the work of a first-century AD Christian author, or Christian authors, writing from knowledge of the life and times of a Jewish prophet living in the Roman province of Syria in the first half of that century, and published in the second half of that century.

Even more, Dodd has helped us to verify that the traditions the author had to hand were early, and independent of the other three canonical Gospels Matthew, Mark, and Luke. But here we arrive at what appears at first sight to be a *cul-de-sac*. We must ask, were these traditions reliable? Dodd hands the question over for further research. Using a document as ancient as the Fourth Gospel, and lacking contemporary records to check its reliability, how *can* we verify those traditions?

As we outlined in *Bad, Mad or God?*,[94] by the use of the criteria of historical credibility evolved by historical Jesus researchers, we can sometimes achieve reasonable certainty that a given saying or deed of Jesus was authentically his, whoever might or might not have been the author of the particular Gospel in question. But it is surely common sense to realise that our investigation would be much more successful if at least we have some possible knowledge of whom the author might be.

Thus we pass on to consideration of evidence as to the actual author of the Fourth Gospel. But first, a brief reference must be made to the relationship between Paul and the Fourth Gospel.

Paul and John?

There is no clear evidence of significant influence by St Paul or his writings, even though the author clearly shares the same Christian faith.

C.K. Barrett[95] summarises well the evidence for the relationship between Paul and John, and the reader is referred to that commentary for the relevant biblical texts. Barrett concludes:

> When all these differences, which of course are by no means sufficient to outweigh in importance the substantial similarities between Paul and John, are borne in mind, it seems easier to believe that Paul and John wrote independently of each other than that John was expressing Pauline theology in narrative form. John was not one of the deutero-Pauline writers; both he and Paul were dependent upon the primitive Christian tradition.[96]

NOTES – CHAPTER SEVEN

1   ODCC, 108.
2   Dodd, 1953, 10.
3   "Manes' system was a radical offshoot of the Gnostic traditions of Eastern Persia... uncompromisingly dualistic, consequential, and deeply conscious of having 'unveiled' truths of universal validity." ODCC, 864.
4   Westcott, 1958, xv.
5   ODCC 1100-1102.
6   Dodd, 1953, 10.
7   ODCC, 1312.
8   ODCC, 1083.
9   Cf. NJBC, **68: 62-78**, 1091-1093.
10 Dodd, 1953, 69.
11 Dodd, 1953, 276-277.
12 Brown, I, LVIII.
13 Brown I, LVIII.
14 Dodd, 1953. 11.

15 Brown, I, LIX. Dodd, 1953, 53, concludes "It seems clear that as a whole (the Hermetic literature) they represent a type of religious thought akin to one side of Johannine thought, without any substantial borrowing on the one part or the other".

16 Schnackenburg, I, 136-138.

17 Brown, I, LIII.

18 Brown, I, LIII.

19 Schnackenburg, I, 143-149.

20 Schnackenburg, I, 145.

21 MJ1, 157, n.87. cf. *L'Évangile selon Thomas.* NHS 3; Ed. M. Krause. Brill, Leiden 1975, 3.

22 Dodd, 1953, 115-130.

23 Dodd, 1953, 115.

24 Dodd, 1953, 116.

25 Dodd, 1953, 116-7.

26 Dodd, 1953, 119 (G.R. 1.200 sqq. 28-9).

27 Dodd, 1953, 120.

28 Dodd, 1953, 122.

29 JN, 220.

30 Schnackenburg, I, 141-2.

31 Cf. BMG, 144-146 on Mark 14:64.

32 On the whole question of the historicity of the Atonement in Christian thought, cf. OC, 107-126.

33 Brown, I, LXIV.

34 Brown, I, LXII.

35 Brown, I, LXIII-IV.

36 Brown, I, LXIII.

37 ODCC, 471.

38 Fredriksen, 2000, 5.

39 Brown, INT, 831-835.

40 Barrett, 262.

41 BMG, 147-150.

42 ODCC, 726.

43 Dodd, 1953, 75, lists the main sources concerning Rabbinic Judaism available to him.

44 Cf. McNarmara, M., *Targum and Testament: Aramaic Paraphrases of the Hebrew Bible: A Light on the New Testament,* Irish University Press, Shannon 1972,

45 Dodd, 1953, 79.

46 Dodd, 1953, gives further examples as to how the author of the Fourth Gospel knew his Rabbinic theology, 79ff.

47 Dodd, 1953, 85 (Pesahim 54a Bar.)

48 Dodd, 1953, 86.

49 Westcott, 1880, xvi.

50 Westcott, 1880, xvi.

51 Dodd, 1953, 92.

52 Dodd, 1953, 91.

53 Dodd, 1953, 93.

54 Dodd, 1953, 95.

55 JN, 236.

56 Barrett, 1978, 30.

57 NJBC, 60:3, 920.

58 Barrett, 1978, 30.

59 Dodd, 1953, 274-275.

60 Dodd, 1953, 263.

61 (1:3,6,9,14,20,24,26,29), corresponding to the acts of creation of God, his active word. Also this is joined three times with the word "call" (*qara'*) [1:5,8,10]. God calls into existence by naming his creation. Thus the author of the Prologue of John has cleverly drawn out of the Creation account the concept of God's active Word, a most Hebrew concept, and given it personality by turning the verb into a noun; which as we have seen already, could have been originally part of the oral Rabbinic tradition, calling the Word Memra.

62 Cf. above 35, "Thus Mark, in putting together his Gospel...", note 16, "It is my opinion that..."

63 Cf. NJBC, **40:1-36**, 587-595.

64 NJBC, **41:2**, 596.

65 NJBC, **42:4**, 630.

66 NJBC, **43:3**, 675.

67 NTI, 231.

68 "The most important item in the development of the 'new look' on the Fourth Gospel is, beyond any doubt, a small book written by P. Gardner-Smith in 1938 on the relationship of John with the Synoptics. In a carefully reasoned analysis he established the independence of the Fourth Gospel so firmly that subsequent critical comment was in the position of either accepting his conclusion or using much space in an attempt to refute it." Temple, 1975, 10.

69 Smith, D.M., 1965, 243, n.86.

70 Barrett, 1978, 44.

71 Barrett, 1978, 45.

72 Barrett, 1978, 43.

73 Barrett, 43.

74 Barrett, p.43, Transposed in John. "The transposition does of course weigh against the argument that John was aware of the Marcan order, but each incident remains in the same order in relation to the other members of the list, and a reason for the transposition can be suggested (see p.409)." I would add myself that, if the transposition was made in John because of the eye-witness's historical memory that would be at least another possibility.

75 Barrett, 44.

76 BMG, 211-232.

77 Brodie, 57.

78 Brodie, 145, thinks that they are: "But the historical tradition found in John is not independent. The reliance on the synoptics is pervasive. What is independent is John's reshaping of the tradition, his reworking of it in order to develop his theological vision. In his own way he was just as closely involved with Matthew, Mark, and Luke as they were with one another. Thus the idea of an independent historical tradition is left without its foundation". But it is clear as we have seen, e.g. with the Cleansing of the Temple, that there is no comparison between on the one hand the close similarities between Matthew, Mark, and Luke, and the great differences despite the similarities between any one of them or all three and John. It is this phenomenon which led Dodd to his concept of the independent historical tradition of John.

79 Brown, I, 378-9.

80 Dodd, 1965.

81 Dodd, 1965, 8 .

82 Dodd, 1965, 8-9.

83 Dodd, 1965, 423.

84 Dodd, 1965, 424.

85 Dodd, 1965, 424. However, Dodd does not give any evidence for the existence of oral tradition; nor do other authors. As we have just seen, Dodd in his *Historical Tradition in the Fourth Gospel* has clearly argued for Synoptic type pericopes in the Fourth Gospel yet independent of the Synoptic tradition. But Dodd has not given any reasons why the original sources of the tradition should be oral or written. He just assumes it is oral. Indeed, it is difficult to see how one could prove that a given source was originally oral rather than written; since the first evidence for it is always written. Obviously, the original preaching of Jesus was oral; but we have no idea when or at what stage this preaching, and other Gospel material, was first written down. Cf. BMG, 68-75, where we outline the debate between Gerhardsson, in favour of early memory controls, and the form-critical movement. The form-critical movement has favoured major shaping by oral tradition because there are apparently less controls on the tradition if it is oral; but again, where is the evidence?

86 Dodd identifies this distinctively Johannine oral tradition such as John's use of an Aramaic tradition. He tends to use *Messias* [John 1:41] and *Képhas* instead of *Christos* and *Petros*. There are allusions to well attested Jewish beliefs (Dodd, 1965, 425) such as the fact that the Messiah would remain unknown until Elijah identified him (Dodd, 1965, 266. John 1:26), and the High Priest's gift of prophecy by virtue of his office (Dodd, 1965, 425, John 11:47-53). So also, the date of the crucifixion agrees with the Tractate Sanhedrin (Dodd, 1965, 109-10). The tradition also knew of the Hebrew or Aramaic names of places for which the evangelist supplies sometimes a Greek equivalent (Gabbatha, *lithostroton,* [John 19:13]. This tradition was well informed, concluded Dodd, about the political situation "which

existed in Judea in the half-century preceding the outbreak of the great rebellion, and which had entirely passed away at any date to which the composition of the Fourth Gospel may be reasonably assigned".

87   Dodd, 1965, 426.

88   Dodd, 1965, 430.

89   "The basic tradition, therefore, on which the evangelist is working was shaped (it appears) in a Jewish-Christian environment still in touch with the synagogue, in Palestine, at a relatively early date, at any rate before the rebellion of 66 AD" (Dodd, 1965, 426). This tradition, Dodd claims, preserved the schema of short narrative which we find in the Synoptic Gospels of "action-dialogue-pronouncement" (Dodd, 1965, 427).This independent tradition sometimes supplemented the Synoptic account, John making Mark's account of the Feeding of the Multitude clear (Dodd, 1965, 428, cf. 213-5). Jesus was frightened of the crowd trying by force to make him king. [John 6:15]. Dodd contends that this historical detail of John "fits perfectly what we know of the situation in Palestine, and the popular mood, about the time" (Dodd, 1965, 214).

90   Dodd, 1965, 7-8.

91   Cf. the teaching of the Second Vatican Council regarding the formation of the Gospel tradition, DV19. The reader is also referred to *The Instruction of the Pontifical Biblical Commission Concerning the Truth of the Gospels,* 21 April 1964. This latter document, influential on DV of Vatican II, referred to the three stage process of the formation of the four Gospels (Christ's preaching – The Apostles' Preaching – The Four Gospels), yet implied clearly that the Gospels did not lose their essentially historical character in this process, which the Biblical Commission freely admits began with oral preaching.

92   Dodd, 1965, 10-18.

93   Dodd, 1965, 17.

94   BMG, Chapter 6, *The Critical Minimum,* 113-124.

95   Barrett, 1978, 54-59.

96   Barrett, 1978, 58.

CHAPTER EIGHT

THE EVIDENCE FROM TRADITION

> • External evidence that the author was John the intimate disciple of the Lord is explicit, early, and virtually unanimous.
>
> • It is possible, as Bauckham argues, that the beloved disciple John was not an apostle, one of the Twelve, but an intimate disciple of Jesus. But it is more likely, in my opinion, that the traditional ascription of authorship to John the Son of Zebedee is correct.
>
> • Objections to John the Son of Zebedee being the author of the Fourth Gospel are not decisive.

In the second half of the twentieth century, not all critical scholars dismissed the question of authorship of the Fourth Gospel out of hand. Raymond Brown, in his masterly summary of the evidence for and against the Christian tradition concerning the authorship of the Fourth Gospel, concludes:

> Thus it is fair to say that the only ancient tradition about the authorship of the Fourth Gospel for which any considerable body of evidence can be adduced is that it is the work of John son of Zebedee. There are some valid points in the objections raised to this tradition, but Irenaeus' statement is far from having been disproved.[1]

We must be clear immediately concerning any "proof" from tradition. Methodologically, all we need to show is that the tradition has not been *disproved*. If it has not been disproved, then it can become a piece of *converging evidence* for the authorship of the document named by tradition. The argument would run: the Fourth Gospel was at least possibly written by John the Son of Zebedee, as Christian tradition tells us.

What would be fatal to such an argument would be the view expressed by Walter Schmithals, who wrote the Introduction to Bultmann's Commentary on John for the English translation of the original German,[2] and whose devastatingly negative judgement we have quoted above. Schmithals concludes "The author remains unknown to us".[3] For our argument to have any force, there must be some possibility based upon concrete evidence for the traditional authorship, and Schmithal's objections above must be countered.

The Testimony of Irenaeus

We agree with Schmithals when he states: "The first clear testimony to this tradition [i.e. of John's authorship] is offered by Irenaeus III, 1.2." This ancient text, to be dated at the end of the second century of our era, states "Afterwards [*sc.* after the writing of the other gospels] John, the disciple of the Lord, who also reclined on his bosom, published (*exedóké*) his gospel, while staying at Ephesus in Asia".[4]

Irenaeus' statement is as clear as it is brief. The author of the Fourth Gospel was John the Son of Zebedee, who was also the person named in the Gospel as the "Beloved Disciple". But to put flesh on the rather bare affirmation as quoted by Schmithals, we will provide the full quotation, which shows that Irenaeus was conscious of a close contact with the authorship of the Fourth Gospel through a second hand witness Polycarp Bishop of Smyrna (c.69–155).[5] Irenaeus wrote a letter to a certain Christian Florinus, quoted by the historian Eusebius (c.260–c.340). The authenticity of this letter from Irenaeus to Florinus, as quoted in Eusebius Bishop of Caesarea, (c.260–c.340) the "father of church history", has never been questioned by scholars.[6]

> For when I was a boy, I saw thee in lower Asia with Polycarp, moving in splendour in the royal court, and endeavouring to gain his approbation. I remember the events of that time more clearly than those of recent years. For what boys learn, growing with their mind, becomes joined with it; so that I am able to describe the very place in which the blessed Polycarp sat as he discoursed, and his goings out and his comings in, and the manner of his life, and his physical appearance, and his discourses to the people, and the accounts which he gave of his intercourse with John and with the others

who had seen the Lord. And as he remembered their words, and what he heard from them concerning the Lord, and concerning his miracles and his teaching, having received them from eyewitnesses of the 'Word of life', Polycarp related all things in harmony with the Scriptures. These things being told me by the mercy of God, I listened to them attentively, noting them down, not on paper, but in my heart. And continually, through God's grace, I recall them faithfully.[7]

If we are to believe Irenaeus, therefore, his testimony to the authorship of the Fourth Gospel by John the Son of Zebedee, the beloved disciple, is not only certain but also intimate. The line of tradition goes:

JESUS OF NAZARETH (c.4 BC to c.32 AD)
|
JOHN SON OF ZEBEDEE (c.10–105)
|
POLYCARP OF SMYRNA ((c.69–155)
|
IRENAEUS OF LYONS (c.130–c.200)[8]

Irenaeus then becomes himself a third-hand witness of the life of the historical Jesus, and a second-hand witness after John the Son of Zebedee. As traditions go, this is very strong. Stemming from the same period, the end of the second century, there are other early witnesses to authorship by John who back up the testimony of Irenaeus: the Muratorian Fragment (c.170-200); the Latin anti-Marcionite Prologue (c.200) and Clement of Alexandria (c.150-c.215).[9] However, during the past two hundred years, this testimony has been subjected to constant critical questioning.

Which "John"?

Most recently the distinguished New Testament scholar Richard Bauckham has revived a minority opinion in

Johannine scholarship that the "John" referred to by Irenaeus was not one of the Twelve, but John the Presbyter, the second "John" mentioned in Irenaeus' famous letter to Florinus.

This view must be distinguished from the more common opinion that this second John, John the Elder, wrote the Gospel, but that the beloved disciple was the Apostle John, Son of Zebedee, who was the witness to the events which were written down by John the Elder.

The text which gives credence to those who think that the "John" referred to in Irenaeus is not the Son of Zebedee, is testimony of Papias:

> I shall not hesitate also to put into properly ordered form for you (sing.) everything I learned carefully in the past from the elders and noted down well, for the truth of which I vouch. For unlike most people I did not enjoy those who have a great deal to say, but those who teach the truth. Nor did I enjoy those who recall someone else's commandments, but those who remember the commandments given by the Lord to the faith and proceeding from the truth itself. And if by chance anyone who had been in attendance on the elders should come my way, I inquired about the words of the elders – [that is,] what [according to the elders] Andrew or Peter said *(eipen)*, or Philip, or Thomas, or James, or John, or Matthew, or any other of the Lord's disciples, and whatever Aristion and the elder John, the Lord's disciples, were saying *(legousin)*. For I did not think that information from books would profit me as much as information from a living and surviving voice (Eusebius, *Historia Ecclesiastica* 3.39.3-4).[10]

Regarding the testimony of Irenaeus above, Bauckham notes that the early church father does not explicitly refer to him as "John the Son of Zebedee, one of the Twelve", but rather according to Eusebius' quotation as "John, the disciple of the Lord, who also reclined on his bosom".[11] And even when second-century testimonies to the authorship of the Fourth Gospel, as with Justin Martyr, refer to the author as "John the

Apostle", Bauckham concludes "We cannot tell whether Justin thought John, the author of the Gospel, was a member of the Twelve", since, Bauckham argues, *apostle* had a meaning not necessarily restricted to the Twelve.[12]

Bauckham argues that this John the Presbyter was also the author of the three letters of John as well as being the beloved disciple who wrote the Fourth Gospel.[13] Indeed, the second and third letters of John address their readers "From the Elder…" [2 John 1:1,3; John 1:1]. Most of the second-century references to "John" as being the author of the Fourth Gospel refer to him as "one of the disciples", as does the second century Muratorian Canon.[14]

Bauckham's intriguing view needs wider discussion, and must be considered a plausible interpretation of the evidence of tradition. We intend to spend a whole chapter on the identity of the beloved disciple. There we shall examine more closely Bauckham's opinion from the text of the Gospel itself.

However, it needs immediately to be said that Bauckham has to reject the testimony of the second century apocryphal works, possibly *The Acts of John*[15] and certainly *The Epistle of the Apostles*,[16] which assert that John the Son of Zebedee was the author of the Gospel. We must also say that all the texts from early tradition quoted by Bauckham which refer to "John the disciple of the Lord" *could* equally be a reference to John the Son of Zebedee. If he was not one of the Twelve, and was one of the most intimate disciples of Jesus, why could not early tradition more clearly identify him? Bauckham has to enter into a long and complex argumentation to explain why it was that this other John, John the Presbyter mentioned by Papias, and who lived at Ephesus after John the Son of Zebedee died, was unknown to the rest of the early witnesses of tradition.

But Bauckham must be willingly credited with at least presenting us with a seriously argued case from the evidence, as distinct from many views about the authorship of the Fourth Gospel and about the identity of the beloved disciple which must be adjudged pure speculation.

In my opinion, however, the more simple explanation, that "John, the disciple of the Lord, who also reclined on his bosom" was John the Son of Zebedee, has not been convincingly disproved, and thus remains as the most likely interpretation of the external evidence of the authorship of the Fourth Gospel. It is this interpretation which we shall follow in discussing the issues in this chapter. However:

Was John the Presbyter the author but was not the beloved disciple?

Papias, therefore, mentions another "John". Is it possible that Irenaeus confused this John the Presbyter, not an apostle, with the Son of Zebedee? In this view, as distinct from Bauckham's view that John the Elder was the beloved disciple, John the Son of Zebedee one of the Twelve was the beloved disciple; and John the Presbyter was the author of the Gospel.

John the Presbyter in this view therefore was not the beloved disciple, but rather the one who testified in 21:24 "This disciple is the one who vouches for these things and has written them down, and **we**[17] know that his testimony is true." Those who hold this view would necessarily also conclude that the "we" referred not to the beloved disciple himself, but to those others, one of them at least being John the Presbyter, who testified to the truth of what the beloved disciple had said. We will be looking more closely at Bauckham's view when we try to tackle the question of the identity of the beloved disciple in the next chapter.

The argument of Schmithals concerning the possible authorship of the Gospel of John by John the Presbyter, which we have quoted above, states:

> Now the much discussed testimony of Papias (in Eusebius, H.E. III, 39.3f) refers not only to John the son of Zebedee but also to the Presbyter John, who may have written the Book of Revelation. Probably Irenaeus and the whole later tradition confused the Ephesian Presbyter with the son of Zebedee of the same name. Prior to Irenaeus, then, the Presbyter John could have been regarded as the author of the Fourth Gospel, and possibly this was already the view of the redactor of the Gospel.

157

This is one of the most popular opinions of those who wish to hold to some kind of traditional authorship of the Fourth Gospel, but cannot accept that John the Son of Zebedee was himself the beloved disciple and the author of the Gospel. Contrary to Bauckham's view that Irenaeus never actually refers to John as the Son of Zebedee, this opinion would claim that Irenaeus was mistaken. He thought that the author was John the Son of Zebedee, but the author actually was John the Presbyter.

Many critical scholars, in addition to Bultmann and Schmithals, thus contend that Irenaeus simply mixed up John the Apostle with John the Elder. Recently, Martin Hengel has added his own prestigious name to their number.[18] He builds up a complex and fascinating case for this problematic figure "John the Elder" being the principal figure in the Johannine community at the turn of the first and second century:

> So we can make a provisional assessment. Behind the 'Johannine community' and the Johannine corpus, letters, Gospel (and Apocalypse) there is one head, an outstanding teacher who founded a school which existed between about 60 or 70 and 100 or 110 in Asia Minor and developed a considerable activity extending beyond the region and who – as an outsider – claimed to have been a disciple of Jesus, indeed – in the view of the school – a disciple of a quite special kind. This teacher, who bore the common Jewish-Palestinian name John, must have attained an extremely great age and therefore was known as 'the elder' in the school and in the communities connected with it; special hopes for the parousia were also associated with his person.[19]

The hypothesis is intriguing and presented with the weight of Hengel's enormous scholarly authority. His view has now the huge support of the present occupant of the Chair of Peter who, in *Jesus of Nazareth*, supports entirely Hengel's view that this "John the Elder" was the head of a Johannine school, out of which was written the Fourth Gospel.[20]

Furthermore, (and this is important for the Pope's

argument) if it turned out that John the Elder was the author of the Fourth Gospel, then he would certainly have been early enough to be an eye-witness of the historical Jesus, or at least early second generation, even if he was not the beloved disciple reclining on the breast of his Lord at the Last Supper. But we must judge that the theory that Irenaeus has mistaken John the Son of Zebedee for John the Elder must remain always a hypothesis, based upon a reconstruction of the evidence rather than upon the evidence itself.

On the contrary, with respect to Hengel as indeed to the Holy Father, while it is possible that Irenaeus was wrong, his testimony is still evidence, not hypothesis, that an early Christian Father was sure that the Fourth Gospel was written by John the disciple of the Lord, and therefore, as we assume as the more likely opinion, John the Son of Zebedee one of the Twelve. Brown concludes his study, to which the reader is referred for full details of the discussion on this matter:[21] "Once again, there is not the slightest positive evidence in antiquity for making John the Presbyter the author of the Fourth Gospel. Indeed, the evidence after Papias that mentions John the Presbyter affirms that John son of Zebedee was also at Ephesus and was the author of the Gospel. That the evangelist was John the Presbyter is a modern theory."[22]

OBJECTIONS:
Did John the Son of Zebedee suffer an early martyr's death?

The tradition that the Apostle John the Son of Zebedee suffered an early death is without value historically.

Nevertheless, Schmithals is convinced by this counter tradition. In the quote from Bultmann's commentary above, we read "But John the son of Zebedee must have been killed by the Jews very early, as Mark 10.39 shows, and as is indicated by several witnesses of the ancient Church".[23] But Brown has an entirely different opinion. He says "This argument against Irenaeus' tradition is very weak".[24] This weakness is exposed briefly but cogently by Barrett, as follows[25]:

159

- First, Mark 10:39 does not say that the apostle James and his brother John the Sons of Zebedee will be martyred at the same time. When the disciples answer the Lord's question as to whether or not they are able to drink the cup that he will drink, they replied, "We are able." Then Jesus said to them, "The cup that I drink you will drink; and with the baptism with which I am baptized, you will be baptized" [Mark 10:39]. All that the Lord says is that they will both be martyred. John's brother James was killed early [Acts 12:2]. But there is no mention of John the Son of Zebedee being killed at the same time.

- An epitomist of the historian Philip of Side (c.430) and Georgius Monachus Hamartolus (ninth century) quote Papias to the effect that both John and James were martyred "by the Jews".[26] Furthermore, a Syriac martyrology dating from 411 at Edessa commemorates John and James the apostles both martyred in Jerusalem on 27 December. But even here it is not said that James and John were martyred at the same time. It is possible that John was killed by the Jews, but much later in Asia. In any case, as Barrett says regarding Philip and George, "Neither was an accurate historian".[27] Barrett adds, "In fact, we are almost compelled to choose between the veracity of Irenaeus and Eusebius on the one hand, and the intelligence and accuracy of Philip and George on the other. It is a comparison which does credit to the earlier writers. If however Philip and George are discredited, the other evidence falls to the ground". The counter tradition emerged probably as a misinterpretation of Mark 10:39. Jesus said that James and John were both to be martyred; and one tradition in the Church drew the false conclusion that they were martyred together.

Why do other important sources not refer to John at Ephesus?

The failure of some contemporary sources to mention John at Ephesus is possibly problematic, but is countered by very early texts supporting Irenaeus.

This argument is not mentioned by Schmithals, yet it probably bears more weight than the spurious counter-tradition that John the Son of Zebedee was martyred at the same time as his brother John. The New Testament does not mention that John went to Ephesus at all. Paul does not mention John when he goes to Ephesus in 58[28] [Acts 20:18ff.]. Brown mentions other early fathers, Ignatius, Papias, and Polycarp, also who are silent about John being at Ephesus when a mention might have been expected.[29] But, as Brown says, arguments from silence are notoriously difficult to press. And he also mentions positive testimony that John was at Ephesus, of Justin the Martyr (c.135) and the apocryphal Acts of John (150). We must conclude that the silence of expected witnesses is strange and difficult to explain. But it is not strong enough as evidence to overturn the tradition originating with Irenaeus, that John the Son of Zebedee wrote the Fourth Gospel in Ephesus; although, in fact, the Ephesus tradition is not essential to our argument that the Gospel was written by John the Son of Zebedee."

What of other early sources denying authorship by John?

The presence of other groups who denied that John was the author of the Fourth Gospel proves only that the Fourth Gospel's authenticity needed to be defended, as Irenaeus in fact defended it, by the testimony that it was authentically apostolic.

At the close of the second century, one Gaius, a learned and orthodox Roman priest, rejected both the book of Revelation and the Fourth Gospel "which he attributed to the heretic Cerinthus because it apparently contradicted the Synoptic Gospels".[30] Irenaeus mentions that the Alogoi, who denied the divinity of the Logos and the Holy Spirit, also attributed the Fourth Gospel to Cerinthus.[31]

Some have tried to suggest that this proves that the Fourth Gospel was already suspect. But a counter-argument could be used here. Irenaeus and those who supported him at the close of the second century insisted that the Fourth Gospel presented the right Christology and indeed Pneumatology, precisely because the author was the beloved disciple himself.

Lindars makes much of the heretical use of the Fourth Gospel in the early centuries and one of the "formidable" objections to the authorship of the Fourth Gospel by John the Son of Zebedee:

> However, the Gospel was already known and valued by the Valentinian Gnostics, who found in it much to support their heretical views. Irenaeus *(Adv. Haer.* I.viii.5) quotes Ptolemaeus' exposition of the Prologue, which he ascribes to 'John, the disciple of the Lord'. This is clearly an allusion to the beloved disciple, and suggests that the identification of the author was derived from the internal evidence of the Gospel itself. It has been plausibly suggested that the Valentinians were the first to make the identification of him with John the Apostle, as the authority of the Apostle's name would naturally strengthen their case. They were so successful that some Christians rejected the Fourth Gospel as a heretical work. Thus Hippolytus speaks of the 'Alogi', who ascribed both the Gospel and the Apocalypse to the Gnostic Cerinthus. The *Acts of John* (a heretical popular work of the mid-second century) however appears not to know that John was the author of the Gospel, though apparently making some use of it. It is the earliest work to link John with Ephesus.[32]

But Lindars' objections begin to lose some of their heavy weight when looked at more closely. First, our information about the Valentinian Gnostics,[33] we have to emphasise, comes from Irenaeus himself (c.180),[34] Tertullian (160-225),[35] and Clement of Alexandria (150-215).[36] Thus it is second-hand information, and none is earlier than Irenaeus himself.[37] There is no evidence, even at second hand, that Valentinus or the Valentinians thought that John the Apostle had written the Fourth Gospel. Therefore, the suggestion that Valentinus was the source of Irenaeus' claim that John the Son of Zebedee was the author of the Fourth Gospel is pure guess work and nothing more. Moreover, it is puzzling that Lindars should imagine that, because Irenaeus refers to the beloved disciple (if indeed "John the disciple of the Lord" necessarily refers to the beloved disciple), that this must imply that Irenaeus had received his information only from intelligent reading of the Fourth Gospel itself. Why should he not have received his information down the line of tradition, only three generations as we have seen?

The final argument advanced by Lindars in this connection is the silence (and no more than the silence) of the *Acts of John*, in the middle of the second century AD. But that is a weak argument indeed. First, Lindars casts doubt on the author of the *Acts of John*[38] Leucius Charinus when he gives *positive testimony* that John the Son of Zebedee was at Ephesus only decades after the Apostle's death. Then Lindars throws doubt on Irenaeus' testimony because Leucius Charinus is silent about who was the author of the Fourth Gospel. This is a bizarre combination of extreme scepticism regarding evidence in favour of the tradition combined with unsubstantiated hypothesis accepted in favour of arguments contrary to that tradition. It is a combination by no means unknown in Johannine criticism.

Conclusion

I suggest, at the end of this section on the external evidence for the authorship of St John's Gospel, that we have fulfilled our project: to demonstrate that the tradition of antiquity that the author of the Fourth Gospel was John the Son of Zebedee the beloved disciple *has not been overturned by criticism*. It remains a genuine possibility. Indeed, that could be even an understatement of the case:

- The testimony of Irenaeus is clear and unambiguous, that John the "disciple of the Lord" wrote the Fourth Gospel, thus an eye-witness of the events recorded.
- It is most plausibly evidence based upon second-century texts that this John was John the Apostle, one of the Twelve, Son of Zebedee.

- The counter tradition that the apostle John suffered a martyr's death early is without value historically.
- The silence of other sources contemporary is possibly problematic, but is countered by very early texts supporting Irenaeus.
- The possibility that Irenaeus mistook John the Son of Zebedee for John the Elder remains only an hypothesis.
- The presence of other groups who denied that John was the author of the Fourth Gospel proves only that the Fourth Gospel's authenticity needed to be defended, as Irenaeus in fact defended it, by the testimony that it was authentically apostolic.
- Schmithals' view therefore that the author of the Fourth Gospel is "unknown" to us is not correct. There is evidence, not to be lightly dismissed, that John the Son of Zebedee was at least possibly its author.

NOTES – CHAPTER EIGHT

1 Brown, I., XCII. In his later work *An Introduction to the New Testament,*, London, Doubleday, 1997, Brown is much more sceptical about the Irenaeus tradition: "it is now recognized that such late-2nd-century surmises about figures who had lived a century before were often simplified; and that authorship tradition was sometimes more concerned with the *authority* behind a biblical writing than with the physical writer". INT, 368. Brown gives no reason why the Irenaeus testimony should be in particular rejected. It is surely not sufficient for such a distinguished exegete simply to concur without reason regarding John that "As with the other Gospels it is doubted by most scholars that this Gospel was written by an eyewitness of the public ministry of Jesus", 368-9. It is somewhat strange that Brown in his *Introduction to the New Testament* accepts conclusions rather than discusses them rationally, as he did in the Anchor Bible Commentary.

2 Cf. Bultmann, 3. As we have stated earlier, the German Edition, Göttingen, Vandenhoeck and Ruprecht, 1941, has no introduction, but simply begins on p.1 with commentary on 1:1-18, *Der Prolog.*

3 Bultmann, 12.

4 Barrett, 101. Irenaeus, *Adv.Haereses,* 3.1.1. Quoted in Eusebius *H. Eccl.*, viii, 4. Cf. Bauckham, 2006, 453.

5   DCC, 1107. "He appears to have been the leading Christian figure in Roman Asia in the middle of the 2nd century, and his long life (about which unfortunately little is known) is thus an important link between the Apostolic Age and the great Christian writers (e.g. St. Irenaeus) who flourished at the end of the second century."

6   ODCC, 481.

7   Barrett, 101. From Eusebius H.E. v., xx, 4-8.

8   ODCC, 713.

9   ODCC, 302.

10 Quotation as in Bauckham, 2006, 417. Who explains, cf. note 10: "Apart from the first sentence and the translation of "*parekolouthekos tis*" as "anyone who had been in attendance on", this translation is from J. B. Lightfoot, J. R. Harmer, and M. W. Holmes, *The Apostolic Fathers* (Leicester: Apollos, 1990) 314, with the words in square brackets added."

11 Bauckham, 2006, 458.

12 Bauckham, 2006, 466

13 Bauckham, 2006, 420-423.

14 Bauckham, 2006, 426.

15 As we shall see later, Lindars denies that the *Acts of John* affirms the Son of Zebedee as the author of the Fourth Gospel. Bauckham, 463, clearly thinks it does, presumably because the *Acts of John* is familiar with the Ephesus tradition regarding John the Apostle, thus assuming that the author of this apocryphal letter thought that John the Apostle also wrote the Gospel at Ephesus.

16 Bauckham, 2006, 465-6.

17 Bold text mine.

18 Hengel, 1989.

19 Hengel, 1989, 80

20 JN, 225-226.

21 Brown, I, XC mentions also the view that John Mark might be the "John" who wrote the Fourth Gospel, but again, there is no evidence for this whatsoever, unless, as Brown says, "it stems from internal evidence…"

22 Brown, I, XCI.

23 Bultmann, 11.

24 Brown, I, LXXXIX.

25 Barrett, 103-4.

26 Barrett, 103.

27 Barrett, 104.

28 Paul does not give the impression, in any case, that he was particularly friendly with his fellow apostles. Cf. Galatians 2:11ff. He does not mention any other apostles by name in any of his letters, to recognise their authority. He was himself an authoritarian figure, not particularly happy when anyone else might challenge it.

29 Brown, I, LXXXIX.

30 NTI, *Introduction,* p.285.
31 Adv. Haer. III 11:9, Brown I, XCII.
32 Lindars, 28-9.
33 ODCC 1423.
34 ODCC 713.
35 ODCC 1352.
36 ODCC 303.
37 The discoveries at Nag Hammadi have brought us no closer to the historical Valentinus. Barrett notes "It is possible that Valentinus was the author of the *Gospel of Truth*, one of the Coptic texts found at Nag Hammadi and certainly an early Valentinian work which shows more definite connection with John than do the Odes of Solomon." After noting certain passages with some affinities with the text of the Fourth Gospel, Barrett concludes "It seems probable, though perhaps not quite certain, that the author of the *Gospel of Truth* had read John." Barrett, 113-4.
38 Brown, I, LXXXIX.

CHAPTER NINE

THE BELOVED DISCIPLE

- The Gospel itself testifies that its author was an eye-witness of the events he narrates.
- The Gospel affirms that its author was "the beloved disciple".
- That "beloved disciple" was most likely John the Son of Zebedee.
- The beloved disciple was the disciple who stood at the foot of the cross, was known to the High Priest [John 18:15], and who testifies to the truth of what he has witnessed [John 19:35].
- He was the disciple who "testifies to these things" [21:24].
- He wrote the whole of the Gospel.
- He was the actual author, although he might have used a scribe.
- Alternative possibilities as to the identity of the beloved disciple are hypothetical at best.
- That the beloved disciple does not name himself is no decisive objection to the conclusion that he was the Son of Zebedee.
- He might originally have been a "simple fisherman" (sic), but that again is no barrier eventually to him being able to write a work of such literary and theological genius as the Fourth Gospel.
- That he was a high priest is an intriguing hypothesis, but again only an hypothesis.

The author of the Gospel was an eye-witness

Now we are in a position to ask what evidence there is in St John's Gospel itself for the authorship of the Fourth Gospel. First, there seems to be evidence that the author of the Gospel, or at least the author of its introduction, claimed to be an eye-witness. The verse, "We have seen his glory", John 1:14, appears to be an obvious statement from eye-witnesses, who claim to have seen the glory of the Word become flesh,

Jesus of Nazareth. This is part of the Prologue of the Fourth Gospel, 1:1-18. As compared to Luke 1:1-4, it is a much more theological introduction. It is perhaps the most discussed text in the whole of scripture, and such discussion is not relevant to our purpose at present. Sufficient it is to say that all scholars agree that, whether it originally contained sources[1] or was written as one piece,[2] in its final shape it serves as an introduction to the whole Gospel."[3] As Schnackenburg says, "it is indissolubly linked with the Gospel itself",[4] or as Carson says "The Prologue is a foyer to the rest of the Fourth Gospel".[5] Perhaps best of all, Lightfoot:

> These verses give the key to the understanding of this gospel, and make clear how the evangelist wishes his readers to approach his presentation of the Lord's work and Person; and equally the rest of the book will throw light on the contents of these verses.[6]

1:14 itself provides us with the obvious climax of the Prologue. The Prologue begins with a statement about the eternal pre-existence of the Logos, as the principle of life of everything that has come to be. There is a constant contrast in the Prologue between the Logos who is (*én*) existent permanently and eternally, with created beings, who only came to be (*egeneto*) through the Logos. So John the Baptist was a man who came to be (*egeneto anthrópos*). He came only "to bear witness concerning the light". [1:6] because he was (*én*) not that light himself. That was the Logos, which was (*én*) the true, the genuine (*aléthinos*) light which was coming into the world. This Logos was now coming into the world; but coming to his own, his own did not receive him. But to those who did receive him, he gave power to become (*genesthai*) children of God..."And the Logos became (*egeneto*) flesh". It is a superb climax. That Word which ever was (*én*) with God has now come to be (*egeneto*) with creation as flesh (*sarx*). Flesh for John simply means weak human nature; "the sphere of the human and the worldly as opposed to the divine".[7] The Logos, eternal with God through whom all things came to be, actually entered the sphere of the human and the worldly, became flesh.

But do the words "And we beheld his glory" refer to the physical seeing of original eye-witnesses of the life on earth of the divine Logos? Westcott asks, "Are we to understand this beholding of the historical sight of Christ, so that the writer claims to have been an eye-witness of that which he records? Or can it be referred to a spiritual vision, common to all believers at all times?"[8] If the former, if "we" refers to the eye-witness writing this work (perhaps an author's plural), or perhaps the group of apostolic witnesses as a whole, then the writer is claiming that the whole work as a whole is the work of eye-witnesses. That is if we take seriously the agreement among scholars that the Prologue refers to the whole work of the Fourth Gospel, and links inextricably with it. Brown in particular accepts this interpretation: "This (we) is a more confined use of the first person, for the "we" is not mankind but the apostolic witnesses, as in the Prologue of 1 John".[9]

Brown here is at one with Westcott. Westcott, as Brown, refers to the text parallel with this, which seems clearly to refer to eye-witnesses:

> We declare to you what was from the beginning, what we have heard, what we have seen with our eyes, what we have looked at and touched with our hands, concerning the word of life; this life was revealed, and we have seen it and testify to it, and declare to you the eternal life that was with the Father and was revealed to us [1 John 1:1-2].

All Christians can believe. But only eye-witnesses can see with their eyes, look at and touch with their hands, the word of life which has become flesh. Westcott is quite sure. "Language cannot be plainer. The change of tense moreover emphasises the specific historical reference (we beheld and not as of that which ideally abides, we have beheld [1 John 4:14, John 1:32n.]...) The whole point of the passage is that the incarnation was historical, and that the sight of the Incarnate Word was historical. The words cannot without violence be made to give any other testimony".[10] Therefore, says Westcott, the whole of the Gospel of John is about eye-witness testimony concerning the coming of the Word made flesh.

Is "we" rather a reference to all Christians?

However, as so often in biblical scholarship, what is certain to one scholar is by no means necessarily so to another. The distinguished Liberal Protestant philosopher and historian Adolf von Harnack was convinced that both the Prologue of John and the First Epistle of John were referring to all Christians. In this sense, "We beheld his glory" would mean "All Christians have shared in the glory of Christ by faith". Harnack's view has been followed most recently by H.M. Jackson in an intriguing article written in 1999.[11] Jackson goes back to Harnack's view.[12] For the purposes of this argument, it does not matter if there was a different author for the epistle as for the Gospel. The language is the same, and discussion of its meaning likewise. Harnack claimed that there were three possibilities regarding the "we" in the Johannine writings:

1. An *authoritative* plural or plural of majesty

2. A *collective* plural, either:
    a. Associative, including the readers in its purview.
    b. Dissociative, excluding the readers and referring only to a closed group testifying to the document in question.

Of these possibilities, Jackson supports Harnack in preferring the Associative that "we" refers to the readers as well as to those testifying. This is because Harnack argues to associative references in the First Epistle of John, [e.g. 1 John 5:14], which intends to rally the collectivity of Christians to true Christianity against Docetism, which denied Jesus Christ truly coming in the flesh. It looks quite likely that "And this is the boldness we have in him, that if we ask anything according to his will, he hears us" [1 John 5:14] does refer to all Christians.

But does this mean that the "we" in 1 John 1:1-2 refers to the generality of Christians likewise? Harnack thinks so, because "if the first person plural either is or can be argued on good grounds to be crucially associative in the rest of the letter, it is not likely to be dissociative here". This point is compelling for Jackson "because the author's primary purpose in writing is precisely to admonish the readers to maintain their Christological solidarity with him against the dissenters".[13]

Of course, the author of 1 John was concerned to maintain the Christological fidelity of his readers against the threat of Docetism, the belief that Jesus' humanity was not real, but only an appearance. But what better way of maintaining this fidelity was there than to emphasise that a group of people among them, namely the apostles and eye-witnesses, had actually seen Jesus with their very eyes, heard him with their ears, touched him with their hands, and been with him during his life on earth? That is why 1 John 1:1-2 wishes so strongly to emphasise that these eye witnesses touched the word of life with their hands. He truly was flesh and blood among them.

Jackson sees a serious problem for this interpretation, as does Harnack, regarding 1 John 4:14, "And we have seen and do testify that the Father has sent his Son as the Savior of the world". The words used, "seen and testify" (*tetheametha kai marturoumen*) are Johannine expressions used elsewhere it seems for eye-witness testimony. Surely, argue Harnack and Jackson, "No one, not even a group of apostolic eyewitnesses, could ever say that they 'have seen' with physical eyes 'and bear witness that the Father has sent the Son to be saviour of the world'."[14] This is a fair point. But, in what we may call the "witness theology" of John, the eye-witnesses are not without faith. They need faith to appropriate what they have seen with their eyes. For them, as with Thomas, believing is linked to seeing, because they see, they believe [John 20:29]. But believing is still necessary. Many people, unbelievers, in Jesus' time, saw yet did not believe. One could say that they were not eye-witnesses in the Johannine sense of the word. But nor were those who did not see, were not eye-witnesses, but believed through the testimony of those who did see and believe. Lightfoot again expresses it well:

171

> In the last sentence the speakers are obviously not merely
> eye-witnesses, in the obvious or legal sense of the word.
> The Jews were such, but they saw in the Lord only an
> opponent [6:16]. The sight-and this includes, but must
> not be confined to, physical sight-is sight of the Logos
> 'become flesh', become historical; and the last words must
> always be borne in mind.[15]

It is not surprising therefore that the majority of commentators
do interpret these verses as referring to eye-witnesses, as Jackson
says,[16] but of course as eye-witnesses who also believed. The
same must surely be true regarding John 1:14. "We beheld
his glory" must refer to the eye-witnesses of Jesus' life, death,
and resurrection, who also believed in him. Jackson is quite
right in seeing the "we" of John 1:16, "From his fullness
we have all received, grace upon grace", as referring to all
Christians. But he sees this as proof that 1:14 must likewise
have a similar generic reference. But again, is a shift of meaning
here from eye-witnesses in 1:14 to all Christians in 1:16 so
far-fetched?

I suggest, it is even demanded. The expression, "We beheld
his glory" (*kai etheasametha tén doxan autou*) in 1:14 is very
Johannine, and very biblical. The glory of God is that which
appears of God to human sight, terrible to behold. In the
book of Exodus, Moses wishes to see God's glory:

> Moses said, "Show me your glory, I pray." And he said,
> "I will make all my goodness pass before you, and will
> proclaim before you the name, 'The LORD'; and I will
> be gracious to whom I will be gracious, and will show
> mercy on whom I will show mercy. But," he said, "you
> cannot see my face; for no one shall see me and live." And
> the LORD continued, "See, there is a place by me where
> you shall stand on the rock; and while my glory passes by
> I will put you in a cleft of the rock, and I will cover you
> with my hand until I have passed by; then I will take
> away my hand, and you shall see my back; but my face
> shall not be seen." [Exodus 33:18-23]

Notice that a person who sees God's glory sees that glory with
his physical eyes. God has to turn the other way, because if he

showed Moses his face, Moses would die from the terrible sight. The same is true in John. Jesus said to Martha concerning her brother Lazarus who has just died, "Did I not tell you that if you believed, you would see the glory of God?" [John 11:40] The phrase is similar to that used by Moses, who wanted to see God's glory. John even makes specific reference to Isaiah, who in Isaiah 6:1 saw the Lord seated on his throne in the Temple, and according to John 12:41 "saw his glory". This is precisely the argument of Pope Benedict XVI in *Jesus of Nazareth*, who sees the testimony of the Fourth Evangelist precisely as a fulfilment of the vision of the glory which Moses saw of old.[17]

Now Lazarus steps forth from the tomb alive, the grave-clothes still on him. Martha has, as Jesus promised, seen the glory of God; seen it, that is, with her physical sight.

This aspect of seeing the glory as being a physical experience becomes even clearer when we compare John 1:14 with John 2:11, the evangelist's comment on the miracle of the turning of water into wine, Jesus' first miracle as recorded in the Fourth Gospel. The author of the Fourth Gospel comments, "Jesus did this, the first of his signs, in Cana of Galilee, and revealed his glory; and his disciples believed in him" [John 2:11]. His first miracle was then a revelation of his glory. We must surely see an intended reference, here, by the evangelist back to the Prologue 1:14. "We beheld his glory", now the first time was when Jesus turned water into wine. Then it says, "His disciples believed in him". Faith followed the sight of the extraordinary power of Jesus. Jesus performed that miracle precisely so that his disciples should be eye-witnesses of his glory, much more than Moses and Isaiah, to see the glory of God with their physical eyes, but the glory of the incarnate Word in its full power.

Bultmann says "The 'eye-witnesses' as such are considered not as those who stand guarantee for some later generation for the truth of the revelation, but as those who confront every generation anew with the offence that the doxa must be seen in the one who became sarx".[18] But that is precisely what John says they are, in saying "we beheld his glory".[19] Those first eye-witnesses are saying to all Christians reading that

Gospel "We did actually see his glory, and believed. You have not seen his glory, because you did not have a physical sight of him. But you can believe through our testimony and above all through the testimony of the Spirit in you." This of course is an offence, but only an offence for those who will not accept their testimony. Bultmann must avoid any recognition of the value of the miraculous in his *theologia negativa*. But in this case, as so often regarding John, Bultmann is just running away from the obvious.

The cosmic trial

Most recently, Richard Bauckham has compiled a strong defence of the view that the Fourth Gospel is based upon eye-witness testimony. He builds upon the work of Andrew Lincoln, who sees the witnesses in John in terms of the metaphor of a cosmic trial.[20] He first notes that there are seven witnesses, "in order of appearance are, John the Baptist (1:7, etc.), Jesus himself (3:11, etc.), the Samaritan woman (4:39), God the Father (5:32), Jesus' works or signs (5:36), the Scriptures (5:39), and the crowd who testify about Jesus' raising of Lazarus (12:17). In the second phase of the trial, the phase that lies in the future from the perspective of the narrative, there are only two witnesses: the Paraclete (15:26) and the disciples (15:27), of whom the beloved disciple is one (19:35; 21:24). This is how the beloved disciple's witness fits into the Gospel's much wider metaphorical motif of the cosmic trial".[21]

Bauckham argues that the testimony is to historical events, not to a metaphysical truth. Comparing "witness" in John with Acts 1:21-22:

> (b) If we take John 15:27 seriously, it is clear that for this Gospel the role of witness to Jesus in the period of the Paraclete is strictly limited to a specific group defined by their relationship to Jesus in the time of his ministry. John never suggests that "witness" is something else that later Christian believers also do. Similarly Luke confines

the vocabulary of witness almost entirely to those who have been personal disciples of Jesus, with the single major exception of Paul, who is a witness on the basis of his own special experience of the exalted Christ. For both John and Luke witness is something that requires firsthand contact with the events of Jesus' history.[22]

We may conclude this particular discussion as to the nature of the Fourth Gospel as being in the genre of history, precisely because it is rooted in eye-witness testimony of "the glory", with the persuasive words of Ridderbos in his excellent commentary:

> Here we have to restrict ourselves to what seems to be the essential point in this entire complex of problems, which is the meaning the Evangelist attributes, in his interpretation of the Christ-event, to history. And in this connection it seems that only one answer finally fits: The Evangelist views the real miracle of the coming and work of Jesus, the Christ, as the in-carn-ation of the Word or, as he states in no less pivotal pronouncement, as the descent of the Son of Man (3:14).

> This is in total contradiction to any idea that in the development reflected in the Fourth Gospel the meaning of history is pushed back, blurred, spiritualised, or even simply fabricated. In 1:14, "flesh" refers precisely to that which is human, natural, and historical, and that neither as the unreal though visible world over against a real though invisible world nor as the concealment of the glory of the only begotten of the Father (in which case humanity and the world are supposed to be confronted with the great challenge to believe despite how things appear) but as the life in which and the means by which his glory was made visible to every eye and, as it were, palpable to every hand (cf. 1 John 1:1ff.). Hence, to have "beheld" the revelation of that glory in the flesh and to witness to him who thus dwelled among us forms the foundation and content of the Fourth Gospel.[23]

The Prologue, therefore, must refer to those behind the authorship of the Fourth Gospel ("we beheld his glory") as

175

eye-witnesses. But can we conclude that such a claim refers to the whole of the Gospel, and not only to its introduction? Bauckham's analysis of the theme of "witness" in John leads us now to consider the role of the beloved disciple himself. Bauckham insists that his role as "witness" was to be the author of the Gospel.

The Gospel affirms that its author was "the beloved disciple"

What we call "the anonymous disciple" is not always in John called "the beloved disciple". First, let us assemble together all the texts in the Gospel, gathered by Brown, where there is such an anonymous disciple:

THE ANONYMOUS DISCIPLE[24]

Who is this disciple whom Jesus loved? There are three types of reference to anonymous disciples in the Fourth Gospel:

a. In 1:37-42 two disciples of John the Baptist follow Jesus. One is named: Andrew; the other is unnamed. In the immediate context other disciples appear: Simon Peter, Philip, and Nathanael

b. There are two passages that mention "another disciple" or "the other disciple":

18:15-16: Peter and another disciple follow Jesus, who has been taken captive, to the palace of the high priest. The other disciple is known to the high priest and gets Peter into the palace.

20:2-10: Mary Magdalene runs to Peter and to the other disciple (the one whom Jesus loved) to tell them that Jesus' body is not in the tomb. The other disciple outruns Peter to the tomb. Peter enters first; then the other disciple enters, sees, and believes.

---

c. There are six passages that mention the disciple whom Jesus loved (the verb "to love" is *agapan* in all the instances except 20:2 where *philein* is used):

13:23-26: The disciple whom Jesus loved leans back against Jesus' chest during the Last Supper, and Simon Peter signals to him to ask Jesus about the betrayer.

19:25-27: The disciple whom Jesus loved stands near the cross, and Jesus gives Mary to this disciple as his mother.

20: 2-10: The "other disciple" mentioned under (b) above is parenthetically identified as "the one whom Jesus loved". For the content of the scene see above.

21:7: The disciple whom Jesus loved is in a fishing boat with Simon Peter and the other disciples; he recognises the resurrected Jesus standing on the shore and tells Peter.

21:20-23: The disciple whom Jesus loved is following Peter and Jesus; the writer parenthetically reminds us that he is the same disciple spoken of in 13:23-26. Peter turns and sees the disciple and asks Jesus about him. Jesus says that possibly the disciple will remain alive until he himself returns. The writer says that this statement of Jesus created confusion among the Christians who began to believe that the disciple would not die. Reading between the lines, we may assume that the disciple has died, whence the need of explanation.

21:24: The writer tells us that this disciple is the source of the things that have been narrated.

Westcott, by a process of elimination, attempts to demonstrate that the unnamed disciple in the Fourth Gospel can in reality be none other than John the Son of Zebedee. His arguments are worth reading in full:[25]

> If the writer of the fourth Gospel was an apostle, does the narrative indicate any special apostle as the writer? In the Epilogue (21:24) the authorship of the book is assigned, as we shall see afterwards, to the disciple whom Jesus loved (*hon ēgapa ho Iēsous*). This disciple appears under

the same title twice in the narrative of the Passion (13:23, 19:26), as well as twice afterwards (21:7,20), and once in connection with St Peter under a title closely resembling it (20:2 *hon ephilei ho Iésous*).

He is known to the high-priest (18:15), and stands in very close relationship with St Peter (13:24, 20:2, 21:7; comp. 18:15, Acts 3). Though his name is not mentioned, there is nothing mysterious or ideal about him. He moves about among the other apostles quite naturally, and from the enumeration (21:2; compare 1:35 ff.) of those present at the scene described in the last chapter, it follows that he must have been either one of the sons of *Zebedee*, or one of the two other disciples not described more particularly.

If now we turn to the Synoptic narrative we find three disciples standing in a special sense near to Jesus, Peter and the sons of Zebedee, James and John. There is then a strong presumption that the Evangelist was one of these. St Peter is out of the question. Of the two sons of Zebedee, James was martyred very early (Acts 20:2), so that he could not have been the author of the Gospel. John therefore alone remains; and he completely satisfies the conditions which are required to be satisfied by the writer, that he should be in close connection with St Peter, and also one admitted to peculiar intimacy with the Lord.

Does then this definite supposition that St John was the anonymous disciple who wrote the Fourth Gospel find any subsidiary support from the contents of the history? The answer cannot be doubtful. St John is nowhere mentioned by name in the Gospel; and while it appears incredible that an apostle who stands in the Synoptists, in the Acts (3:1, 4:13, etc.), and in St Paul (Galatians 2:9), as a central figure among the twelve, should find no place in the narrative, the nameless disciple fulfils the part which would naturally be assigned to St John. Yet further, in the first call of the disciples one of the two followers of the Baptist is expressly named as Andrew (1:40); the other is left unnamed. Andrew, it is said, found *first his own brother Simon* (1:41). The natural interpretation of the words suggests that the brother of some other person, and if so, of the second disciple, was also found. A reference to the last scene at the Sea of Galilee (21:2) leads to the certain inference that these two brothers were the sons of Zebedee, and so that the second disciple was St John. Another peculiarity of the Gospel confirms the inference.

The Evangelist is for the most part singularly exact in defining the names in his Gospel. He never mentions Simon after his call (1:42f.) by the simple name, as is done in the other Gospels, but always by the full name Simon Peter, or by the new name Peter. Thomas is three times out of four further marked by the correlative Greek name Didymus (11:16, 20:24, 21:2), which is not found in the Synoptists. Judas Iscariot is described as the son of a Simon no where else (7:71, 12:4, 13:2, 2:26). The second Judas is expressly distinguished from Iscariot even when the latter had left the eleven (14:22). Nicodemus is identified as *he that came to Jesus by night* (19:39, 7:50). Caiaphas on each of the two separate occasions where he is introduced is qualified by the title of his office as the *high-priest of that year* (11:49, 18:13).

But in spite of this habitual particularity the Evangelist never speaks of the Baptist, like the three other Evangelists, as "John the Baptist," but always simply as "John". It is no doubt to be noticed that in most places the addition of the title would have been awkward or impossible; but elsewhere such an identification might have been expected (1:15 and 5:33, 36 comp. Matthew 3:1, 11:11ff.) If however the writer of the Gospel were himself the other John of the Gospel history, it is perfectly natural that he should think of the Baptist, apart from himself, as John only.

To summarise, therefore, Westcott argues:

• That this unnamed disciple stands in a close relationship with Peter, and yet is not mentioned, as he is in Acts, and indeed in the Synoptic Gospels, which one would expect regarding a disciple having such importance.

- Three disciples stand in the Synoptic Gospels in close relationship with Jesus, Peter, James and John. Peter is frequently mentioned in the Fourth Gospel, therefore presumably is not the anonymous Beloved Disciple. James was already martyred. This unnamed disciple stands in a close relationship with Jesus and with Peter.[26] Therefore the natural assumption is that it is John the Son of Zebedee.

- In the first call of the disciples, one of two followers of the Baptist is called Andrew, "his own brother" [1:41]. This suggests someone else's brother, i.e. the brother of James who was called at the same time.

- While the evangelist gives close attention to the detail of names, he refers to John the Baptist simply as 'John' implying that he himself is 'John the Evangelist'. As Carson says, "The simplest explanation is that John the Son of Zebedee is the one person who would not feel it necessary to distinguish the other John from himself".[27]

Westcott's arguments from internal evidence are very strong, indeed ruthlessly logical. Standing alongside the external evidence of Ireneaus *et al*, we seem to have now a strong case for saying that the author of the Fourth Gospel is the beloved disciple, and the beloved disciple is John the Son of Zebedee.

More sceptical scholars point out that there is no explicit statement in the Gospel to the effect that the author is John the Son of Zebedee. Westcott has had to come to this conclusion from a skilful reading of the text, drawing out the implications of hints and suggestions in the Fourth Gospel account. There is no way in which Westcott could be accused of reading too much into the text. But the ambiguities in the texts in question have led Johannine criticism to throw doubt on this simple identification of the beloved disciple, the other disciple, with John the Son of Zebedee.

Could the beloved disciple have been John the Presbyter?

Westcott's line of argument is sufficient reason, in my opinion, to settle the question against Bauckham's view that the beloved disciple was not the Son of Zebedee but rather John the Presbyter. We have discussed earlier the external evidence for the author of the Gospel named as "John the disciple" by Irenaeus and the early tradition, and found that, while Bauckham's case that "John" is hardly ever explicitly John the Son of Zebedee in the patristic quotations, it is always at least possible that "John the disciple" means "John the Son of Zebedee" the apostle, one of the Twelve.

It is when we look at the Gospel itself that it seems to me, that the only realistic candidate for the beloved disciple is revealed as John the Son of Zebedee, one of the Twelve. As we see immediately above, this Beloved Disciple is in a close relationship with Peter, but is not mentioned. He reclines next to Peter at the table of the Last Supper, and again is not named. He is part of the call of the disciples. Every reference to this anonymous disciple is consistent with his being an apostle; and the only prominent apostle who is not named throughout the Gospel is John the Son of Zebedee.

For this same reason Westcott is completely right, it seems to me, in concluding that the anonymous disciple throughout the Fourth Gospel is the same man, however that is expressed as "the other disciple" or "another disciple"; and that man is always the beloved disciple. Westcott's argument is a presentation of a coherent confluence of probabilities that all the quotations make sense together in the identification of the anonymous disciple as the beloved disciple.

There is one text which could conceivably be against this interpretation. Bauckham claims that John the Son of Zebedee could not have been the beloved disciple because in 21:2, the "the sons of Zebedee" are part of the list of disciples meeting by the Sea of Tiberias. Bauckham asserts:

> When readers or hearers discover that the beloved disciple
> is one of this group (21:7), the natural assumption, in

view of his anonymity throughout the Gospel up to this point, is that he is one of the two anonymous persons in 21:2. The fact that John the son of Zebedee appears as one of "the sons of Zebedee" in 21:2 actually excludes the possibility that he is the beloved disciple.[28]

This view was also proposed by Haenchen, who concludes that because an unnamed pair of disciples in addition to the Sons of Zebedee is listed "makes it impossible for us to determine the beloved disciple's name".[29] Carson quite correctly accused Haenchen that he "overstates the matter", although Carson admits that naming the "Sons of Zebedee" complicates the matter.[30]

Barrett does not see the problem. He says "This is the first and only reference in John to the Sons of Zebedee (see among several synoptic passages Mark 1:19). The beloved disciple is mentioned a little later (v.7), and therefore may have been James or John". In this case, then, there would be no problem in the naming of the Sons of Zebedee (in Greek *hoi tou Zebedaiou* "those of Zebedee"),[31] since the reference is far enough away from 12:1 to make such an identification with the beloved disciple not impossible.

In calling those two disciples "the sons of Zebedee", John the Son of Zebedee is still actually unnamed in the text. We might assume that he is one of the anonymous disciples in 21:2; but why could we not equally assume that he was one of the Sons of Zebedee? He is explicitly called "the disciple whom Jesus loved" in 21:7, again close to Peter. There seems to be no reason at all why that should not be a reference to one of the "Sons of Zebedee" any less than a reference to one of the other unnamed disciples.

After all, scholars are quite convinced that the anonymity of the beloved disciple is not a code to avoid recognition by a hostile reader, or at least not necessarily so. We will discuss reasons for the anonymity of the beloved disciple later. It is most likely a literary technique whereby the author of the Fourth Gospel refers to himself. It would not matter if the knowing reader was fully aware that it was John the Son of Zebedee; any more than the visitor to the Birmingham Oratory might well realise that references to "the Cardinal" were not references to the present incumbent of Archbishops House, Westminster, but to their founder John Henry Newman. In this case, the author of the Fourth Gospel just wants to make clear that both he and his brother were there at the lakeside together with other disciples.

There perhaps may be some reason for concluding that by using the expression "Sons of Zebedee", the writer of that chapter might be referring *in the third* person to the beloved disciple. In that case the beloved disciple will not be the author of Chapter 21, even if he was the author of Chapters 1-20. This raises the whole question as to whether Chapter 21 was an Appendix to the whole work, perhaps written by another author. It also raises the question as to who the "we" refers to in 21:24, "we know that his testimony is true". Is the "we" a reference to a group of Christians testifying to the truth of what has been written, or a literary device whereby the single author of the Gospel refers to himself alone? But before we look at that question in detail, we must look at other texts apparently identifying the beloved disciple.

Was the beloved disciple a Jewish High Priest?

This is an extension of Bauckham's view that the beloved disciple was an actual person, an eye-witness, and close to the events of the life of Jesus, but not John the Son of Zebedee one of the Twelve.

Bauckham is even more specific in identifying the beloved disciple. He claims that he was a Jewish High Priest at the time of the tragic events of Christ's last days in Jerusalem. This comes from a statement by Polycrates, bishop of Ephesus, 189-98 AD. He writes to Pope Victor (*apud* Eusebius, *H.E.* in, xxxi, 3, also v, xxiv, af.):

> In Asia also great lights have fallen asleep, which shall rise again on the last day, at the coming of the Lord, when he shall come with glory from heaven and shall seek out all the saints. Among these are Philip, one of the

twelve apostles,[32] who sleeps in Hierapolis, and his two aged virgin daughters, and another daughter who lived in the Holy Spirit and now rests at Ephesus; and moreover John, who was both a witness (*nap-rus*) and a teacher, who reclined upon the bosom of the Lord, and being a priest wore the sacerdotal plate (*petalon*). He also sleeps at Ephesus.[33]

Bauckham is convinced that Polycrates meant by *petalon* (a leaf of metal)[34] as it does in the LXX (e.g. Exodus 28.32, 36) as the rendering of *tsits*, "shining thing, *plat*, constituting the diadem on front of high priest's mitre". Bauckham concludes:

It is impossible to tell whether, when Polycrates refers to the petalon worn by John, he is referring to the whole of the high priest's golden crown or only to that part of it that formed a band across the forehead and on which the Tetragrammaton was engraved. What is important is that in either case the reference is to a distinctively high-priestly, indeed the distinctively high-priestly, item of headdress.[35]

If we assume with the generality of the tradition that Polycrates like the other early witnesses is referring to John the Apostle, the Son of Zebedee was high priest, following Bauckham's view that the author of the Gospel was once high priest. This would be the precise view of Rigato.[36] It would not be impossible that John the Son of Zebedee served as high priest; but if so, it is strange that the Gospel itself does not mention the fact, but rather says that the beloved disciple was intimately associated with the high priest, 18:15.

Bauckham and others make significant mention of Acts 4:6, which states:

[5]It happened that the next day the rulers, elders and scribes held a meeting in Jerusalem [6]with Annas the high priest, Caiaphas, Jonathan, Alexander and all the members of the high-priestly families.

Robert Eisler even "identifies John the author of the Gospel with the John who appears as a member of the high priestly family in Acts 4:6. Going further than Delff, he claims that this John actually was the high priest, by identifying him with Theophilus the son of Annas (Josephus, Ant. 18.123), who was high priest from 37-41 CE."[37] Again, if John the beloved disciple, whether John the Son of Zebedee or another John if we follow Bauckham, was a high priest, then it is strange that there is no other mention of that in the tradition.

This view is depending much too heavily upon what might be even be granted the most plausible interpretation of *petalon*, a speculative interpretation of Acts 4:6, and even more too much credibility on the single testimony of Polycrates. As Barrett comments: "Polycrates appears to confuse Philip the Apostle with Philip the Evangelist – an error which does nothing to increase confidence in his other remarks."[38]

Barrett's conclusion is, to my mind, judicious: "What Polycrates meant by the word is uncertain. It is conceivable that he thought that John had been high priest (or perhaps a priest); he may have used the word with reference to the Christian priesthood; or he may have used it in some sense which now escapes us."[39]

If we are no longer convinced of Polycrates' testimony as being specifically referring to the beloved disciple as high priest, or if we conclude that Polycrates was not reliable in his reference to John wearing the petalon, then there is little to persuade us that either John the Apostle the Son of Zebedee or, if we follow Bauckham, another intimate disciple of Jesus, was a high priest. We might even judge that it is a speculation which does not have too much importance in the debate.

Who was the disciple at the foot of the cross?
"This is the evidence of one who saw it – true evidence, and he knows that what he says is true – and he gives it so that you may believe as well [19:35], and known to the High Priest [18:25]".

Westcott claimed that there were only two realistic alternatives; that "The Evangelist either makes an appeal to an eye-witness separate from himself, but not more definitely described, who is said to be conscious of the truth of his own testimony; or he makes an appeal to his own actual experience, now solemnly recorded for the instruction of his readers".[40]

Westcott says that it is crystal clear that the second alternative is the only possible one, because the beloved disciple stands alone at the foot of the cross with the mother of Jesus in 19:25-28, where that disciple and the mother of Jesus are united as mother and son by the word of Jesus. This argument of Westcott is also convincing for Brown: "There can be little doubt that in the writer's mind this witness was the beloved disciple mentioned in vss.26-27... The beloved disciple is the only male follower of Jesus mentioned as present at the foot of the cross; he is a true eyewitness on whom the writer depends (21:24). Are we to think that at the foot of the cross there was another disciple, otherwise unmentioned, who was also a true witness on whom the Johannine writer depends in a special way?"[41]

This is one instance; it seems to me, where exegesis is simple. The one standing at the foot of the cross was the beloved disciple, and he was known to the high priest. But we now have to discuss a text whose meaning is continually hotly debated among Johannine scholars:

> **This disciple is the one who vouches for these things and has written them down, and we know that his testimony is true. [21:24]**

This text bristles with questions, which we will now proceed to discuss:

1. Did the beloved disciple write the whole of the Gospel?

The argument seems to be clinched with the identification of the "he" of "and he knows that he tells the truth" [19:35b]. Westcott is convinced that the Greek for "he", *ekeinos* "that man", is a reference to the eye-witness to whom reference has already been made. Others, for example Bultmann, take *ekeinos* to refer to a person other than the eye-witness. Various authors even consider that *ekeinos* refers to Christ or even God as a solemn testimony to the truth of what is said.[42] Clearly, we are not dealing at this point with exegetical certainties. We can most aptly summarise with Brown, "Probably the best explanation is that, despite objections, *ekeinos* refers to the eyewitness".[43] And even if *ekeinos* refers to one other than the eye-witness, it still seems certain to me, with Westcott, that "the one who saw" (*ho heórakas*) can be none other than that apostolic eye-witness.

But, even granted that the person testifying is the beloved disciple, whom Westcott argues is John the Son of Zebedee, to what is he testifying at this point? His testimony seems limited specifically to the blood and water flowing from the side of Christ.[44] He does not seem to be testifying to the truth of the whole of the Fourth Gospel. For such apparent testimony we have to look at John 21:24, "This is the disciple who is testifying to these things and has written them, and we know that his testimony is true".

21:24 is the only verse in the whole of the Fourth Gospel which appears to identify the author of the Fourth Gospel. But exegetical battles are continually being fought over each word of this verse:

1. Who was the "disciple who is testifying to these things and has written them"? Is it the beloved disciple?

2. What are the "things he has written"? Is it Chapter 21, or the whole of the Gospel?

3. What does it mean that he "wrote these things"? Was he the actual author, or could he have authorised someone else to write the Gospel? Or does it mean that the beloved disciple was the author of the tradition behind the Fourth Gospel, but that he did not actually write it?

4. Who is the "we" of "we know that his testimony is true"? Is it the writer himself? Or the Elders at Ephesus?

In each case, we shall discover, there is much to be said in favour of Westcott's argument, namely that the beloved disciple was the actual author of the Fourth Gospel complete and entire, and the beloved disciple was John Son of Zebedee just as Irenaeus said.

1. Did the beloved disciple himself "testify to these things"?

In the narrative, it seems clear that the reference is to the beloved disciple, who testifies to the truth of what he has written. The context is plain enough:

> Peter turned and saw the disciple whom Jesus loved following them; he was the one who had reclined next to Jesus at the supper and had said, "Lord, who is it that is going to betray you?" When Peter saw him, he said to Jesus, "Lord, what about him?" Jesus said to him, "If it is my will that he remain until I come, what is that to you? Follow me!" So the rumour spread in the community that this disciple would not die. Yet Jesus did not say to him that he would not die, but, "If it is my will that he remain until I come, what is that to you?" This is the disciple who is testifying to these things and has written them, and we know that his testimony is true [John 21:20-24].

Even if we hold that 21:24 is a subscript to 21:20-23, the disciple who is "has written these things" is the beloved disciple mentioned in 21:20. As Bultmann says, 21:24 is integral to the whole of 21:20-23. "On the contrary, one should hesitate before striking out verse 24, because if this is done it is not at all plain what interest the author of Chapter 21 and especially of verses 15-22 has in the beloved disciple. In fact it can only be to adduce him as a guarantor for the truth of the Gospel – precisely as verse 24 says".[45] 21:24 is therefore integral to the whole narrative of Chapter 21, even if inserted later by the one(s) testifying to the truth of the Gospel; and consequently the disciple attesting to "these things" must be the beloved disciple.

Now, if we accept Westcott's argumentation, as accepted of course also by the present Pope, that the beloved disciple was in fact John the Son of Zebedee, then firstly, was this beloved disciple truly the author of the whole of the Gospel?

2. Do "these things" refer to the whole of the Gospel?

This is a separate question from whether Chapter 21 is an addition to Chapters 1-20, a view which is widely held, and which we will be looking at later.[46] A scholar could hold that 21 is a later addition, while at the same time claiming that the "things he has written" was intended by the editor who added Chapter 21 to refer to the whole of the Gospel.

Morris is convinced that "these things" refers to the whole Gospel:

> Some hold that "these things" refer to no more than this final chapter. This seems unlikely. The words seem like a reference to the witness of 19:35. Again, there seems no reason for a solemn attestation that the beloved disciple had written a few paragraphs to be tacked on to the end of someone else's Gospel. It is much more probable that "these things" refers to the whole book.[47]

In Morris' view, therefore, "These things" (*tauta*) mean that the beloved disciple was claimed to be the author of the whole of the Fourth Gospel in this final note in 21:24.

Others consider that this phrase refers to the words of Jesus in vv.20-23, countering a false report to the effect that the beloved disciple would not die.[48] In this view, 21:24 does not claim that the whole of the Gospel had been written by the beloved disciple, even though this is the more natural meaning of *tauta*, "these things". Rather *tauta* is a reference only to what is contained in Chapter 21 seen as the supplement of the Gospel.

But it seems to me that Morris' view is more impressive, particularly regarding the solemnity of the statement that the beloved disciple wrote these things, which would surely more likely refer to the whole of the Gospel rather than a small piece of it.

But what does it mean that he "wrote these things"? Was he the actual author, or could he have authorised someone else to write the Gospel? Or does it mean that the beloved disciple was the author of the tradition behind the Fourth Gospel, but that he did not actually write it?

189

3. Does "wrote these things" mean that the beloved disciple was the actual author and writer of the Fourth Gospel?

The most natural meaning of, "he [the beloved disciple] wrote these things (*ho grapsas tauta*)" is that the beloved disciple is actually the author of the Fourth Gospel, that he wrote it himself. But there is a strongly held opinion that *ho grapsas tauta* refers not to the act of writing itself, but to authorship in the most general sense. This has been eloquently argued by Moloney:

> *who has written these things*. This affirmation lies behind all claims, so consistently maintained by Christian tradition, that the beloved disciple (John, the son of Zebedee?) penned the whole Gospel (for an elegant defence of this position cf. W. Sanday, *The Criticism of the Fourth Gospel* (Oxford: Clarendon Press, 1905, 74-108)). This need not necessarily be the case. The aorist participial form of the verb (*ho grapsas*) could have a causative sense: "he had these things written" (cf. Bernard, *Commentary* 2:713). Most modern scholars (cf. Brown, Gospel 2:1123) would follow Gottlob Schrenk, who looked to Paul's use of the verb in 1 Corinthians 4:14 and 14:37 where he is clearly dictating his message to a community to suggest that "in the light of this incontrovertible fact it might be asked whether the *ho grapsas tauta* of John 21:24 might not simply mean that the beloved disciple and his recollections stand behind this Gospel and are the occasion of its writing. This is a very possible view so long as we do not weaken unduly the second aspect. Indeed, it would be difficult to press the formula to imply other than an assertion of spiritual responsibility for what is contained in the book" (TDNT 1:743). Playing on the possibilities of the English language one could say that the beloved disciple is "author" insofar as he is "authority" for the Gospel.[49]

It is very difficult to prove that *ho grapsas tauta*, "he wrote these things", does not have a wider meaning than that the beloved disciple actually set pen to paper. It certainly could mean that someone "caused to be written" something in the sense that a scribe took down a dictated document. Not the scribe, but the dictating person, would be the true "writer" of the document. This is the case in 1 Corinthians 4:14 and 14:37, where it is most likely that Paul used a scribe. The fact that Paul says "I, Paul, write this greeting with my own hand" [1 Corinthians 16:21], is an obvious signal that he used a scribe for the main body of the letter.

On the other hand, using a scribe is a much more active relationship between the scribe and the author than in the sense described by Moloney above, where the "writer" simply would mean the "authority" for the Gospel; as, for instance, Moses was the authority for the Pentateuch, the "books of Moses", and Solomon the authority for the Wisdom literature. We have no evidence from the Greek world in which the primitive Church was launched that *graphó* meant anything other than "I write" or at the very least "I get someone else to act as scribe for me".[50] We have no instance where it simply meant "I am the authority behind this document".

As Barrett says, "The most natural meaning of these words, and therefore the meaning to be adopted unless very strong reasons are brought against it, is that the disciple himself not only bore witness to but also wrote down *tauta*".[51]

Bauckham is even more categorical, insisting "It must be stressed that no one has produced any evidence that *graphein* can be used to refer to a relationship between author and text more remote than that of the dictation of a text to a scribe". Why do so many scholars still insist upon the possibility that the meaning is wider than even that of a scribe? Bauckham answers "This must be because they have found it so hugely improbable that the beloved disciple could himself be the author of the Gospel that they have grasped like a dying man at the straw of possibility that 21:24 does not say that he was".[52]

We are back again to the central question addressed in our first Part, namely the credibility of the Fourth Gospel as history. If that is granted, as we have attempted to demonstrate together with the Pope, then it is easy to accept what is the clear evidence of the text itself that the beloved disciple actually wrote the whole of the Gospel.

It is sometimes objected that the beloved disciple would not have referred to himself in the third person singular. He would have said something like "I am the beloved disciple and I wrote these things". But recently, Howard M. Jackson has shown that, from the early Roman period onwards, following "the precedent of Homer's *Odyssey*" the first person singular was used where "the author's primary purpose was to entertain the reader".[53] But for serious works, the author referred to himself in the third person singular.

Thucydides, for instance, only rarely refers to himself in his historical writings in the first person singular. He mainly refers to himself as "Thucydides",[54] "as if it were a different person, in order by this self-distancing and self-objectification to preserve the posture of objectivity which his view of proper histiographic method demanded... This is exactly, I suggest, what the author of the Gospel of John has done in *houtos estin ho mathétés... ho grapsas tauta* in 21:24 (and equally in 19:35 to which I shall return later), and it is under similar circumstances and for the same reasons".[55]

Jackson reinforces his point later. "The author wants his narrative accepted as a factual and accurate presentation of events in which he himself participated or to which he was himself an eyewitness; his anti-docetic programme demands that it be accepted as such, for otherwise his testimony to the earthly, fleshly Jesus is not credible. To help achieve this goal he has adopted the tried-and-true practice, however it was mediated to him, of distancing himself as narrator from himself as direct participant in the events he recounts."[56]

The preferable meaning of 21:24 is therefore that the beloved disciple was the *writer* of the whole Gospel not simply the *authority* behind it. The question remains entirely open as to whether the writer of the Gospel used a scribe. We have no evidence for that either way, unlike in St Paul's writings as we have seen. Nor does that really matter too much.

4. Who are the "we" testifying?

This is a hotly disputed clause of 21:24. It contains startling change of grammar, from the third person singular "he", referring to the beloved disciple to "we know that his testimony is true". This led Westcott himself, normally cautious before positing redactors and sources, to consider that 21:24 was part of an added note "preserved when the completed Gospel was added to the Church".[57]

The change of person to "we" also causes Brown to see further reasons for his theory of composition of the Gospel. For him, "the 'we' represents the Johannine writer responsible for the addition of Chapter 21 and his fellow Johannine disciples":[58] "We know therefore becomes a further testimony of the circle of the community to the veracity of the testimony of the tradition of the beloved disciple."

On the other hand, there are other scholars who think that the use of *oidamen*, "we", is a reference to the beloved disciple himself, almost a plural of majesty. Carson quotes parallels in the Fourth Gospel to people describing themselves individually as "we" (3:2, 22, 20:2). But Carson is cautious, "Despite these parallels, the use of 'we' in John 21:24, if taken as a self-reference by the Evangelist, remains a somewhat awkward form when the writer is understood to be attesting the truthfulness of his own witness".[59]

Some would therefore revisit the old view that the "we" represented the Elders of Ephesus who were giving their own solemn testimony behind that of the beloved disciple. As with a legal document such as a will, the elders were saying implicitly "We, the undersigned add our testimony to this testimony of the beloved disciple…"

Carson comments: "Yet the view is not without difficulty. It is hard to imagine in what context other church leaders would be providing a character reference for an apostle".[60] But these church leaders would be testifying both that the beloved disciple was truly the author of the Gospel, and that his Gospel was authentic, against false gospels which come from the Docetists. All agree that Docetism (from the Greek *dokeó*, "I imagine"),[61] the refusal to believe in the true humanity of Jesus, was a problem towards the close of the first century AD for the Johannine Christians. The author's own self-designation was the ratification of the Gospel together with the apostle himself. This was especially important if, as we shall see, it is more likely that the Evangelist was not yet dead, but was old and considered close to his eternal reward.[62]

So *oidamen* refers either to the beloved disciple himself, giving solemn backing to his own testimony. Or "we" refers more likely to the Ephesian elders (or, if we do not accept the Ephesus tradition, any other companions of the author) witnessing together with the beloved disciple to the truth either that Jesus did not promise that the beloved disciple would not live until the Parousia, or the truth of the whole of Chapter 21, or to the truth of the whole of the Fourth Gospel. The Elders were not necessarily themselves eye-witnesses. But they could have known that the author was, and were ratifying both that they knew he was an eye-witness, and that they themselves accepted the truth of his testimony.

I would emphasise finally at this point that whether or not we conclude that Chapter 21 was an appendix – a view which as we shall see is not entirely convincing to me – we could nevertheless conclude that at least 21:24 was an appendix. It was from the literary point of view a subscript, a testimony from those who knew the beloved disciple (who was either already dead or even present to add his signature) to the truth of what he had written immediately above. That is even if, as Bultmann says, 21:24 is integral to the whole of the chapter. It could have easily been made integral by the individual or the group who inserted it as a subscript.

Our conclusion to this investigation is therefore that the most plausible theory is that of the tradition; that the Fourth Gospel was written by John the Apostle, one of the Twelve, one of the three intimate disciples of Jesus, Son of Zebedee; and that he wrote the whole of the Gospel. If we hold to this conclusion, which seems to me to be the most consistent with the evidence, then we do not need to speculate as do the scholars whose views we will now consider of another reconstructed solution to the problem.

Other views as to the identity of the beloved disciple

Here are some of the main proposals regarding the identity of the beloved disciple from those who cannot accept the simple solution that he was none other than John the Son of Zebedee:

An ideal figure

This is one of the most popular candidates for the title of "The disciple whom Jesus Loved". For Loisy,[63] he is the perfect Christian disciple, close to Jesus at the Last Supper and the hour of death, the first to believe in the risen Christ. For Bultmann, in several scenes the beloved disciple represents the Hellenistic branch of the Christian Church. "And the beloved disciple therefore represents Gentile Christianity-not of course with regard to its ethnic character, but in so far as it is the authentic Christendom which has achieved its own true self-understanding".[64] As Brown says, this is actually a revival of ancient symbolism: "Gregory the Great[65] found the same symbolism that Bultmann finds, only in reverse order, for the beloved disciple in Gregory's thought represents the Synagogue and Peter represents the Church".

Bultmann cannot accept that the beloved disciple is a real figure because the evangelist does not speak of him by name.[66] There are a good number of explanations for this anonymity, which we will encounter when we deal with this particular objection. Of course, the beloved disciple does have a symbolic value; but, as Brown says, "that does not reduce these characters to pure symbols. The obvious import of the passages in John that describe the beloved disciple is that he is a real human being whose actions are important on the Gospel scene. And so we do not believe that the recognition of the secondary, symbolic dimension of the beloved disciple obviates the quest for his identity".[67]

A deeper issue for Bultmann is that he cannot accept that the beloved disciple could be an eye-witness; and that, as we have already seen, goes back to the fact that Bultmann is unable to accept the historicity of the Fourth Gospel.[68] If he could accept its historicity, he would be inclined to consider the possibility that the beloved disciple was an eye-witness, and then he would further reflect on the possibility that the beloved disciple might be an historical figure of flesh and blood, at least a possible candidate being John the Son of Zebedee, or even the problematic John the Elder, the Pope's choice. This is yet another example of how questions of authorship in Johannine scholarship are intrinsically related to questions of its historicity.

Recently, Sandra Schneiders has proposed an ingenious theory concerning the beloved disciple. "I am going to suggest that such a complete and unsuccessful obscuring of the beloved disciple could not have been accidental. The evangelist wanted to insist on the central importance of the beloved disciple while, at the same time, making it impossible to identify the figure conclusively with any particular individual in the Johannine community. The question of motive, therefore, is crucial".[69]

She continues: "Johannine scholars are as divided over the identity of the 'other disciple' and the possible identification of this disciple(s) with the beloved disciple as they are over the identity of the latter. Part of the hypothesis I will finally offer is that the 'other disciple' is the evangelist's creation of an 'empty set' into which the reader, who is called to become a beloved disciple, is intended to insert him or herself. In modern critical terminology we might say that the 'other disciple' is a cipher for the implied reader who is called to be a beloved disciple."[70]

Sandra Schneiders connects this theory of the beloved disciple with a new feminist approach to the Fourth Gospel. Schneiders clearly is right to emphasise the fact that in St John's Gospel, women play an important role as witnesses. The woman at the well in Samaria in Chapter 4, Martha in Chapter 11, Mary the Mother of Jesus and Mary Magdalene at the foot of the cross, John 19:25, and most of all the role of Mary Magdalene on the first Easter morning, John 20:18, may have much more significance for feminist theology than has up to now been acknowledged. Also, the role of the beloved disciple may also be exemplary, in that his fidelity and closeness to Jesus can form a pattern for all Christians, whether men or women. One feels that the Fourth Gospel is more feminine, for instance, than the very masculine Pauline letters.

But Schneider's theory is highly speculative. It seems to be stretching the symbolism to suggest that the beloved disciple at the foot of the cross was female; and that the author was the Samaritan woman.[71] In exegesis few hypotheses are impossible; but there is surely more evidence that the beloved disciple was John the Son of Zebedee than that she was the Samaritan woman.

Lazarus

Lazarus has become a scholarly candidate for the title of the Disciple whom Jesus loved because of 11:5: "Jesus loved Lazarus". This is the view of Filson,[72] Sanders[73] and Eckhardt.[74] Indeed, Lazarus is the only male figure in the Fourth Gospel of whom it is said specifically that Jesus loved him apart from the beloved disciple himself. Filson argues that the person of Lazarus would have been intelligible to any one reading the Gospel without any prior knowledge. Lazarus was not anonymous; therefore Lazarus was the beloved disciple. But, as Brown says,[75] those reading the Gospel at the time would most likely have been aware of the identity of the beloved disciple if he was a famous apostle like the Son of Zebedee, even if we are not. Eckhardt thinks that Lazarus was a pseudonym for John the son of Zebedee after he had been brought back from the dead by the power of Jesus! Sanders thinks that the basis of the Fourth Gospel was a work written in Aramaic by Lazarus, which was then edited by John Mark, who was the evangelist. This view is highly tentative, even if fascinating.

As Brown says, "it is hard to believe that the same person is spoken of anonymously in chapters 13-21 and is mentioned by name only in chapters 11 and 12". He concludes "...we wonder if it is not more logical to suppose that the beloved disciple is someone who is not named in the Gospel but was known to the readers".[76] Finally, Lazarus in no way fulfils all the qualifications listed above by Westcott for being the beloved disciple. The latter was one of the Apostles, and close to Jesus and to Peter. Lazarus appears in the Gospel just as a friend, but not with any position in Jesus' itinerant following. We have found Westcott's view most plausible, that the anonymous disciple and the beloved disciple are identical, and are both John the Son of Zebedee.

John Mark

John Mark, traditionally the author of the Second Gospel,[77] does appear at first sight as a more serious candidate than Lazarus. This is Parker's view,[78] because of the attribution of the Gospel to John, and for the following reasons listed by Brown:[79]

- Because his house seems to have been the headquarters of the early church in Jerusalem (Acts 12:12).

- He seems to have had relatives in the priestly class; the disciple of John 18:15 was known to the High Priest, who Westcott argues was the beloved disciple. Cf. Colossians 4:10, Acts 4:36.

- Through Paul, Mark seems to have been acquainted with Luke (Philemon 24) and this would account for cross-influence between Luke and the Johannine tradition.

- John seems to have had contact with Peter (Acts 1 2:12, 1 Peter 5:13), the beloved disciple knows Peter, and the Fourth Gospel gives Peter an important role.

John Mark of course has been associated more with the writing of the Gospel of Mark. But Sanders has the fascinating idea, that Mark used Lazarus' notes, which were in Aramaic.[80]

But a basic objection to the whole theory that John Mark was the author of the Fourth Gospel, apart from the fact that there is no evidence in the tradition for it, is that, as Brown says, John Mark was not one of the Twelve. But the beloved disciple was, and indeed sat next to Jesus at the Last Supper, which he shared with the Twelve [Mark 14:17, Matthew 26:20]. "How then could the beloved disciple have been John

Mark (or for that matter Lazarus), who is never mentioned in the Synoptic account of the ministry? This would mean that the disciple who was closest to Jesus was not even remembered in the lists of his specially chosen disciples! The whole Christian world was waiting in expectation for Jesus to return before the death of the beloved disciple [John 21:23]; yet if the beloved disciple was John Mark, the Christian records do not even record that Jesus ever knew the man".[81]

Lindars says in frustration, "But there is no evidence for his [John Mark's] connection with the Fourth Gospel. It only adds to the confusion to bring in yet another John on such slender grounds".[82] We would judge that, whatever the difficulties of the traditional view that the author of the Fourth Gospel was John the Son of Zebedee, there is much more evidence to support that view than for any of the alternatives offered.

But could John the Son of Zebedee have actually written the Fourth Gospel? We will now look at some of the major objections to his being the author of the Fourth Gospel, and to his being the beloved disciple.

Why does the beloved disciple not name himself?

This is perhaps the most frequent and most obvious objection to attributing the authorship of the Fourth Gospel to John the Son of Zebedee. After all, we have the example of Paul, who has no objections to naming himself as the author of his letters. [Romans 1:1; 1 Corinthians 1:1, etc] Bultmann uses this anonymity to dismiss the possibility that the beloved disciple was a real person. He argues that "it cannot be maintained that the beloved disciple, as the Evangelist uses the term, is a particular historical figure. If he were, there would be no accounting for the fact that the Evangelist does not speak of him by name, as he does the other disciples, but refers to him in that mysterious way".[83]

As with any argument from silence, however, the fact that the author withheld his name proves little, and cannot in the end be decisive. Names are withheld for a number of reasons.

Even today, novelists use pseudonyms, for reasons which are by no means always clear to the general public. They are nevertheless real people.

There may have been a number of reasons why the author of the Gospel, albeit an apostle, did not put his name to the work, indeed, studiously avoided the use of his name. R.H. Strachan[84] thought that the "we" of 1:14, "We beheld his glory" implied that, although the Apostle John the Son of Zebedee was the author of the Fourth Gospel, there were others associated with him, who are mentioned by name in the "we" of 21:24. Strachan claims "In conclusion, the Gospel is a genuine Johannine work from the pen of the Apostle, who wrote from Ephesus. We cannot, however, overlook the undoubted fact that the writer is concerned to hide his own identity, and thereby to impress the fact that the Gospel is not the work of a single individual, but the testimony of a group of eye-witnesses. With John's as the guiding mind, they conjointly made themselves responsible for the statements contained in the book. This is at once the oldest and simplest solution of the problem of authorship".[85]

We may, however, wonder why the author, conjointly with his consort of eye-witnesses, did not say "I John, and the following eye-witnesses…" Jackson thinks he has solved the age-old problem of why the beloved disciple chose to remain anonymous throughout the Fourth Gospel. His opinion is that the expression "the disciple whom Jesus loved" serves the Gospel author's anti-Docetic agenda. Jesus was human, flesh and blood, he actually had a friend. Jackson thinks that it is significant that the title "the disciple whom Jesus loved" occurs only late in the Gospel account: at 13:23 (at the Last Supper, in conjunction with reclining on Jesus' breast), 19:26 (Jesus on the Cross), then 21:20 (retrospectively looking back on reclining on Jesus' breast). Jackson thinks that, rather than a title, this late usage of the term in the narrative "suggests that the author has chosen this *ad hoc* self-designation because it so perfectly serves to further his anti-docetic Christological agenda, an agenda which so intimately concerns his own person and his personal relationship with the bodily Jesus".[86]

It is still not clear why anonymity has to be preserved.

Could not the author of the Gospel have said, "I, John, was the special friend of Jesus"? Perhaps we can combine this view of Jackson with that of Roloff.[87] As we have suggested earlier,[88] the beloved disciple is standing with the other witnesses to the Gospel. 21:24 is as it were a statement of their counter-signature. In such a case, the use of the first person plural "we", *oidamen*, and even more the third person singular "his", *autou*, is the only possible. "The beloved disciple" would then be a title, like, *mórah hassedeq*, "The Teacher of Righteousness" in the Dead Sea Scrolls. In my opinion, therefore, the "beloved disciple" was, as Jackson and Bauckham claim, a self-designation of the author of the Fourth Gospel; but it still came to have a meaning for the community of the beloved disciple as a statement of his apostolic authority as one close to the Lord.

Communities often do not refer to persons especially dear to them by name. The Oratory community in Birmingham, as we have mentioned earlier,[89] still refer to John Henry Newman, their founder, as "The Cardinal", which can be somewhat disconcerting for a visitor who might first be thinking of the current Archbishop of Westminster under that title. Likewise, "the disciple whom Jesus loved" was both a title which elevated the leader of the Johannine Community, and (perhaps even more important) gave a special weight to his authorship of the Gospel. This was not simply to provide sound historical information about the historical Jesus, but also to guarantee *the perspective* on Jesus which was special, from one who was so close to Jesus and understood not only his mind but his heart. It was particularly important, as Jackson insists, because of Doceticism. The anonymity, therefore, represented the community's respect for its leader as the one closest to the Lord. All reading the Gospel at that time, whether in the Johannine Community or not, would have known that it referred to their leader and apostle John the Son of Zebedee.

The anonymity of the beloved disciple remains a difficulty in accepting as author John the Son of Zebedee; but is not a decisive one. It could be argued that we simply do not know the explanation, yet other evidence leads us to accept apostolic authorship, leaving some mysteries unsolved. There is certainly more solid evidence, both from early tradition and from the text of the Gospel, for authorship by John the Son of Zebedee, than for any of the other speculative alternatives proposed.

The author of the Fourth Gospel: a simple fisherman?

John the Son of Zebedee might originally have been a "simple fisherman" (sic), but that again is no barrier eventually to him being able to write a work of such literary, spiritual, and theological genius as the Fourth Gospel.

Jesus chose the majority of his disciples, including the two sons of Zebedee, James and John from the fishing industry on the Sea of Galilee. Is it possible that one of these, with no formal education, could eventually have written the Fourth Gospel with its profound theology?

This objection has a habit of reappearing in the most unlikely places. Dodd has great respect for the arguments of Westcott for the traditional authorship of the Fourth Gospel by John the Son of Zebedee, which he judges to be "impressive, though far from conclusive".[90] He does not fall into the trap of imagining that fishermen are "simple". After all, they follow a dangerous trade, which still registers the largest number of industrial accidents in this country. They have to have their wits about them in order to stay alive in a choppy sea, and indeed to sell their fish. Perhaps Jesus chose fishermen precisely because of their quick wit, their physical strength, ability to survive inclement weather, and ability to face danger and to live dangerously. All these qualities would be needed in abundance for their apostolate.

Dodd, at least implicitly, recognises all this. He admits that John could have learnt Hellenistic culture, living in the northern "Galilee of the Gentiles". He could also, Dodd admits, have learnt some Judaism, but not a great deal. What makes Dodd sceptical is "the *combination* of Rabbinic and Hellenistic motifs, their combination at a deep level that should give us pause".[91]

But surely this combination of Greek and Judaistic influences is precisely what we would expect from one who was a "known to the High Priest" [John 18:15]. Could not that *entrée* into the higher reaches of the Judaism of his day have given the Son of Zebedee more than a smattering of Jewish theology? Could not also his closeness to Jesus himself have made him acquainted with intra-Jewish debates, which were in the end to lead to the death of his Master? His fisherman's sense of danger could have led him to ask who Jesus was and what his fate would be. Even *before* the death and resurrection of Jesus, John would have had three years' intense adult education during Jesus' public ministry. He would then have had half-a-century afterwards to develop his own theological ideas.

Furthermore, J.A.T. Robinson gives a typically new and provocative twist to this whole question. He insists that:

> The evidence therefore for the person we are seeking, so far from ruling out a relatively poor and uneducated Palestinian, points suspiciously towards the kind of man that John, son of Zebedee, might have been. There is in fact no reason to suppose that his family was particularly poor and uneducated. His mother Salome (cf. Mark 15:40 with Matthew 27:56) was among those who ministered to Jesus in Galilee (Mark 15:41) as Luke adds (8:3) 'out of their possessions'. In Zahn's words, "As regards its prosperity and social position, the family of Zebedee is to be compared with that of Chuza (Luke 8:3), the financial officer of Herod, or even of Joseph of Arimathea, rather than that of Joseph and Mary (Luke 2:24, cf. 2:7)."[92]

Robinson also makes the valid point that "the lack of education attributed to John and Peter by the 'Jewish rulers, elders and doctors of the law' in Acts 4:13 need indicate no more than that in their professional eyes these were 'untrained laymen' (NEB) a view shared by the authorities both of Jesus (John 7:15; cf.9:29) and Paul (Acts 21:37f.) The astonishment was that despite this they showed themselves so articulate". Robinson goes on to emphasise that John the Son of Zebedee began his career as the younger of two brothers James and John in Matthew and Mark [cf. e.g. Mark 3:17] "James son of Zebedee and John the brother of James (to whom he gave the name Boanerges, that is, Sons of Thunder)". But after his elder brother James' death [Acts 12:2], John rises in importance to become one of the 'big three' in the Jerusalem church, together with James the Lord's Brother and Peter himself [Galatians 2:9].

Nearly all the objections, and there are many, to the authorship of the Fourth Gospel by John need to be taken seriously, and have been taken seriously. But, in all honesty, I do find it difficult to take seriously the objection that a fisherman could not have written such a superb piece of literature as the Gospel of John. Why not? Dare we suggest that even academic snobbery might underlie this objection?

Those of us with experience of adult learning know how in five years part time study one without any university education can become fully competent in complex discussions at degree level, and write excellent essays showing advanced knowledge and integration of thought. The Open University experience has demonstrated that police, shopkeepers, taxi drivers, in number hundreds of thousands of students, can master degree level work. That mastery can be achieved by part-time study, while the adult student is following his or her own career and with the responsibility of a family.

What kind of fisherman was John the son of Zebedee? If Robinson is right, his father might have had a reasonably large business on the Sea of Galilee. He was therefore a businessman's son. The fact that Jesus called John and his brother James to become his disciples when they were mending nets with their father [Matthew 4:21] does not mean that their father was not successful. A man with three or four boats would not necessarily spend all day in the office.

Similarly, the Pope in *Jesus of Nazareth* agrees with Cazelles that Zebedee the father of John, even though a fisherman, was possibly a priest.[93]

This young disciple spent three years *full time* with Jesus of Nazareth, who, ignoring the fact that he was the Son of God, was a highly intelligent rabbi in the Jewish tradition. As to this fisherman, he had the benefit of both formal and informal daily teaching by Jesus. John was chosen as one of the Twelve, his own special inner council to represent, and eventually, said Jesus, to judge the Twelve Tribes of Israel [Matthew 19:28]. Furthermore, John was chosen by Jesus to be one of his closest disciples, and had the inestimable benefit of the Rabbi's private counsel. Can we doubt that, even before the death of Jesus, John was learning a great deal of Rabbinic theology, through private tuition, and through Jesus' dialogue with the scribes and Pharisees?

Furthermore, this knowledge was not naïve but critical. Jesus, John the Son of Zebedee's Rabbi, was scathing of some of the Pharisaic interpretations of the Torah. If John therefore had some knowledge also of Greek religion and philosophy coming as he did from "Galilee of the Gentiles", then that combination of Jewish and Hellenistic thinking which we find in the Fourth Gospel which, as we have seen, was fully cognisant of the world of contemporary thinking yet not a slave to it, was already formed most plausibly in the mind of John the Son of Zebedee possibly even during Jesus' lifetime on earth.

That, as we have said, was true even before the death and resurrection of Jesus. After that death, and after the Day of Pentecost [Acts 2], John assumed a position of high responsibility in the Jerusalem church. He had to preach the new faith, and adapt that faith to a growing number of Gentile converts. If, as seems clear, the Fourth Gospel was not written until between 68 and 100 AD John had more than a whole generation, between thirty and sixty years, to develop as an adult theologian. How can we take seriously the objection that he could not have developed his own theological understanding sufficiently to write a work such as the Fourth Gospel linked as it was with his preaching of the Gospel?

Added to this, as Robinson argues, the career of John seems to have centred on the Jewish rather than the Gentile mission.[94] If we combine his knowledge of the Greek world through living in Galilee, which Dodd is more than prepared to admit, together with his three year induction by Jesus himself in Judaism, his knowledge of the High Priest, and his years of preaching to his fellow Jews, how seriously can we take the objection that he could not have acquired sufficient knowledge of both Hellenism and Judaism to write the Fourth Gospel?

Naturally, there is a question as to how anyone could have written such a work as the Gospel of John, whatever their background or personal history and education, a work so simple in its language and yet so profound so as to baffle philosophers and theologians down the centuries. But how could anyone have painted the Mona Lisa portrait or written the novels of Dostoevsky? The writer of the Gospel of John must have been a genius, as well as inspired by the Holy Spirit.

As we all know, there are no rules about genius. Gray's *Elegy in a Country Churchyard* laments on how in that village cemetery may lay the corpse of some "mute inglorious Milton"; some farm labourer who, if he had had the chance, might have become a great poet or playwright, but who never progressed any further than his plough. If we insist on the humble origins of John the Son of Zebedee (and, as we have seen, perhaps they were not all that humble) we have an example in a "Milton" who was neither "mute" nor "inglorious", but who achieved his true potential in writing perhaps the greatest piece of religious literature in the history of the world, the Fourth Gospel.

Finally, what of Dodd's objection that "a work proceeding directly from the hand of one of the Galilean disciples should show such indifference to the Galilean ministry, should minimise its importance, and should betray all through what can only be called a metropolitan outlook"?[95] Perhaps the fact that Dodd relegates this objection to a footnote betrays some implicit lack of confidence in its cogency. As Robinson counters, the word Galilee occurs more frequently in John than in any other Gospel.[96] Also, we read in John that "leaving Nazareth he [Jesus] went and settled in Capernaum" [4:12]. The Gospel therefore gives us a clear signal that much of the ministry took place there. Robinson gives us an almost bewildering number of Galilean geographical citations, demonstrating that the Fourth Gospel sees Jesus apparently centring his Galilean ministry at Capernaum [cf. John 6:59]. Robinson concludes "I cite these connections, however inferential, because at any rate they do not show indifference to or ignorance of Galilean detail".[97]

Surely, we must also pay attention to the whole purpose of the writing of the Gospel of John. As we have already seen in our Part One[98], much more than in the Synoptics, the Fourth Gospel focuses the drama in Jerusalem, precisely because the key events which determined "the hour" of Jesus [John 13:1], his death and resurrection, took place in Jerusalem; his curing of the man on the Sabbath, his dialogue with the Jews, 7-10, the raising of Lazarus, 11-12, and his discourse with his disciples 13-16. If the Fourth Gospel had a mainly Jewish Christian readership (which Robinson thinks it had[99]) this would give an added reason for the Jerusalem focus.

And even if, as Brown thinks, the audience was much more general than Robinson admits,[100] the Jerusalem focus is still important at the close of the first century, as the separation between Church and Synagogue becomes wider and more distinct than in the earliest days of the infant Church. The Galilean ministry is therefore of necessity telescoped; yet it is the occasion of Jesus' own self-revelation as the Bread of Life and the promise that he would give his flesh for the life of the world, [John 6]. The writer of the Fourth Gospel, as Robinson demonstrates, knows Galilee; but for him, Jerusalem is literally where the action takes place.[101] And, we repeat, John as the beloved disciple has connections in Jerusalem with the High Priest [John 18:16], which might also add to the Jerusalem interest for him.

Conclusion

It is obvious to everyone that the question of the authorship of the Fourth Gospel is a complex question, with many solutions proposed in this post-critical age. All we have been attempting to argue in this chapter is that *the ancient tradition that John the Son of Zebedee was the actual author of the whole of the Gospel traditionally bearing his name has not been overturned, and rather that it is the most consistent and coherent interpretation of all the evidence.*

We have argued that the Gospel was written by an eye-witness; that its author was the beloved disciple; that he was none other than John the Son of Zebedee, one of the Twelve; that he testified to the truth of what he wrote; that he wrote the whole of the Gospel; that he was the actual author, although he might have used a scribe.

Other solutions are possible, such as the view of the Pope that the beloved disciple was the son of Zebedee, but the author was the second John mentioned by Papias, John the Elder. We also took very seriously the theory of Richard Baukham, which was argued in full detail, that the author was indeed the beloved disciple, an intimate disciple of Jesus, but that he was not John the Son of Zebedee, but that other John mentioned by Papias.

All these views would be totally compatible with the author being a close eye-witness of the events he records. The positing of the writer of the Fourth Gospel other than the beloved disciple one of the Twelve the Son of Zebedee would also seem to be more compatible with a view of 21:24, whose use of the third person plural "we" ("we know that his testimony is true") suggests to some that these witnesses could have had something to do with the writing of the Gospel.

But this means that we interpret *ho grapsas tauta* ("who wrote these things") that the beloved disciple "caused to write" the Gospel through someone else, perhaps a scribe. We have concluded that Bauckham is quite correct in excluding the possibility suggested by many that *ho grapsas tauta* might refer to the beloved disciple as the source of the historical tradition underlying the writing of the Gospel rather than the author in the strict sense. The beloved disciple was the actual author, *per se* or through a scribe.

Yet other theories as to the identity of the beloved disciple and the identity of the author are even more hypothetical, whether as an ideal figure (which we agree with Hengel and Bauckham is most unlikely) possibly Lazarus, John Mark; but the evidence for them is much less than for authorship by John the Son of Zebedee; although any of these figures could have been an eye-witness of Jesus' life, death and resurrection as recounted in John.

This *likelihood* of authorship by John the Son of Zebedee is all we need to argue for a post-critical apologetic for the incarnation. What we are really concerned to argue with reasonable certainty is the likelihood of the Fourth Gospel being rooted in the eye-witness testimony of the life, death, and resurrection of Jesus of Nazareth. The various nuances proposed by critical scholarship – for example the identity of the beloved disciple being other than John Son of Zebedee, the identification of the "we" as being the collective testimony of the Ephesian elders – would not nullify the possibility that there is a strong relationship with eye-witness tradition. That is what is essential in order to provide a justification for Pope Benedict who wishes to argue in *Jesus of Nazareth*, namely that the Gospels, and particularly that of John, are reliable when they recount words and deeds of the historical Jesus that demonstrate his divinity.

A simple comparison will illustrate the importance of this conclusion. Tradition held that Moses was the author of the Pentateuch, the first five books of the Old Testament. This position has been abandoned by scholars apart from Fundamentalists, because there are no historical grounds for this tradition. The text of the Pentateuch itself gives no evidence whatsoever that Moses was the author. Critical scholarship concludes that much of the book was written centuries after Moses' time. The tradition of Mosaic authorship is accounted for by the fact that Moses was the originator of the laws of the Israelite community, not that he was the actual author.

Where the Fourth Gospel is concerned, however, it is entirely a different case. The Gospel is demonstrably written within the span of eye-witness testimony. The external evidence of Irenaeus is itself credible even if not indisputable. The text of the Gospel itself gives some grounds for thinking that the author might well have been John the Son of Zebedee, the intimate disciple of Jesus. This is therefore *historical evidence* for the possible veracity of Christian tradition regarding the Fourth Gospel. This real possibility can therefore become part of a developing argument for the substantial historicity of the Fourth Gospel, and its central message that in Jesus of Nazareth the Word has become flesh.

We have already noted how in Johannine scholarship, indeed in any historical research, questions are interconnected. I suggest that the cavalier dismissal by Schmithals of any possibility of apostolic authorship of the Fourth Gospel is based first and foremost upon historical scepticism regarding the content of that Gospel. We have seen in this chapter, that, taken on their own, the arguments in themselves for apostolic authorship are at least very much stronger than the nineteenth-century critical movement would allow. This scepticism within German criticism, as we have seen, goes back to Strauss' *Leben Jesu*, who rejected the historical character of the Fourth Gospel because that Gospel promoted the doctrine of the Incarnation.[102]

If the incarnation was to be rejected in post-Enlightenment exegesis, then it would be hardly possible to support the traditional authorship of the Fourth Gospel, with the clear implication that the Incarnate Word had been encountered as such by an intimate disciple, an eye-witness of the events he described. However, on the contrary, if we assumed that the incarnation was at least a possible event, that Jesus of Nazareth at least might be God the Son, then the arguments favourable to apostolic eye-witness authorship which we have discussed in this chapter only confirm that possibility.

Therefore, as in the twentieth century it became more and more obvious that the Fourth Gospel is not essentially a Hellenistic document, but rather that it is truly a Gospel rooted in first century Semitic thought, then those who wished still to deny historicity have to produce redaction theories which remove the authorship of the Gospel more and more from the direct testimony of an eye-witness. In a radical redaction theory, it would not matter if the first author in the process was an eye-witness. In the process of redaction, the work would evolve into a reflection of what the author, or still more what the "Johannine Community" believed, rather than what the historical Jesus actually said and did. It was a reflection of the "Christ of faith" rather than of the "Jesus of history".

Has St John's Gospel been so thoroughly reworked by later editors that it can no longer be called the product of any author or authors with possible eye-witness contact with the historical Jesus? It might be argued that this is the most important issue regarding the authorship of the Fourth Gospel ever since the publication of Bultmann's first edition of his commentary *Das Evangelium des Johannes* in 1941. We must now, therefore, consider the question, again most complex, of the literary composition of the Gospel of John.

Just as we have found that anti-incarnational tendencies have confused the question of authorship of the Gospel of John, so now we will discover that similarly graduitous theological presuppositions have produced speculative redaction theories with little or no evidence to support them.

NOTES – CHAPTER NINE

1 The view of Bultmann, 16ff.
2 The view of Barrett, 151.
3 Bultmann, 13, Barratt, 149.
4 Schnackenburg, I, 221.
5 Carson, 111.
6 Lightfoot, 78.
7 Bultmann, 62.
8 Westcott, 1958, xxv.
9 Brown, I, 13.
10 Westcott, 1958, xxv.
11 Jackson, JTS, 1999.
12 Harnack, A. von. *Das "Wir" in den Johanneischen Schriften.* 97 n.4. SPAW phil.-hist. Kl., (1923) 96-113, with the review by J. Behm, TLZ 49 (1924), 252-5.
13 Jackson, JTS, 1999,15.
14 Jackson, JTS, 1999, 14.
15 Lightfoot, 84.
16 Jackson, JTS, 1999, 15.
17 JN, 6.

18 Bultmann, 70.

19 I make this same point in BMG, 349-352, concerning *Miracles and Faith in John.*

20 Lincoln, A.T., *Truth on Trial: The Lawsuit Motif in the Fourth Gospel.* Peabody, Hendrikson, 2000. And by the same author *The beloved disciple as Eyewitness and the Fourth Gospel as a Witness.* JSNT 85 (2002), 3-26.

21 Bauckham, 2006, 387.

22 Bauckham, 2006, 389-390.

23 Ridderbos, 13.

24 Brown, I, XCIII-XCIV. I have changed Brown's system of biblical referencing to conform to that in this book.

25 Westcott, xxi-xxii. I have retained Westcott's spelling and his system of quoting biblical texts in italics, but changed the system of biblical reference from his to that adopted in this book.

26 Lindars, 33, says that the unnamed disciple's close relationship with Peter "proves nothing either way". But, as Westcott argues, it certainly proves a great deal if that unnamed disciple stands in a close relationship with both Peter *and* Jesus.

27 Carson, 72.

28 Bauckham, 2006, 415.

29 Quoted in Carson, 669.

30 *Ibid.*

31 Cf. Brown, II, 578. "Lagrange, p.512, proposes that the original text of John mentioned only five disciples and that this phrase was a very ancient marginal gloss identifying the 'two other disciples', a gloss that found its way into the body of the text."

32 Barrett, 101. "Polycrates appears to confuse Philip the Apostle with Philip the Evangelist – an error which does nothing to increase confidence in his other remarks."

33 Quotation from Barratt, 101.

34 Bauckham, 2006, 445.

35 Bauckham, 2006, 446.

36 Bauckham, 2006, 451.

37 Bauckham, 2006, 449.

38 Barrett, 101.

39 *Ibid.*, n.2.

40 Westcott, xxvi.

41 Brown, II, 936.

42 *Ibid.*, cf. Abbott, Lagrange, Strachan, Hoskyns, and Braun. The use of *ekeinos* is strange here for those commentators. Westcott draws attention to 9:37 where *ekeinos* is used by a speaker of himself (in this case Jesus). *Ekeinos* is not grammatically impossible, or un-Johannine. Westcott also argues that if the writer were someone else other than the eye-witness, he would have used the Greek Aorist tense, "he that saw bore witness" and not "he that hath seen hath borne witness".

Westcott, xxvii. Cf. Barrett, 557 *ad loc.*

43 Brown, II, 937.
44 So Hoskyns, 533. "The beloved disciple does not merely bear witness against the Docetists to the evident proof of the actual death of Christ, nor merely to the miraculous occurrence which followed his death, but rather to the significance of that occurrence. He perceived that purification (water) and new life (blood) flow from the completed sacrifice of the Lamb of God…"
45 Bultmann, 715-6, n.6 Carson agrees with Bultmann here. "v. 24 is better seen as part of the answer to Peter's question in v. 21 'Lord, what about him?' All disciples live under the commission of 20:21. After that, there are distinctions: Peter serves by tending the flock of God and by glorifying God in his death; the beloved disciple serves by following Jesus through a long life, and as the trustworthy disciple who testifies to these things and who wrote them down. That means v.24 has to be read as part of vv. 20-23, and v. 20 establishes that the beloved disciple is none other than the beloved disciple who appears throughout the Fourth Gospel. By the same token, these things to which the disciple testifies must not be the contents of ch.21 alone, but the entire Fourth Gospel." Carson, 683. Cf. Barrett, 587-588.
46 Below, 259-267.
47 Morris, 880-881. So also Barrett, 588. More speculative is Pheme Perkins view that "*these things*. They need not refer to the whole Gospel, but may imply that the oral tradition stemming from the beloved disciple and perhaps some written embodiment of that tradition underlie the Gospel". NJBC, **61:244**, 985.
48 Brown, II, 1123-4, summarises the position: "*these things*". Dodd, Note, suggests that this phrase refers to the words of Jesus in 20-23 and their correct interpretation, so that the writer is marshalling support for his contention that an inaccurate report has been spread among the brothers. However, Dodd allows the possibility that the whole of ch.xxi is included under the phrase, a view held by many of those who hold that the chapter was appended as a unit. A more widely held view is that vs.24 is a type of colophon indicating the writer's outlook upon the authorship (in the broad sense) of the entire Gospel. Verse 25 would imply that the "these things" of 24 included all the recorded deeds performed by Jesus.
49 Moloney, 561.
50 VGT, 132-133.
51 Barrett, 587.
52 Bauckham, 2006, 361.
53 Jackson, JTS, 1999, 24.
54 Although it is worth remembering that Lagrange, M.-J, *L'Évangile Selon Saint Jean*, Paris, Gabalda, 1936, XIX, had already noticed the use of the third person in Xenophon and Caesar!
55 Jackson, JTS, 1999, 27.

56 Jackson, JTS, 1999, 29.

57 Westcott, xxviii.

58 Brown, II, 1125.

59 Carson, 684.

60 Carson, 683.

61 ODCC, 413.

62 "J. Roloff (NTS 15 (1968-9, 129-51) has shown that the anonymous figure of the Teacher of Righteousness in the Dead Sea Scrolls serves a similar function, as the authoritative teacher of the Qumran Community."

63 Brown, I, XCIV. Loisy 128.

64 Bultmann, 484.

65 Brown, I, XCIV-V. *Hom. In Evang.* II 22; PL 76:1175.

66 Bultmann, 484.

67 Brown, I, XCV.

68 Bultmann, 484.

69 Schneiders, 516.

70 Schneiders, 519-20.

71 Brown, I, XCV.

72 Filson, 1949.

73 Sanders, 1962.

74 Lindars, 33.

75 Brown, I, XCV.

76 Brown, I, XCV.

77 For discussion of the Authorship of Mark's Gospel, cf. NJBC, **41:2**, 596.

78 Parker, 1960.

79 Brown, I, XCVI.

80 Sanders, 1968, cf. Lindars, 33.

81 Brown, I, XCVI.

82 Lindars, 33.

83 Bultmann, 484.

84 DCG, I, 881.

85 DCG, I, 881.

86 Jackson, JTS, 1999, 31. Bauckham, 2006, 401, agrees with Jackson that "it was not a title used by others but precisely a self-designation adopted by the author of the Gospel specifically for the purpose of referring to himself in his own narrative".

87 Roloff, 1968-9, 129-51.

88 Above, 192, "4. Who are the 'We' testifying?…"

89 Above, 182, "the visitor to the…"

90 Dodd, 1965, 14.

91 Dodd, 1965, 16.

92 Robinson, 1976, 300.

93 JN, 224.

94 Robinson, 1976, 303.

95 Dodd, 1965, 16, n.2.
96 Robinson, 1976, 301.
97 Robinson, 1976, 302.
98 Above, 85, "The Synoptic Gospels do not contain this historical information..."
99 Robinson, 1959-60, 117-31.
100 Brown I, LXXVIII.
101 Cf. Above, 86, Part One. "Jesus goes up to Jerusalem privately..." and BMG, 267-295.
102 Cf. Part One, 97, "who shattered the Christian world..."

CHAPTER TEN

THEORIES OF COMPOSITION

- Redaction theories proposing a radical discontinuity between the life, teaching and self-consciousness of the historical Jesus and the final edition of the Gospel are speculative and exegetically defective. In particular, they proceed from unjustified scepticism regarding the historical veracity of the content of the Gospel.

- The view still held by some scholars that there was a single author of the Gospel is scientifically most plausible, particularly noting the fact that there is no significant stylistic difference in order to identify different authors.

- Likewise, there is no evidence apart from speculation for R.E. Brown's Stages in the formation of the Fourth Gospel.

- A single author, according to tradition John the Son of Zebedee, could have written the whole work using his own sources gathered over the years – liturgical texts, homilies, accounts of miracles, etc. He could have used a scribe. All the evidence we have is consistent with the view that the author was John the Son of Zebedee, as ecclesiastical tradition states.

We carry vitally important conclusions over from the previous chapter. With critical agreement that the Fourth Gospel cannot have been written later than the turn of the first and second century AD, and from our conclusion regarding its Semitic origin in present day Syria, Jordan, or Israel, it cannot be denied that it could have been written by an author in eye-witness contact with the time of the historical Jesus in the first half of the first century AD.

Our conclusions regarding authorship are no less positive. The tradition that John the Son of Zebedee, the intimate disciple of Jesus, was the author of the Fourth Gospel, and that he was the "beloved disciple" of the Gospel narrative, has still not been overturned after two centuries of intense critical study, even though other more complex solutions are possible, such as the theory that John the Presbyter was the beloved disciple, as Bauckham claims, or that that John the Presbyter was the author of the Gospel and a close friend of John the Son of Zebedee, as the Pope proposes in *Jesus of Nazareth*. In these more complex theories, the Fourth Gospel was either written by an eye-witness, or one who was in close contact with that eye-witness.

But now we must examine the question of the composition of the Gospel. Is there evidence of a single author at work? Was the work written in stages, or all in one piece? Is there evidence of later editing (redactions)? These questions are related, as we shall see, to the historical reliability of the Fourth Gospel. An exegete who proposes a particular source theory may contend that the particular source proposed was influenced, not by the author's intention to write a reliable account of the history of Jesus, but e.g. to propose or even counter Gnosticism, or perhaps ideas about the end of the world (eschatology). In this scenario, we might conclude that the Gospel had as its source an eye-witness, but that later redactions have turned the Fourth Gospel into theological fiction.

On the other hand, a work which went through an editorial process could present a substantially reliable account in its later stages of redaction as well as at the earlier stages. Indeed, it is not impossible that a later redactor, in contact with the historical Jesus, could see it necessary to correct possibly false impressions in other Gospels, or in earlier editions of the Fourth Gospel, and to provide an account closer to the historical reality. Too often the impression given (again, influenced by the post-Bultmannian tradition) is that any later redaction will take us further away from the historical Jesus. But this is by no means necessarily so, if, as we have demonstrated, the Fourth Gospel in its final edition is not to be dated later than the beginning of the second century, within the possible lifetime of the possible author, John the Son of Zebedee, or at least by one who knew the author personally, and who was careful to preserve the authentic tradition of the historical Jesus.

It is difficult even to attempt to describe the state of Johannine studies regarding redaction theories. Martin Hengel,

217

in his provocative and stimulating study *The Johannine Question*[1] puts the matter succinctly and eloquently:

> 'Once upon a time', as we must say now, David Friedrich Strauss, the founder of radical gospel criticism in the nineteenth century, compared the Fourth Gospel to 'Christ's seamless robe'. Nowadays, even a conservative theologian would no longer dare to say anything like that; 'Christ's seamless robe' has long become a patchwork 'coat of many colours'. So sometimes scholars hardly dare to speak of a real author of the Gospel, but concern themselves rather with a multiplicity of redactors and sources. Its linguistic and stylistic unity is no longer attributed to an author but to a community. The literary critics, who seek to dissect layer upon layer, redaction upon redaction, have been reinforced by the constructors of a history of the Johannine circle, who combine literary-critical work and the reconstruction of this community. Here Raymond Brown has produced the most impressive hypothesis in his book *The Community of the beloved disciple*,[2] which traces the history of this supposed community through seven or eight phases up to the division into the orthodox Christians and the heretical Gnostics.[3]

How has Strauss' "seamless robe" become Raymond Brown's patchwork quilt of successive redactions all woven together into a bewildering pattern of stages or sources? We will begin by outlining the history of the literary criticism of the Fourth Gospel, and then attempt to discuss those who have offered contrary solutions.

Julius Wellhausen, 1844-1918[4]

Julius Wellhausen was most famous for putting the standard theory about the evolution of the sources of the five first books of the Bible, Genesis to Deuteronomy, the "Pentateuch",[5] into its definitive shape in his *Prologomena to the History of Israel*.[6] Wellhausen, as Roland Murphy says, presented "a brilliant synthesis of previous efforts".[7] It is not perhaps surprising, therefore, that, as Ashton comments, "Julius Wellhausen's earlier triumphs in Old Testament studies (though not the first, he is the most famous pioneer of Pentateuchal source theories) evidently stimulated him to look for evidence of similar restitching elsewhere".[8]

Wellhausen went from his Old Testament studies to look at the Fourth Gospel, where he was the first scholar to think that he found similar evidence of strands of sources as he had discovered in the Pentateuch.[9] John Ashton[10] praises Wellhausen for his seminal researches, even if qualifying his praise by asserting "There is no doubt that Wellhausen's observations and his methods are of more significance than his rather precipitate conclusions".[11] But we believe that we must question Wellhausen's methodology even more than his conclusions.

Wellhausen began by noting that John's narration does not always flow as the reader would expect. Thus, for example, Jesus' call "Rise, let us be on our way" [John 14:31], and instead we have a continuing homily by Jesus together with a dialogue with his disciples, which takes us right up to the story of Jesus' arrest in 18:1. Wellhausen concluded that the whole passage from "Rise, let us be on our way" to the arrest, i.e. Chapters 15-17, were a later addition.

Similarly, Chapters 4, 5, 6 and 7 seem to be out of order. The narrative sequence is apparently awkward:

- Chapter 4: Jesus is in Samaria and Galilee.
- Chapter 5: Jesus is in Jerusalem
- Chapter 6: Jesus is back in Galilee.
- Chapter 7: Jesus goes again to Jerusalem.

Wellhausen concluded here that the logic of the narrative demanding a sequence of Chapters 4,6,5 and 7.

Finally, Chapter 21 appears in effect to be an epilogue, the Gospel already having been properly ended in the last verses of Chapter 20:

Thomas answered him, "My Lord and my God!" Jesus said to him, "Have you believed because you have seen me? Blessed are those who have not seen and yet have come to believe." Now Jesus did many other signs in the presence of his disciples, which are not written in this book. But these are written so that you may come to believe that Jesus is the Messiah, the Son of God, and that through believing you may have life in his name. [John 20:28-31]

Wellhausen therefore concluded that Chapter 21 was also a later addition.

It is to Wellhausen's credit that Johannine scholarship has at least acknowledged that there is a problem regarding these examples of unevenness in the Gospel narrative. His statement of the problem has now become classical, even though scholars have proposed different literary – critical solutions to the problem.

However, in addition, Wellhausen posited that there is a lack of *theological coherence* in the Fourth Gospel, and this was for him proof of a primitive strain in the text which had been added to later. So he considered that the eucharistic passage in 6:51-59 was a later addition, as also the sacramental allusions in 19:34, 35 and 37. Finally, Wellhausen considered that the early Church had no expectation of the final return of Jesus, but believed in his constant presence with them now. This, for Wellhausen, is revealed in part of 5:21-24):

> Very truly, I tell you, anyone who hears my word and believes him who sent me has eternal life, and does not come under judgment, but has passed from death to life. [John 5:24]

But the very next verse is evidence of belief in the future Parousia, the Second Coming of Jesus. For Wellhausen, this is clear evidence that this text, 5:25-29, is a later addition:

> Very truly, I tell you, the hour is coming, and is now here, when the dead will hear the voice of the Son of God, and those who hear will live. [John 5:24-25]

Wellhausen regarded the Fourth Gospel's original author therefore as unorthodox, since he apparently denied the Second Coming of Jesus, and indeed taught that Jesus was waiting in heaven for his disciples. Thus Wellhausen again dismisses as secondary the hypothetical clause at the beginning of 14:3, "if I go and prepare a place for you":

> And if I go and prepare a place for you, (*ean poreuthó kai etoimasó*) I will come again and will take you to myself, so that where I am, there you may be also. [John 14:3]

Ashton explains: "This verse, Wellhausen continues, consorts ill with the context and is omitted by one or two of the early versions. If this clause is left out the result is a natural sequence: 'otherwise I would have told you [*hypothetical affirmative*] that I was going to prepare a place for you and that I would come again and take you to myself'. Read in this way the sentence becomes a denial of the parousia, not an assertion of it." [12]

Wellhausen is performing mental contortions not unfamiliar with those attempting to uncover redactional additions, and is building castles on sand. As Ashton complains, "Wellhausen was wrong to build upon the hypothetical nature of the *ean* clause, since this word may be used in contexts where it has to be translated 'when': for example 12:32." [13]

We must ask, furthermore, whether Wellhausen has illicitly transferred Pentateuchal methodology to a very different piece of work, the Fourth Gospel. In the first five books of the Bible, there is a gap of more than a thousand years between the events they record (Patriarchal period eighteenth century BC) and the final form of the Pentateuch according to the Documentary Hypothesis, produced in the fifth century BC. But it is now unanimously agreed that there were at the most, eighty years (32-110 AD) between the events in the life of Jesus and the final form of the Fourth Gospel. We have already quoted J.A.T. Robinson's graphic presentation of this remarkable consensus among Johannine scholars concerning the dating of John in his *Redating the New Testament*. [14]

But, on any assessment, the view that in the seventy years of the development of Christianity, the Johannine camp came to believe that Christ would not return, a view which is solely based upon textual surgery, indeed some might say textual butchery, must be considered as hypothetical in the extreme. Wellhausen has just become drunk with source analysis, and produced no historical evidence. At least where his evolution of the Pentateuchal sources is concerned we do have some evidence of the ethical teaching of the prophets and the Davidic theology of 2 Samuel 7 (J theology) in the eighth century, and we do have some evidence of developing Judaism in the post-exilic period in the sixth and fifth centuries BC. But there is no historical evidence whatever for evolution of belief in the Johannine community from 40 to 110 AD apart from the reconstructions of redaction criticism.

Philosophically, Wellhausen was a devotee of the Romantic philosopher Vatke,[15] who saw human history as beginning with natural and innocent happiness, and becoming more and more legalistic and institutionalised. In Wagner's *Der Ring des Nibelungen*, the Rhine Maidens' gold, which they guard under the river with simple joy at its glowing beauty, is stolen by the lovelorn and avaricious dwarf Alberich; so Wellhausen sees Israelite history as the story of how its early, more natural religion was "stolen" by the eighth century prophets with their "ethical monotheism" (J), and even more, the legalistic Priestly author (P) of the sixth century BC. Wellhausen was therefore tempted to see a similar development (for him a downward one) in the primitive Church, from a simple acceptance of Jesus the Messiah to the sacramental ecclesial institution of the Johannine Church.

We may question Wellhausen's assumption that institutionalisation necessarily represents a downward path in history. But at least there is some historical evidence which Wellhausen can interpret where the Old Testament is concerned. But we have no historical evidence for what Wellhausen claims has happened in the early church. The first New Testament document is the First Epistle to the Thessalonians, 51 AD,[16] which has the clear belief that Jesus will return [I Thessalonians 4:1-13]. It cannot be considered naïve harmonisation to conclude that the evangelist believed *both* that Christ was with his disciples here and now, 5:21-24, *and* that Jesus will come again to judge the world in the future, 5:25-29. We must rightly conclude that Wellhausen is simply bringing in his philosophical and theological prejudices to write his own literary history of the Fourth Gospel; but it is his Gospel, not John's.

This is not to say that the problems uncovered by Wellhausen do not have a real foundation, as outlined by Zumstein,[17] for example the apparent unevenness and repetitiveness of the Final Discourse 13-17, the difficulty of the original order of the narrative as in the canonical text Chapters 4,5,6 and 7, and finally Chapter 21 itself. These problems must have our serious consideration later. What Wellhausen leaves as a question mark as to methodology is the validity of applying *one's own subjective theological and philosophical prejudices* as the criteria of source and/or redactional analysis, together with some arguments based upon literary criticism. The problems inherent in this subjective approach become even more marked in those who followed Wellhausen on this redactional path as a key to understanding the Fourth Gospel.

Rudolf Bultmann, 1884-1976

We have already examined Bultmann's theological and philosophical presuppositions,[18] and will not be surprised to see them underpinning once more his literary-critical studies. Bultmann's approach is close to that of Wellhausen.[19] For instance, he changes the order of Chapters 4,5,6 and 7 to what he considered to be the primitive order, 4,6,5 and 7:15-24. He likewise shifts the ordering of the Final Discourse, placing 14 after 15 and 17. Zumstein, who wrote a stimulating and original essay on redaction in John[20] states: "The conclusion which the sage of Marburg draws from his study is that the traditional and canonical order of the gospel is the result of a final redaction, and not of the evangelist, a redaction which is expressed fully in Chapter 21."[21]

This redaction, subsequent editing, reveals itself also in dogmatic corrections and glosses. Like Wellhausen, Bultmann finds 6:51-58, then 19:43b-35, which outline the foundations of the sacraments, were the work of the ecclesiastical redactor, and are not part of the original Gospel. Likewise, references to future eschatology, Christ appearing again at the last times, 5:28-29, 6:39-40, 44, 54 and 12:48 must come from the ecclesiastical redactor, because, for Bultmann, the original writer of the Gospel did not believe in futurist eschatology, but only in the Christ here and now. Bultmann was strongly of the opinion that the final editor was worried about ecclesiastical orthodoxy and saw it necessary to insert passages which emphasised the sacraments, and the coming of Christ in the future.[22]

The same difficulty attends Bultmann's view as it does Wellhausen's. Bultmann has imposed his own theological ideas on the Fourth Gospel. Why again is it not possible for the same Gospel writer to believe both in a futurist and a realised eschatology? Has not Bultmann injected his own existentialist view of Christianity, emphasising the here and now decision of faith rather than a future heaven, to make it a principle of redaction criticism? In other words, have we not here *eisegesis* (reading a meaning into the text) rather than *exegesis* (reading out the meaning in the text)?

According to Bultmann, some ecclesiastical redactor set out to "dampen down" the original author's Gnosticism,[23] expressed in the *Offenbarungsreden* or "Revelatory Discourse Source".[24] Evidence of this redaction is to be found in many of the discourses of Jesus in John. The theology of this source was an early Oriental Gnosticism as professed by a group like the followers of John the Baptist and later by the Mandean writings. We have already noted Dodd's objections to Bultmann's Mandean hypothesis,[25] which are surely decisive.

Brown's four objections against Bultmann's source theory are likewise telling:

- In John signs and discourses are woven together. Bult-mann proposed a Signs Source, a collection of miracle stories which was used by the Fourth Evangelist, an analysis which many have followed. But the problem, as Brown says,[26] is that in John signs and discourse are closely woven together. In Chapter 6, for instance, the Bread of Life Discourse interprets the multiplication of the loaves.

- As Dodd argued in his *Historical Tradition in the Fourth Gospel*,[27] embedded in the discourses are sayings of Jesus, which by comparison with those in the Synoptics, have every reason to be considered as belonging to a primitive tradition of the words of Jesus. Bultmann's poetic Revelatory Discourse is therefore superfluous.

- The stylistic differences are not verifiable. As Brown says, "Now, we grant that in incorporating the sources into one work, the evangelist would introduce common elements of style. However, if we remember that, according to Bultmann's hypothesis, one of the sources was originally in Aramaic poetry and another was in Semitizing Greek, and the evangelist himself wrote in a less Semitized Greek, the commonness of Johannine peculiarities in all three is inexplicable. As P. Parker[28] has remarked, 'It looks as though, if the author of the Fourth Gospel used documentary sources, he wrote them all himself'."[29]

- Brown argues that there are no parallels in antiquity for the kind of sources Bultmann has postulated. The *Odes of Solomon* are not really paralleled to the discourses of Jesus at all, as Brown says, but only to the Prologue 1:1-18. Brown concludes that "We cannot help but judge that the theory (Bultmann's) suffers from almost insuperable difficulties".[30]

Other Redaction Theories

It is not possible to deal in detail with the large number of possible redaction theories which have abounded since Bultmann's commentary. We can only list below a few examples. Full consideration of each one would entail a book of this size devoted only to that subject.[31] We have already admitted the problems are real:[32] the apparent strange ordering of 4,5,6 and 7, the strange transition from 14:31 to 15:1, and above all the fact that Chapter 21 seems to be an addition after the Gospel has come to a fitting conclusion in 20:31.

But do these breaks and evident unevenness in the narrative require us to believe that the Fourth Gospel is not the work of one author but a compilation by several hands? Leon Morris, in *The Composition of the Fourth Gospel*,[33] is to be commended. He has canvassed the major source theories produced this century, and has shown that the methods used and the results obtained are inconsistent, and that at countless junctures evidence that is adduced to support a source is better understood a different way. We have seen, in the case of both Wellhausen and Bultmann, that to apply theological differences as a criterion of sources leads to reading into the text the exegete's own theological presuppositions.

Thus the source theory of **Georg Richter** [34] is open to the same accusation of subjectivity. Richter posits four stages in the source process. The first two stages are from a low Christology to a high, i.e. they pass from Jesus the Prophet to Jesus the Divine Son of God. Richter's third stage is not represented by any text in John, but is a presupposition of his own; namely that a third redactor injected a Docetic Jesus, emphasising his divinity and ignoring his humanity. The fourth stage, which is represented in the text, corrects the Doceticism of the hypothetical third stage. Richter finds this in the Fourth Stage, for example in 1:14-18.

Richter in effect proposes a quasi-Hegelian dialectic. In his perspective, each action calls forth a symmetrical reaction.[35] Zumstein makes a telling point when he warns against the scholar following Richter's presumption that the evolution of ideas will necessarily be so homogeneous.[36] But still the most telling point throwing doubt on Richter's theory is the total lack of any historical evidence outside of Richter's hypothetical reconstruction to support his supposed development of ideas within the Johannine community.

Like Wellhausen, Bultmann, and Richter, **Hartwig Thyen**[37] has in his mind an imaginary conflict within the early church to which the final redactor of the Fourth Gospel responds. Where Wellhausen and Bultmann had posited a "low Christology", Thyen finds a naïve Docetism. For Richter this was one of the later sources. For Thyen it is the source of the primitive Fourth Gospel.[38] Thus Thyen has again used his imagination to posit a theological movement contrary to the ideas of the Fourth Gospel, in his case anti-Docetism in John, and then – lo and behold! – has found texts which correct the Docetic naïvety of the *Urtext* of John.[39]

It must be a warning against the soundness of the methodology of such as Wellhausen, Bultmann, Richter and Thyen that the theological principles by which the sources are uncovered are so often diverse, even contradictory. For Bultmann, the original is Jesus the prophet and rabbi, for Thyen the early edition of the Fourth Gospel is Jesus the quasi Greek god. The *arbitrariness* and the *subjectivity* of such judgements surely is obvious when set against each other as they are by Zumstein.

Robert Fortna, although indebted to Bultmann, dispenses with Bultmann's "ecclesiastical redactor"[40] and posits a simple Signs Source, consisting of a kind of early hypothetical wonderbook of miracles from which a selection was made by the author of the Fourth Gospel. We have already discussed the feasibility of a Signs Source in detail in our consideration of the miracles of Jesus in *Bad, Mad or God?*.[41] But Carson concludes:

> Hengel rightly questions that it was likely that the Evangelist took over something like the "Signs Source", which all sides admit (if it ever existed) boasted a theology radically different from that of the Evangelist, and incorporated it so mechanically that it can be retrieved by contemporary scholarship.[42] Indeed, if John knew of the Synoptic Gospels (as we have already admitted as a distinct possibility), the one point on which all sides agree is that modern scholarship could not possibly reconstruct any block of Synoptic material from the text of John before us.[43]

Finally, regarding source theories, **John Ashton**'s commands most recent attention, argued as it is with a profound knowledge of the various source theories up to his own work, and an equally profound knowledge of the Fourth Gospel. In a lengthily argued and complex position, Ashton sees the various sources in the Fourth Gospel coming together not as with Bultmann from an external origin such as the *Odes of Solomon*, but rather "after prolonged and sometimes painful reflection in the course of a struggle with the establishment party in the synagogue. Traces of this struggle remain in the Gospel text; the witness motif, for example, mentioned only once in a purely revelatory passage (3:32) was forged in the course of controversies with the Pharisees. Other elements, for example the positive use of the light motif, are more probably the fruit of the prophetic activity of the evangelist and his community".[44]

It is most interesting that Ashton, coming to the fore in the last two decades of the twentieth century, is finding his sources originating in the development of the Christian community itself rather than from outside, from sources alien to Christianity. This is an encouraging trend of modern Johannine criticism, stemming from the conclusions outlined in the previous chapter about the origin of the ideas of the Fourth Gospel, from Dodd onwards. Our difficulty with Ashton's whole position is how early the "high Christology" of the early church actually was,[45] and how much of that early Christology finds its source in the historical Jesus. We could agree with Ashton that Johannine theology developed in the mind of the author influenced by the developing Christian church of the first century. But if, as we are arguing, the author of the Fourth Gospel at least could be John the Son of Zebedee, or even dependent upon him as witness, then the development of thinking will be seen as taking place first and foremost rooted in eye-witness encounter with the historical Jesus. In keeping with our conclusions in Part One, affirming the essential historicity of the Fourth Gospel with the Pope, we would argue that the Christology of St John's Gospel is the result of the author's own memory of the historical Jesus, staying faithful to that memory throughout the process towards the final edition of the Fourth Gospel, unless better arguments for the loss of that historical reliability are provided.

Johannine scholarship moved very much in Ashton's direction in the final decades of the twentieth century. Discussion centred around the evolution of the Johannine

Community, the group of Christians seen as responsible for the Fourth Gospel.[46] The Gospel itself was seen as evidence of the development of the ideas of this Community rather than necessarily an account of the life and times of Jesus of Nazareth. This direction of scholarship received great impetus from acceptance of Raymond Brown's theory of staged development in the writing of the Fourth Gospel. It is more appropriate therefore to leave fuller examination of this trend in Johannine scholarship until later in this chapter, when we will be looking more closely at Brown's theory. However, we shall find that there is as little evidence for such stages in the writing of the Fourth Gospel as there was for redaction theories based upon theological incoherence which we have just examined and found wanting.

The contrary view: unity of style

Martin Hengel draws our attention to the fact that there has always been a view in modern Johannine scholarship which has insisted on the stylistic and theological unity of the Fourth Gospel. Hengel insists that this claim has received additional support first from more recent discoveries of second century manuscripts of John which manifest no evidence of any layers of redaction. De Boer[47] discounts this objection: "The objection that there is no textual evidence for different editions (cf. Carson, 1991, p.45) is worthless, since there are no manuscripts, or scraps of manuscripts, that predate the second century. The hypothesis of several editions over several decades is intended to account for the composition history of the Gospel *in the first century*, when it still belonged to a limited community of Christians".

De Boer is of course correct here. But Hengel's view is justified to the extent that pushing this development within the Johannine community back into the first century telescopes the redaction process more than it would have been had there been demonstrated a second century date for the Fourth Gospel, and emphasises even more the speculative nature of the various redaction theories.

More convincingly, Hengel notes the impressive literary criticism of the Fourth Gospel which has only demonstrated further the literary unity of the Fourth Gospel:

> A second fact which limits the literary 'deconstruction' of the Fourth Gospel is the unity of language and style which is also unique in the New Testament. It had already been brought out in the two volumes by E.A. Abbott, *Johannine Vocabulary* and *Johannine Grammar (1905/6)*. Then E. Schweizer in 1939 showed by means of thirty-three stylistic characteristics which he discovered that the earlier hypotheses suggesting divisions into sources could not in any way be supported 'on stylistic grounds'. E. Ruckstuhl refined Schweizer's method further in 1951 and also applied it to Bultmann's commentary which appeared in 1941 He could point out that from a stylistic point of view there is no justification for Bultmann's numerous literary-critical operations. It is striking that chapter 21 also shares in the unity of the Gospel, while the pericope about the woman taken in adultery, 7.53-8.11, which found its way in at a secondary stage, shows no signs of Johannine style. Granted, Ruckstuhl's conclusions, which are uncomfortable for all literary critics of the Fourth Gospel, have been doubted, but they have never really been refuted. Let me recall them briefly. The Fourth Gospel is 'a unitary work throughout', 'it has a clear ground plan of its own' and forms 'an unusually strong stylistic unity' which includes chapter 21. Its aporias must not be attributed to the involvement of 'several hands', and this unity makes even the hypothesis of an 'ecclesiastical redactor' improbable. 'Style criticism in John does not demonstrate' any underlying literary sources. Glosses cannot be excluded, but they must be demonstrated by textual or stylistic criticism. We should therefore be suspicious of literary criticism based only on 'theological tendencies' and supposed or real inconsistencies in argument and narration. The strongest argument is the stylistic one.

Ruckstuhl developed his older investigation, which is still valid, in his article 'Johannine Language and Style', in it taking apart piece by piece the opposed theses of R.T. Fortna. The detailed investigations of Schweizer and Ruckstuhl suggest a 'normative' figure as author, and who other would this be than the head of the Johannine circle? It is to him that the Johannine corpus owes its unitary language and its main theological ideas, and the Gospel its basic structure. It is a step back in terms of method for modern authors by contrast to postulate a separate Johannine church which simply cannot be demonstrated, with a 'clearly definable history of its own' and its 'own authoritative canon' and even claim, as J. Becker does, that this is an 'undisputed fact'. Justified though the assumption of a Johannine school is, there are doubts about conjecturing the existence of a sect which existed 'in relative separation and with little contact with Christianity'! As though the Johannine school was not an important part of 'Christianity' during the lifetime of its head! And precisely what do we really know about a 'mainstream church' and separated 'sects' or 'groups' in Christianity around 100 CE?[48]

Hengel therefore argues from scientific literary criticism that there was a single author of the Fourth Gospel, whoever he or she was. There is no way in which this view can be characterised as "fundamentalist". Rather, it is based upon solid linguistic and stylistic study of the text of the Fourth Gospel. C.K. Barrett comes essentially to the same conclusion:

Neither displacement theories nor redaction theories are needed to explain the present state of the gospel, in which certain roughness undoubtedly remain, together with an undoubted impression of a vigorous unity of theme. It was not for nothing that the image of the 'seamless robe' was applied by Strauss to the gospel itself. It shows a genuine unity of language and style, which is no more than the outward expression of an inward unity of thought and purpose; but this unity was imposed upon material drawn in the first place from a variety of sources, and composed, it may be, over a fairly considerable period. Much of the discourse material in the gospel can be readily understood as having been originally delivered in sermons. An incident from the life of Jesus was narrated, and the evangelist-preacher expounded its significance for the life and thought of the church. As this process was repeated and prolonged a body of material would grow under his hands until it was capable of formulation in the shape of a gospel. The formulation, however, would be no easy task. Not only would the original sources be disparate; the several sections, or homilies, would not necessarily dovetail into one another. The evangelist was, however, aided in his work by two principles which tended strongly towards unification. In the first place, he possessed an extraordinary grasp of the theological significance of the earlier gospel tradition as a whole. He was able to see its total significance in its parts; to present, not a miscellaneous collection of the deeds and words of Jesus, but a unified conception of his person, which shone out in various ways in the several traditions about him... In the second place, he was impelled by a purpose which gave unity to his work. In an age when the first formulations of the Christian faith were seen by some to be unsatisfactory, when gnosticism in its various forms was perverting the Gospel and adopting it for its own uses, he attempted and achieved the essential task of setting forth the faith once delivered to the saints in the new idiom, for the winning of new converts to the church, for the strengthening of those who were unsettled by the new winds of doctrine, and for the more adequate exposition of the faith itself.[49]

A key part of Bultmann's redaction theory was his view that there was a separate "signs source", a book of the miracles of Jesus upon which the author of the Fourth Gospel referred. I have maintained in *Bad, Mad or God?* that there is no evidence for such a Signs Source in John.[50] In addition, it seems to me that Van Belle's conclusion to his lengthy and exhaustive discussion of this subject in *The Signs Source in the Fourth Gospel: Historical Survey and Critical Evaluation of the Semeia Hypothesis* sums up very neatly in a few lines the truth of the matter:

In general, the two indications, which make it impossible for many critics to regard the Fourth Gospel as a consistent work, namely the "all but intolerable tension between *narrative* and *discourse"* and the presence of the so-called aporias, do not necessarily lead to the acceptance of a signs source. First, it should be noted that a rigid distinction between narrative and discourse does not reckon with the interrelationship and unity of both as a "literary skill of the author". Second, an aporia is not "a sure sign of a source", much less of a recoverable source.[51]

Van Belle's conclusion concerning the inadequacy of the proof of a pre-existing Signs Source would seem to me to apply more generally to the lack of sufficient grounds for positing redactions in the process of the formation of the Fourth Gospel.

One would not wish to deny, any more than do Hengel, Barrett, and van Belle, that the composition of the Fourth Gospel was a complex process. We can easily accept that Wellhausen *et al* at least have demonstrated that any proposed literary process is obviously both complex and speculative, as it must be. But Barrett has already provided for us an example of the type of process of the formation of the Fourth Gospel which is at least plausible, and which takes account both of the *aporias*, i.e. the breaks in the flow of the narrative, and even more importantly, of research of such as Ruckstuhl which clearly demonstrates that throughout its writing a single unifying literary mind was at work.[52]

Jülicher (1857-1938),[53] Professor of New Testament at Marburg, Bultmann's predecessor in that post, who certainly would never be called a Fundamentalist, was firmly convinced that the Fourth Gospel was the unified work of a single hand, apart from the story of the Woman Taken in Adultery, which all accept to be out of place in John 7:53-8:11.[54] Jülicher also included in the original unified literary work Chapter 21, which the majority of scholars think was a later addition. Jülicher dismisses all theories of redactional composition thus:

> These hypotheses must, however, be rejected *in toto*, because they do not take into account the similarity both

in form and matter which extends to every part of the Gospel – for even the miracle stories are indissolubly connected with the discourses that precede and follow them. The Prologue is the most indispensable part of all; it bears the very stamp both of the other explanatory insertions of the Evangelist and of the Johannine discourses of Jesus; but the writer was prevented by the fineness of his tact from putting a Greek philosophical term like 'the Word' into the mouth of Jesus himself or even of his disciples, and wherever Jesus speaks the general term 'grace' is replaced, in accordance with the old tradition, by the more particular 'salvation' *(sózein, sótér, sótéria)*. Add to this that it is impossible to discover any obvious motive for the interpolations. The irregularities and contradictions which are relied upon to support such hypotheses are the very characteristics of John. The critics too often set up the standard of their own logic, their own attention to details, their own demand for a correct succession of events, in short, a Gospel such as they themselves would write it, as their guide, whereas the task which John set himself (that of carrying out his ideal of the Christ in the actual history of Jesus, and of using materials drawn from a tradition still partly entangled in the things of the flesh for the representation of a spiritual Christ) was not attainable without certain inconsistencies, since the form prescribed was far too inflexible for the new matter it was to contain.[55]

Jülicher, as is obvious from the above quotation, does not have a high regard for the historicity of the Fourth Gospel. But he is convinced of its integrity as a literary work; and his conclusions remind us that, while it is most plausible that the composition of the Fourth Gospel was a complex process as we have agreed, we must also take account of the possibility that some of the literary unevenness of the Fourth Gospel may well itself be the consequence of the most extraordinary content and flow of the work itself, which is not easy to fit into a conventional literary pattern. The breaks can often be the expression of the dramatic genius, or at least talent, of the author.

What is most of all unconvincing regarding all the redaction theories is how frequently those who argue to the essential literary unity of the Fourth Gospel can explain the *aporias* and shifts in the narrative without recourse to anyone but to the work of a single author. For example, the ordering of chapters 4,5,6 and 7 can be explained quite easily in terms of the following narrative logic:

1. **Chapter 4** concludes the early ministry of Jesus. It signals the end of the Baptist's ministry, and the beginning of the ministry of Jesus on his own.[56] As Brown says [John 4:4], "Jesus' departure from Judea seems to mean the end of his ministry of baptising; henceforth his ministry will be one of word and sign".[57] Morris has an apt point here:

   John does not say that the Pharisees took any action against Jesus, or even that they were planning any such action. But it is not likely that they would view with equanimity the rapid increase in the number of Jesus' followers. Jesus, however, forestalled any action on their part by withdrawing from Judea and setting out for Galilee. He would not precipitate a clash until the right time. Probably also He did not wish to enter into a controversy on baptism.[58]

This explains the narrative of Chapter 4 in its present sequence. Jesus goes on a journey through Samaria and Galilee, but Jesus waits until Chapter 5, when he goes up to Jerusalem, to manifest himself in his own language and in his own terms.

2. **Chapter 5** narrates that Jesus goes up to Jerusalem again. He speaks as if the Baptist's ministry is over [5:33], indeed as if the Baptist is dead already. Jesus, in Chapter 5 for the first time manifests who he is, the transcendent Son of Man who will judge all people at the end of time. His hearers think he is making himself God, this self-manifestation of Jesus again taking place significantly in Jerusalem [John 5:18]. And he must first manifest himself

in Jerusalem, precisely because, as he has already said, "salvation is of the Jews"[John 4:22].[59]

3. **Chapter 6**. Jesus goes back to Galilee to perform the miracles of the walking on the water and the multiplication of the loaves. This parallels with the Synoptic sequence of events, which we have argued earlier is at least possibly historical.[60] In the context of the Fourth Gospel narrative, Chapter 6 is another major disclosure from Jesus as to whom he is, the Bread of Life. This is ideally placed here because it is a prelude to Jesus' ultimate self-disclosure on his final visit to Jerusalem.

4. **Chapter 7**. Now follows the whole climax of the public ministry of Jesus. He goes up to Jerusalem for the last time, and manifests himself as the Light of the World, as the I AM of the acting God of the Old Testament [8:58]. All is now prepared for the raising of Lazarus [John 11-12], and the passion, death and resurrection of the Word become flesh [John 13-21].

The narrative sequence of Chapters 4-5-6-7 makes perfect sense of the Gospel, viewing its agenda as the gradual self-manifestation of Jesus as the Word become flesh.[61] There is no need to posit that the original ordering of the chapters was any different.[62] However, even if the original ordering of the Gospel narrative was e.g. 4-6-5-7, then how do we know that the first edition was not by the single author of the Fourth Gospel, who himself or herself made the changes later? It is here that redaction theories have been most unconvincing, trying, as we have seen, unsuccessfully to uncover different sources by means of criteria such as theological incoherence.

If there is a case where the criterion of presumption is most clearly to be applied, it is in the case of a redactor. Regarding a literary work, it is presumed that it is by a single author unless reason can be found that other authors were demonstrably employed. It is a case of Occam's razor ripe for application, to cut off unnecessary multiplication of beings,[63] which must be eliminated in any objective enquiry. Redactors are unnecessary beings, unless they can be proved to be present. As we have seen, it has proved difficult if not impossible to provide criteria for redactors based upon theological incoherence, and based upon literary-critical criteria.[64] But Johannine scholars persist in seeing more than one hand at work in the process of writing the Fourth Gospel. Indeed, the establishment of these theories has become more and more complicated, in particular beginning with the Staged Theory of Raymond Brown combined with redaction hypotheses.[65] Thus we must now examine some of those more recent views.

Raymond Brown

As with redaction theories, we find Raymond Brown's posited five stages in the composition of the Fourth Gospel, from the First Stage, the primitive preaching identified by C.H. Dodd in his Historical Tradition of the Fourth Gospel to the final fifth stage with a redactor, equally unproven.

Raymond Brown, in his Anchor Bible Commentary 1966, set out his theory of five stages in the composition of the Fourth Gospel.[66] His theory has had great popularity in the biblical world, no doubt because of Brown's own acknowledged high level of competence as a Johannine scholar, and also perhaps because it seemed to be a position moderately between the "conservative" defence of authorship of the Son of Zebedee, and the more radical views of the form-critical school which rejected the historicity and apostolic authorship of the Fourth Gospel.

Brown summarises his theory thus:

> To sum up, although we have spelt out our theory of the five stages of the composition of the Gospel at some length, we would stress that in its basic outlines the theory is not really complicated and fits in rather plausibly with what is thought about the composition of the other Gospels. A distinctive figure in the primitive Church preached and taught about Jesus, using the raw material of a tradition of Jesus' works and words, but shaping this

material to a particular theological cast and expression. Eventually he gathered the substance of his preaching and teaching into a Gospel, following the traditional pattern of the baptism, the ministry, and the passion, death, and resurrection of Jesus. Since he continued to preach and teach after the edition of the Gospel, he subsequently made a second edition of his Gospel, adding more material and adapting the Gospel to answer new problems. After his death a disciple made a final redaction of the Gospel, incorporating other material that the evangelist had preached and taught, and even some of the material of the evangelist's co-workers. A theory of two editions and a final redaction by a disciple would not be extraordinary among the theories of the composition of biblical books – a very similar theory is proposed for the Book of Jeremiah.

We believe that the theory we have proposed solves most of the difficulties discussed above. It explains why Schweizer and Ruckstuhl find a rather uniform style throughout the Gospel, for in Stages 2, 3 and 4, one dominant figure has shaped, phrased, and edited the material, and even in 5 much of the added material stems from this same figure. Yet, while preserving the substantial unity of the Gospel, this theory explains the various factors that militate against unity of authorship. The redaction in Stage 5 accounts for the presence of Johannine material of different style[67] and also for the presence of duplicate discourses, the insertions that seem to interrupt, the seeming rearrangement of some scenes (without, however, positing elaborate displacements).

There remain many inadequacies and uncertainties in such a theory. In Stage 2, where the material from Stage 1 was developed in Johannine patterns how much personal contribution did the evangelist make? What precisely was in the first edition of the Gospel, and what was added in the second? How can one infallibly distinguish between the hand of the re-editing evangelist and the hand of the redactor? All that we pretend to have done is to have given a working hypothesis for the study of the

Gospel, a hypothesis that combines the best details of the various theories narrated at the beginning of this discussion, and avoids the more obvious difficulties."[68]

Brown differs from the source theorists we have discussed in speaking of stages and development rather than editorial redactions with their own agendas. Thus Brown has to depend less on proven theological incoherence, as with the redaction theories. But Carson's comment is the most challenging. He names the greatest problem with Brown's theory its lack of any control. In fact, he says, it is "utterly untestable".[69]

> But as influential as is, say, the five-step theory of Brown, it is important to see that it too is a kind of source theory, compounded with speculation about the *Sitz im Leben* ('setting in life') of each source – only in his case the sources are much fuzzier around the edges than the source postulated by Fortna. Brown of course prefers to talk about the development of 'traditions' rather than the delineation of 'sources'. Still, someone has to enter John's text with a literary scalpel and retrieve those traditions. It transpires that some of these lie on the surface, and are tied to certain words and expressions (which make them very similar indeed to literary sources) while others are the reconstructions Brown offers to explain what he thinks must have generated this or that bit of text.[70]

Carson has a point. Brown can isolate his stages only by stylistic criteria, which are lacking, or by theological development; which makes his theory like a source theory.

Firstly, regarding **Stage One**, Brown finds support in Dodd for the existence of a first level of Gospel tradition independent of the Synoptic accounts. But we must bear in mind Dodd's purpose here, which he outlines in the Introduction, namely to provide eventually some evidence that John provides a primitive historical tradition of Jesus' words and works which had validity independently of the Synoptic Gospels.[71] Dodd did not intend in general to use criteria to isolate texts from within the Fourth Gospel to provide a *Grundschrift* which might represent Brown's Stage One. Sometimes, Dodd considers that he has identified such a *Grundschrift,* as for instance regarding *Sayings Common to John and the Synoptics*[72] and *Parabolic Forms,* i.e. primitive forms of parables, for example John 12:24 about the "grain of wheat.[73] But usually, we can use his methodology only to isolate a core oral tradition of Jesus' words and works, not in order to isolate Stage One texts from the rest of the Fourth Gospel. Brown has to do more than provide criteria to posit a possible oral tradition for his Stage One. He must show that there was an early written stage. This he does not do.

If Brown's Stage One is difficult to discern, his **Stage Two** is virtually impossible to identify. This stage is what we might call a "Johannisation" of Synoptic style material; by adding discourse Synoptic style account. But how is it possible to isolate this material? Brown says "That this preaching and teaching was the work of more than one man is suggested by the existence of units of Johannine material, like chapter xxi, that are different in style from the main body of the material".[74] We have already seen that Johannine exegetes of distinction have maintained the unity of style in John's Gospel, and we shall see later that this applies even to Chapter 21. Hoskyns view, that Chapter 21 is integral to the whole of the Fourth Gospel, is very much a minority opinion. But what he has said about the style of Chapter 21 would seem to be unchallenged by Johannine scholarship. "The narrative (of Chapter 21) is Johannine in structure, in phraseology, and, most important of all, in the subtle references to passages in the main body of the gospel, the clear recognition of which is necessary for any true exegesis".[75] What is true of Chapter 21 is even truer of the rest of the Gospel, as Ruckstuhl's researches have indicated. The Fourth Gospel has a single style according to all the sophisticated literary criteria which have been employed to test it.[76]

Whoever wishes to identify Brown's later Stages must have recourse to redaction theories such as Bultmann's or Fortna's.[77] As Carson says, someone has to enter John's text with a literary scalpel and retrieve those traditions. However, as Brown has himself said earlier, this runs up against the difficulty consequent upon all John's Gospel redaction theories, in that, in Parker's terms, "It looks as though, if the author of the Fourth Gospel used documentary sources, he wrote them all himself".[78] This also presumes that the Johannine critic has already been successful in dissecting Stage One, the primitive Synoptic-style tradition. We have seen above that this will be by no means an easy task.

Stage Three is perhaps even more hypothetical than any other of Brown's Stages. As we have seen above, Brown sees this stage as putting into Gospel format what had so far existed only in separate literary or even oral pieces. Obviously, the writer must have put the Gospel into Gospel narrative framework at some stage in the writing process, as it is in Mark and in the other Gospels. But the only possible evidence for this stage being an *editing* rather than a *writing* stage is the Gospel outline, which is roughly similar to the Synoptic Gospel outline, in both the Second and the Fourth Gospel as: *Witness of Baptist – Departure to Galilee – Feeding of the Multitude – Walking on the Lake – Peter's Confession – Departure to Jerusalem – Entry into Jerusalem and Anointing – The Last Supper – The Arrest – The Passion and Resurrection.*

Earlier, we noted that Barrett thought that this common Gospel outline[79] was evidence of John using Mark. But we saw that this conclusion was not the only necessary one. We argued that an historical memory of this sequence of events was possible, which both Mark and John used. Secondly, if the author had before him any one of the Synoptic Gospels, he could have followed that framework with his own variations, whether or not he was using his own eye-witness memory or not.

But again, there is no hard evidence that John did not write his work in Gospel format from the beginning, using perhaps only oral tradition, and perhaps as Dodd has suggested short sayings which may have been in written form. As we have seen above, it is difficult if not impossible to isolate the primitive stages of the Gospel of John from later stages. Earlier, we questioned whether Wellhausen, the first on the redaction scene in Johannine scholarship, was guilty of illicitly projecting a methodology from Old Testament Pentateuchal studies and imagining that the same literary scalpel could be used on the Fourth Gospel.[80] Now we must wonder whether

Brown has been guilty of a similar projection of Synoptic studies into the study of what is a very different literary piece, the Gospel of John.

Stage Four reveals yet greater difficulties, if such is possible. Brown posits that the Fourth Gospel "was intended to answer the objections or difficulties of several groups, for example, the disciples of John the Baptist, Jewish Christians who had not left the Synagogue, and many others... For instance, the parenthetical passage ix 22-23 seems to represent an adaptation of the story of the blind man to the new situation in the late 80s or 90s which involved the excommunication from the Synagogue of Jews who believed in Jesus as the Messiah".[81]

But what if, as we have earlier seen J.A.T. Robinson argue,[82] the excommunication of the blind man as a follower of Jesus actually happened in the life of the historical Jesus? Robinson quotes D.R.A. Hare, who "makes the point that exclusion was already a regular discipline at Qumran, who used very similar language in anathematizing their heretics".[83] If excommunication of followers of Jesus was practised in his lifetime, therefore, then, in this case, there is no demonstration whatsoever from historical development that the dating of Brown's Stage Four is to be placed in the late 80s or 90s; unless perhaps we could argue that the language reflects a later redaction. In the latter case, we would be back to attempting to demonstrate that investigation of stylistic or other literary criteria led to a later date. And it is this diversity of literary criteria which Ruckstuhl shows is also so conspicuously lacking regarding the Fourth Gospel.

Regarding **Stage Five**, for Brown, as we have seen, this was the work of someone else other than the Evangelist, namely a Redactor, who was close to him, and close to his thought. Stage Five is allegedly discernible in passages in the Fourth Gospel which seem a little out of line with the rest of the Gospel; for example 6:51-58 as compared with 6:35-50; Chapters 11-12, the "Lazarus" chapters, which were inserted after the original account of the ministry of Jesus at 10:42; and of course Chapter 21. But again, these sections could have been added later by the same author. There is no need to posit a separate redactor.

Brown's Stages must therefore be judged unproven as any Fourth Gospel redaction theory.

Culpepper and the new criticism

Perhaps not surprisingly, in more recent Johannine scholarship there has been a reaction to the detailed attempt to discover sources and stages by textual surgery. In the past twenty years or so, there has been more than one attempt to view the Gospel of John as a piece of literature rather than as a slab of textual pathology. The more recent approaches to the Fourth Gospel using a literary approach have all discovered once again the essential unity of that work, with a masterful mind behind it. No one has expressed this better than Francis Moloney in his recent *Sacra Pagina* commentary on John. "It is difficult to imagine that such a passionate book as the Fourth Gospel is anything but the communication of a historical person's deeply held and passionate belief in what God has done in and through Jesus".[84]

Leading the field in what Carson calls the "new criticism"[85] has been R. Alan Culpepper's *Anatomy of the Fourth Gospel*, 1984. Culpepper aimed to present a rhetorical analysis of the Fourth Gospel. He was convinced that it would be fruitful to study the Gospel of John as if it were a modern novel. Thus there was a "real author" (who actually wrote the Gospel) and an "implied author", who is there as it were in the secrets of the narrative. Thus, in an Agatha Christie novel, as well as the real author Agatha Christie, there is an implied author who lets us into the evil deeds on the Orient Express to keep our interest, without letting us really know who the actual murderer is, until Hercule Poirot brushes his moustache and calls the parties in at the end of the novel to tell them who really "dunnit". So also there is a "real reader", the one to whom the novel was originally addressed; and there is the "implied reader", the reader who is being addressed beyond the actual circle of actual readers, whom the real author thinks will wish to read what is written.

For Culpepper, there is also the narrator, who in the novel

actually tells the story. Often the narrator is barely distinguishable from the implied author. The distinction would be clear if the novel is an "I" narrative, where the narrator throughout the novel is in the first person singular. But, Culpepper insists, even when the narrator is not in the first person singular, there is a distinction between narrator and implied author. The narrator is the one who tells the story, is the witness to what is going on for those of us who are reading the novel.

Culpepper thinks that in St John's Gospel, the narrator is "omniscient", that is, he is able to provide inside information as to what is going on. Culpepper finds evidence for this, for instance, in the following texts:

- 6:61, But Jesus, being aware that his disciples were complaining about it, said to them, "Does this offend you?"
- 3:28, Now, no one at the table knew why he said this to him.
- 19:8, Now when Pilate heard this, he was more afraid than ever.

We must be grateful that Culpepper has rediscovered and brought to the fore the powerful narrative quality of the Fourth Gospel, which comes alive through his rhetorical criticism, because he is inviting us to listen to the text itself, and to the story told. But Carson is right also in not allowing Culpepper to ignore the question as to the historical truth of the Fourth Gospel.

We encounter at this point a major concern of our discussion in this present book, which is a consideration of the historicity of the Fourth Gospel. Culpepper sees the Gospel as a novel. But what if the Gospel is not a novel? What if the "narrator" was actually an eye-witness? Carson is quite right in insisting that this will change entirely the perspective, even the rhetorical analysis, of the narrative in question. "To take one example, Culpepper subsumes discussion of the eyewitness themes in John under the narrative categories of *narrator* and *implied author*, without seriously considering that if the witness themes are given force within some narrative framework other than the novel, the shape of the discussion *inevitably* swings to *some* consideration of the kind and quality of the *history* purportedly being told, and therefore to truth claims – and not just to the shape of the *story* being narrated".[86]

Carson is also right in challenging Culpepper to think again about whether the aim of a novel is the same as the aim of a narrative which is not fictional but intentionally factual. The Gospel, unlike the novel, is a window not just on us but on the life and ministry of Jesus. A novel's character is a universal, existing in our imagination, whereas, as Carson says, "Biblical Christianity cannot outlive the 'scandal of historical peculiarity'. By contrast, the novel thrives on the universals of human existence".[87]

Culpepper is right to say that there are narrative "mechanisms" working within the text of the Fourth Gospel, and any fruitful approach will attempt to locate those mechanisms. But any discussion of the Gospel's literary *genre* must, as well as finding parallels with other types of literature, do full justice to the Gospel as a unique form of literature dealing with a unique person who actually lived in history in a certain time and place.

Culpepper's fascinating studies, and Carson's further questions about those studies, bring us to consider Schweitzer's important distinction between the *form* and the *origin*[88] of a piece of literature, which we would perhaps prefer to distinguish between its *form* and its *content*. Is there always an identifiable difference between the form of a fictional account and the form of a factual account? Christians down the centuries, before the eighteenth century Quest of the Historical Jesus, would not have denied the dramatic quality of the Fourth Gospel. But they would have read it as an essentially historical account. Could they be demonstrated to be wrong to have so read the Fourth Gospel because of the *form* of the narrative? Or could Culpepper's sophisticated literary analysis apply equally to an essentially historical and factually reliable account, but one written in a dramatic way? At first sight, it would seem that an essentially factual account could well have been written in a form with dramatic mechanisms such as identified by Culpepper.

If this is so, an important consequence follows. Culpepper has identified a masterly literary mind behind the Fourth Gospel with a strong dramatic sense. Ruckstuhl has demonstrated the unity of style throughout this work and Hengel insists on the necessity of a single individual mind rather than an amorphous "community" as author of this Gospel.

We have already demonstrated that there are good reasons at least that this author is to be identified with John the Son of Zebedee, named as such by Irenaeus just over a century after the time of Christ. If the *form* of the narrative is not demonstrably fiction, then we are left with the real possibility that the author of the Fourth Gospel was an apostolic eyewitness, most likely John the Son of Zebedee one of the Twelve; and that what he describes, however dramatically, was in his intention to write as a reliable historical account for us of the actual life, ministry, death and resurrection of the historical Jesus.

Thomas L. Brodie

A recent commentary on John which realises that any approach must take all factors into account is that of **Thomas L. Brodie** in his *The Gospel According to John, A Literary and Theological Commentary*.[89] Perhaps Brodie's most illuminating contribution, in the tradition of Adolf Jülicher, is to see the breaks and apparent contradictions in the Fourth Gospel not as reasons for cutting up the text into sources first and foremost, but as "a spur to reflection".[90] Brodie's comment on the end of Chapter 14, "Rise, let us be on our way" [John 14:31], which critical commentators from Wellhausen onwards[91] have seen as clear reason that the insertion 15-16 is a later addition, challenges us to think more imaginatively:

> At the end of chapter 14, for instance, when Jesus says, "Arise..." and then goes on talking, the reader feels like Nicodemus or the woman of Samaria; this is muddled, contradictory. But there is another possibility – that the gospel is seeking to invite the reader to become aware of

a further dimension, namely that the last discourse as a whole, as well as speaking at an obvious level (concerning Jesus' departure) is speaking also at a further level (concerning a departure or movement which is spiritual, in fact, concerning the whole realm of spirit).[92]

Brodie is not necessarily right in this interpretation. Westcott would see Jesus' "let us go hence" as Jesus' invitation to his disciples to walk with him through the Temple courtyard down to the Kedron valley to his arrest and death.[93] But Brodie is surely insightful in inviting us to see contradiction as challenge, and invitation to further reflection, rather than as necessarily an invitation to rush for the critical scalpel.

Brodie is also helpful in emphasising that there are three dimensions to a study of any Gospel, and in particular the Gospel of John: the theological, historical and literary. In an investigation such as this, we cannot neglect any of those three dimensions. He recommends that "the best starting point seems to be the literary".[94]

However, Brodie's own source theory as expressed in his *The Quest for the Origin of John's Gospel* is a unique development in what might be called the new criticism. Brodie emphasises the unity of the Gospel and its single author. But he firmly considers that John was dependent on the Synoptic Gospels. We have already looked at Brodie's theory in more detail in Chapter Seven.[95] We have argued that Brodie has demonstrated at the most an *association of ideas* between John and Matthew, Mark, Luke/Acts, and Ephesians. Comparison between Mark 8:22-6 and John 9:17, 13, 15 does not amount to dependence in the literary sense of the word, but only a parallelism of ideas. Nothing would prevent John having his own "historical tradition" in Dodd's terms, or in the traditional sense of eye-witness testimony, and then from weaving his narratives using the Synoptics as a kind of warp and woof.

It is not therefore a licit conclusion to say "This implies that in the quest for the historical Jesus, John makes no perceptible contribution. If he reflects the historical Jesus he does so only to the extent that he reflects aspects of whatever may be historical of the Synoptics".[96] This statement clearly goes beyond what he has actually demonstrated in his book, which is at the most John's *use* of the Synoptics, and not his *dependence* on them.

Brodie is encouraging to this extent, however. He would agree with our thesis that, regarding sources and stages, there is no need for this hypothesis. The Gospel can be read as a unity because, if there are sources, and if there are stages of writing, these are simply what the author himself used and mastered completely for his own work, to construct a unified narrative. This narrative unity, represented and demonstrated by its unity of style, also makes the identification of sources and stages an uncertain process, and even of uncertain value.

One author or one community?

Brodie and Culpepper are in agreement regarding the dynamic literary unity of the Fourth Gospel. They disagree in this, that whereas for Brodie (as for Hengel, Barrett and Jülicher) this implies a single *individual* who was the author of the Fourth Gospel, Culpepper is quite prepared to admit the possibility of a multiplicity of authors and redactors. For Culpepper, having accepted Ruckstuhl's conclusions that the Fourth Gospel is a literary unity, the source of that literary unity, both of the Fourth Gospel and of the Epistles of John, is not an individual but a community, the Johannine Community, albeit in the case of the Gospel working with the Fourth Evangelist:

> In short, I would therefore formulate this hypothesis: the Johannine writings were composed within the Johannine community by a group close to the beloved disciple... The Johannine literature is the result of its being rooted in that community. The literary unity of the Gospel could be thus explained as the result of the creative work of the evangelist on the material at his disposal. As to the redactor, his perspectives would have to be close to that of the evangelist. The aporias of the Gospel, as with the

differences which separate it from the epistles, could find their explanation in the plurality of implied authors in the production of the Johannine corpus. There could be divergence between us regarding the role of the collaborators with the evangelist or of the redactor, but we would be perfectly in agreement with the following point: we would have nothing to do with a Gospel which would have been composed from sources without relationship between themselves and emanating from diverse communities, with a Gospel later revised by a redactor whose theology differed sharply from that of the evangelist.[97]

Culpepper clearly accepts our negative thesis; namely, that there is no evidence of sources and redactors in the process of the creation of the Fourth Gospel at variance with each other theologically. If we followed Culpepper's view, nothing would prevent the final published version of the Fourth Gospel being written under the control of an eye-witness. The Johannine community, in this view, could have produced the Fourth Gospel under the control of the "beloved disciple". If the beloved disciple were John the Son of Zebedee, or even one close to eye-witness tradition such as John the Elder, he could have supervised the final edition of the Gospel ensuring its close contact with apostolic eye-witness tradition. Our only point of variance with Culpepper would be that expressed above, as to whether Culpepper has considered sufficiently that, despite its narrative quality, the *genre* of the Fourth Gospel is not that of a fictional novel, but what we might call that of an historical drama.

But we must still press Culpepper to consider how it could be possible to demonstrate the role of the *Johannine Community* in writing the Fourth Gospel. How could one possibly demonstrate the authorship of a work by a community rather than by an individual? Such a demonstration would be still more difficult for Culpepper precisely because he has excluded the hypothesis of separate redactors based upon the principle of theological incoherence. Culpepper's possible multiplicity of "implied authors" could also be accounted for simply from the fact that a single author was writing from his own experience, or at least from an experience second hand, and therefore was able to assume what Culpepper calls "omniscience", but not in reality omniscience at all, but simply eye-witness knowledge of events.

Thus my own inclination would be to agree with Barrett, Jülicher, Hengel, and Brodie, that the *aporias* in the Fourth Gospel do not need to be explained by positing a redactor nor the putative Johannine Community.[98] They can all be explained either by the same author himself writing the Gospel in his own stages, such stages by now almost impossible to detect with any accuracy; or by the literary creativity of the evangelist which appears only at first sight not to be a unified literary creation. Similarly, if there were "sources", not only are they undetectable, but we cannot determine whether they came from the evangelist's own memory (eye-witness?), or from the hypothetical Johannine Community, precisely because those sources have been so well worked over by the evangelist.

Brodie is adamant that the Fourth Gospel was not authored by a committee, or even by the evangelist as representative of the Johannine Community, but rather by a fiercely independent individual:

> Overall, then, the evangelist emerges not as the leader of an independent group but as a prophetic voice from within the church – a voice critical of the world, critical in another way of the Jews, and critical in yet a further way of the church and its leadership (Peter); but a voice which, even amid so much darkness, never failed to reflect a vision of light and life – for the church, for the Jews and for the world.[99]

My own inclination is towards Brodie's view here, even though I would prefer to say that the evangelist appears not so much as a prophet in the Gospel (however much the author of the Apocalypse sees himself as prophetic) as a witness to apostolic tradition, Peter's as well as his own. However, Culpepper's view, based upon his penetrating literary analysis, is important, and we agree with him completely in emphasising the unity of the Fourth Gospel as does Ruckstuhl, and even more in rejecting the views of Wellhausen, Bultmann, Richter, Thyen *et al*, who posit redactors and a patchwork quilt of sources with different theological agendas. This is an important confirmation of Ruckstuhl's researches, whose primary work *Die Literarische Einheit des Johannesevangeliums* began with a searching analysis of Bultmann's source and redaction theory[100] demonstrating that contrary to what Bultmann claimed, the Fourth Gospel possesses a literary unity, and therefore, by implication, a theological unity.

An important conclusion follows for our own discussion of the Fourth Gospel as a prime literary source for the life of the historical Jesus. If the Fourth Gospel, as we have demonstrated, is early enough and comes from the right geographical environment, and from the right circle of ideas, to have been authored by one in eye-witness or at least second hand contact, of the life and times of the historical Jesus, then it is important to have demonstrated also, that this Gospel at least possibly indeed most likely derives from a single author; even if that mind has used sources (no longer detectable), might even have been edited by one redactor no longer identifiable, and was part of a Christian community who believed that Jesus was the only begotten Son of God [John 1:14].

Schnackenburg's Summary

At the close of a lengthy two chapters of investigation, chapter III *Literary Criticism of the Gospel of St. John*,[101] and chapter IV, *Tradition and Redaction*,[102] Rudolf Schnackenburg concludes with this summary. He says, "We may perhaps sum up the results of our investigations as follows." We will take his conclusions point by point:

Schnackenburg (a)

Literary criticism does not enable us to distribute the fourth gospel over various independent literary strata, which were then combined by one or more redactions. It is essentially the work of the evangelist, who relied, however, on diverse traditions, and allowed his gospel to grow and mature slowly, but did not finish it completely.[103]

Response to (a): We would agree that the author of the Fourth Gospel, whom we have argued is most likely John the Son of Zebedee, has not written his Gospel in such a way that sources can be easily isolated. The work appears as a unity. The Fourth Gospel is indeed the work of the evangelist. It is not so easy to demonstrate that he did not finish it completely. Many of the so-called "aporias" can be explained as a deliberate literary technique, for example as Brodie explains the break at the end of Chapter 14. For instance, we can read too much into the fact that the author names the first two signs as the "first" [2:11] and the "second", [4:54] whereas the subsequent five signs (=miracles)[104] are not numbered. Barrett, for instance explains the first sign, the miracle at Cana, as the 'primary sign' (*archén*) "because representative of the creative and transforming work of Jesus as a whole".[105] The second sign is so named, according to Barrett, because the second miracle looks back to the first, and for Barrett, "like the first, ends a division of the gospel".[106] It is even more difficult to determine when the author of any redaction is not the evangelist himself. Chapter 21 is a special case, which we will deal with shortly.

Schnackenburg (b)

It is difficult to point to written sources among the traditions upon which the evangelist worked. Apart from some doubtful cases, direct use of the Synoptics cannot be proved. But he must have had some knowledge of the synoptic tradition by word of mouth, and have taken it for granted in his readers. In the course of their history, his traditions had striking associations with the special tradition of Luke (see above, ch.ii). The use of a written "*sémeia* source" may be maintained with some probability.[107]

Response to (b): We agree that it is difficult to point to any written sources among the traditions upon which the evangelist worked. Direct dependence on the Synoptics cannot be proved, as we have shown above.[108] But we agree also that he must have had some knowledge of the Synoptic tradition. With which of the three evangelists there is most contact, there is no agreement among the scholars. Schnackenburg is impressed with parallels with Luke,[109] and Barrett in particular with Mark.[110] Perhaps the evangelist knew all three, and drew upon them; but not in terms of literary dependence. However, we do not accept the identification of a separate *sémeia* source, as we have argued in *Bad, Mad or God?*.[111] The miracle stories in John are integral to the narrative, and not distinct either in style or in vocabulary from the rest of the Gospel.

Schnackenburg (c)

> For his special traditions, the evangelist could draw on independent and original oral narratives, which may be considered to be of high antiquity and to contain good information. This is a stage of tradition for which efforts have been made to disengage a "basic document" or a "basic Gospel". Though literary criticism is unable to detach and establish such a basic Gospel as an independent piece of writing, it may be presupposed with some assurance as an early stage in the history of tradition.[112]

Response to (c): With Dodd and Schnackenburg, we think that the evangelist could draw on independent and original oral narratives, and perhaps also some written, for example some of the sayings isolated by Dodd in his *Historical Tradition*: "Very truly, I tell you, unless a grain of wheat falls into the earth and dies, it remains just a single grain; but if it dies, it bears much fruit" [John 12:24].[113] The same would apply to short narratives of miracles, such as the Feeding of the Multitude [John 6:1-14].[114] But it is difficult if not impossible to determine whether these were part of the individual memory of the evangelist, as an eye-witness, or whether he was using oral or written traditions which he had

253

to hand. The existence of a basic Gospel, though always possible, has not been demonstrated, as Schnackenburg admits. *Pace* Schnackenburg, and indeed Brown, there is strictly speaking no reason at all why we should presuppose it. It remains possible, therefore, that the evangelist wrote the present Gospel without any such *Grundschrift*.

Schnackenburg (d)

These early traditions must also have contained logia and other utterances already couched in fixed form, which the evangelist made use of for the sayings and discourses of Jesus in his Gospel. A special source for logia or discourses is improbable, but there is reason to think that when shaping the revelation discourses of Jesus, the evangelist utilised formulae which were already fixed, and many established units of discourse. But he inserted them into the dialogues and discourses of Jesus as he constructed them, combining all so well that it is the discourses which bear most clearly the stamp of his mind.[115]

Response to (d): It is very likely that the evangelist used his own "homily notes" to put into writing the discourses. He also must have had some fixed formulae in his mind, both from the Historical Jesus (e.g. John 5:17 "My Father is still working, and I also am working."), and from his own developing theology, for example possibly John 3:32 "He testifies to what he has seen and heard, yet no one accepts his testimony". Again, this can be only conjecture, as Schnackenburg admits; but here we have some likely conjecture, based upon what would be probable in the circumstances.

Schnackenburg (e)

It is also possible that at certain places he incorporated liturgical or kerygmatic matter which was circulated and preserved in the communities. This is true of the prologue in particular, the basis of which may be assumed to be a

Christian hymn to the Logos, and may also be true of the "eucharistic homily" (linked with Ps 78:24) in 6:31-58, or of its last part, 6:51-58.[116]

Response to (e): It is likely also that the evangelist used existing liturgical texts. The existence of a pre-existing Logos Poem prior to the final text of the Prologue 1:1-18 has always been hotly debated. In any case, the remark of Barrett is apt, that "the Prologue stands before us as a prose introduction which has not been submitted to interpolation and was specially written (it must be supposed) to introduce the Gospel – and, it may be added, to sum it up. Many Introductions and Prefaces serve this dual purpose".[117] Thus whatever the evangelist has used has been fully integrated into his own masterful introduction. It is possible also that embedded in the Eucharistic Discourse is a Johannine formula for the Words of Institution.[118] John speaks of "Those who eat my flesh and drink my blood abide in me, and I in them" [John 6:56]. The word for "flesh" may be the Johannine equivalent for "body" (*sóma*) in "this is my body" in the Synoptic and Pauline Institutional formula. There is no Hebrew word for "living body", and thus Jesus might well have used the word *basar* "flesh" in the original Institutional narrative.

Schnackenburg (f)

> The evangelist was unable to give his work its final form, and also left some items among his material – particularly discourses of Jesus – which represented further drafts, as perhaps 3:13-21, 31-36; chapters 15-17. These were inserted into the Gospel only at the final redaction, sometimes not quite relevantly (the "unattached" passages of discourse in chapter 3), sometimes with traces of the secondary addition (farewell discourses and high priestly prayer, chapters15-17).[119]

Response to (f): This is much more difficult to prove, even if it is not beyond the bounds of possibility. Again, the breaks in the text could be explained in another way. However, it is certainly not impossible for instance that 3:13-21 was a later homiletic comment by the evangelist adding to the dialogue with Nicodemus, 3:1-12. This would be perfectly consistent with unity of authorship, and none of these above proposals of later addition necessitate another redactor, certainly not another redactor with a separate theological agenda.

Schnackenburg (g)

The redactors are certainly responsible for chapter 21, where they may have used material from the evangelist, and perhaps the *sémeia* source (for the great catch of fish). They are also responsible for certain collocations of text which do not correspond to the original intentions of the evangelist: the inversion of chapters 5 and 6; the displacement of 7:15-24 to its present place, instead of after 5:47; the insertion of one of the fundamental revelation discourses, 3:31-36, 13-21, at two places in chapter 3; perhaps also 12:44-50 at the end of the first main section. Elsewhere the redactors confined themselves to brief glosses and additions (4:2 or 4:1f, 4:44; 6:22f; 7:39b; 11:2; perhaps 12:16). It seems unnecessary to suppose major interventions or re-arrangements on the part of the redactors; it likewise seems superfluous to postulate several redactions one after the other.[120]

Response to (g): We will be dealing with Chapter 21 in a moment, under separate cover. Regarding Schnackenburg's other suggestions, final glosses and additions are all possible, and do not essentially prejudice unity of authorship, even if one or two verses might have been added by a later redactor. Schnackenburg is quite sensibly economical in his suggestions as to redaction. But the inversion of Chapters 5 and 6 is not necessary, as we have already attempted to demonstrate earlier in this chapter.[121]

Finally, Schnackenburg states:

These results may seem meagre and disappointing after all the sharp sighted criticism which has been done on John. But if they serve to underline the evangelist's predominant role in the making and shaping of the fourth Gospel, and as the distinctive theologian who gave its doctrine its unified character, then the detours and labours of research have not been in vain. At the same time, John no longer appears as the "single-storeyed" work of an author who wrote it in one piece. It displays a pre-history in tradition, just as it can be seen to have undergone a subsequent redaction. Finally, it must be emphasised that the solution offered to this difficult and intricate question is only the personal and debatable view of the author of this commentary. But it had to be definitely outlined, so that the reader could recognise clearly the direction that has been taken.[122]

Response to Conclusion: Schnackenburg is quite right to emphasise the tentative nature of his conclusions, and the conclusions of any investigation into the sources and redactions of the Fourth Gospel must be in the nature of the case. On the other hand, whereas there is some evidence of sources and of redactions, none of these sources and redactions have taken away from the initial impression of so many who have read the Fourth Gospel of the underlying unity of the whole work, dominated by its single author. If the sources and redactions are his own work, and the pre-history of the tradition has been worked over by himself from his own eye-witness knowledge, then this would explain both the unity of style and "feel" of the work, together with the bumps and unevenness which appear to many critics when reading the work.

Summary of our conclusions regarding John 1-20

- The writing of the Fourth Gospel appears at least as likely as not the work of a single dominant mind. All the evidence is patient of this interpretation.

- It is difficult to point to solid evidence for any written sources among the traditions upon which the evangelist worked, for example the *sémeia* (signs) source.

- Direct use of the Synoptics cannot be finally proved. But we agree that the author probably had some knowledge of the Synoptic tradition.

- The author could draw on independent and original oral narratives, and perhaps also some written. But it is difficult if not impossible to determine whether these were part of the individual memory of the evangelist, or whether he was using oral or written traditions which he had to hand.

- The existence of a basic Gospel *Grundschrift*, though always possible, has not been demonstrated. It is possible that the author wrote the Fourth Gospel in its present form using a literary pattern in his own mind, in particular dominated by the sequence of amazing historical events which he was recounting.

- It seems most likely that the discourses of the Fourth Gospel, perhaps already in sermon form, contained sayings of Jesus and also explanatory comments from the evangelist himself prior to the final form of the written Gospel.

- It is likely also that the evangelist used existing liturgical texts.

- All admit breaks and unevenness, *aporias*, in the narrative. But there is no agreement as to whether this requires a separate redactor from the original author. It is quite possible that the evangelist added major sections of the Gospel at a later time than earlier drafts, or even some phrases as an afterthought, for example John 4:2, cf. below, n. 56.

- Some glosses in the text may be at least possibly the work of final redactors, not the evangelist. But again, the author could have added these himself. In any case, they are not decisive in throwing into doubt the general literary unity of the work.

Chapter 21

Chapter 21 is a special case, because there is wide agreement among the scholars it was added as an afterthought. The strongest argument appears to be that the Gospel of John has a superb ending at the close of Chapter 20, as we have seen, with Doubting Thomas' profession of faith, "My Lord and my God", followed by Jesus' exhortation, "Have you believed because you have seen me? Blessed are those who have not seen and yet have come to believe" [John 20:29], with the reader being given a summons to faith. Chapter 21 seems to be an anti-climax.

Zumstein summarises the argument for the later addition of Chapter 21 in *La Rédaction Finale de L'Évangile.*[123]

1. He begins with emphasising the finality of 20:31, adding that the use of the expression "in this book" (*en tó bibló*) in 20:30 is itself a way of closing the book itself. He argues that the revelations in Chapter 21 form an anti-climax to the revelation to Thomas, and are out of place, since, having been told that "blessed are those who have not seen and yet have believed", we go back in the next chapter to those who are seeing as well as believing, namely, the apostolic witnesses!

2. Next, Zumstein sees an anomaly in that, though the disciples had been sent on their mission, [20:19-23], the disciples in Chapter 21 then go back to their fishing. Furthermore, with the appearance of Jesus to the Eleven in Chapter 20, they are all reinstated after fleeing at the arrest and crucifixion. However, in 21:15-19, Peter is reinstated personally as shepherd of the community by the threefold question, followed by the commission three times stated "feed my sheep" This seems at odds with the reinstatement already effected in Chapter 20.

3. Thirdly, Zumstein sees the "we" (*oidamen*) in 21:24, echoing the *oidamen* of the Prologue 1:14 as referring to a group of eye-witnesses wider than the evangelist himself. It is this group of witnesses which refers to the disciple

whom Jesus loved [21:20-23], which beloved disciple is for Zumstein now dead. There was a tradition that he would not die, referred to in 20:23, which has now been contradicted by that beloved disciple's death. They are therefore writing Chapter 21 after the completion by the evangelist of Chapters 1-20, to correct the false impression that the Lord had promised that the beloved disciple would not die.

4. Finally, Zumstein refers to the difference of theological emphasis in the final chapter. Chapters 1-20 are focussed on faith of the person of Christ. This last Chapter has an ecclesial dimension, legitimising the authority of the church and of the Gospel itself.

These are arguments of some weight. Arguments such as these have convinced the majority of scholars that Chapter 21 was added by a later redactor. At the end of the day, if twenty out of twenty-one chapters were written by John the Son of Zebedee, this would not be a bad score. But we ought first to hear the contrary case stated briefly but cogently by Hoskyns in his commentary:

> Since the above exegesis of the concluding verses of the gospel depends upon the assumption that chapter xxi is not the work of a later editor, it is necessary to justify this assumption. The arguments for the conclusion that the record of the miraculous draught of fishes is Johannine have already been stated. The same arguments apply to xxi.15-25. The further definition of the pastoral character of the Apostolic work, and the destiny of the two chief Apostles, form an entirely suitable conclusion to the gospel. The narrative is Johannine in structure, in phraseology, and, most important of all, in the subtle references to passages in the main body of the gospel, the clear recognition of which is necessary for any true exegesis. The rehabilitation of Peter presumes xiii.36-8 and perhaps xvi.32. The name Simon, Son of John, echoes i.42; the martyrdom of the Shepherd recalls x.1-18, its peculiar nature xii.33, xviii.32; the glory of God, xii.24-6, xiii.31,32: the synonymous words for *know* and *love*

are Johannine ... so are the phrases *again a second time*
(iv.54), *verily verily* (i.51 & c.), *by what manner of death*
(xii.33, xviii.32). The intimacy of the two disciples and
their relationship with the Lord (xiii.6 sq., 24, xviii.15,
xx.2,6), the double meaning of the words *follow* (i.43,
xiii.36, & c.) and *abide* (i.33 & c.), the subtle rebuke to
Peter for questioning the Lord (xvi.23), are all characteristically Johannine. *v.* 24 is necessary if the Johannine
canon of evidence is to be maintained (v.31,32, viii.13,14,
xix.35; 3 John 12); *v.* 25 echoes xx.30; and the alternating
and *we* also underline the First Epistle (1 John i.1-4,
ii.12 sq., & c.).[124]

Since Hoskyns' arguments are rarely heard, it is worth setting
them out. He emphasises the stylistic unity of Chapter 21
and 1-20; evidence which the researches of Ruckstuhl have
confirmed, as we have seen,[125] who argued equally for the
stylistic unity of Chapter 21 with the remainder of the Gospel.

Hoskyns would probably reply to Zumstein that the
differences he notes between 21 and 1-20 can easily be
explained without the necessity of a redactor for 21.

Ad 1 – We must admit with Zumstein that Chapter 20 could
have made an ideal climax to the Gospel. But Hoskyns would
argue that it is not therefore necessary to propose a separate
author for Chapter 21, in particular noting the stylistic unity
of 21 *vis à vis* 1-20, and the linguistic parallels he has drawn
between 21 and the remainder of the Gospel.

We could easily accept that the Gospel originally ended
with Chapter 20; but that the beloved disciple, even helped
by the Ephesian Elders, saw the necessity of a final chapter
both to testify the place of the Gospel in the Church after the
beloved disciple died, and to clarify any misunderstandings
which arose from a possible rivalry between the beloved
disciple and Peter.

Westcott's explanation is ingenious:

On the other hand, if we bear in mind that the Gospel
as originally composed ended with xx.31, to which
xxi.25 may have been attached, and that the narratives in

xxi.1-23 were drawn up by the same author at a later time under circumstances which called for some authoritative interpretation of a mistaken tradition, we can readily understand how the note was added to the record by those who had sought for this additional explanation of the Lord's words, and preserved when the completed Gospel was issued to the Church. At the same time, if v.25 (i.e. 20:25) formed the last clause of the original Gospel, it would naturally be transferred to the end of the enlarged record.[126]

In my opinion, if we see 21:24 as a separate subscript from the rest of Chapter 21, as we have suggested above, the testimony of those who authenticate the truth of what has been written, then there is no difficulty whatsoever in seeing Chapter 21 as an afterthought of the writer himself, John the Son of Zebedee. We do not need Westcott's complex solution; provided of course that the remainder of Zumstein's reasons for Chapter 21 have been countered, as I will now go on to do.

Ad 2 – Regarding the "reinstatement" of the apostles first in 20 and then in 21, there is a difference between 20 and 21 in that the apostles are individually *commissioned*, which they have not yet been in 20. "Feed my sheep" in 21:17b is much more specific as a commissioning of Peter than the much more general outpouring of the Spirit in 20:23, with the commission to forgive sins.

We may apply the comment by Jean Manns to being a theological justification for Chapter 21:

> For John, the Christian community must not enclose itself in a ghetto. On the contrary, it must open itself out to its mission, because Jesus sent by the Father now sends his disciples out. He himself has healed the centurion, and had dialogue with the Samaritan woman. Having cleansed the world by the blood of his cross, Jesus has accomplished the expectation of Israel.[127]

Having come to faith in Jesus as Son of God [20:23], the believer is now sent out on that mission led by Peter, and accepting the testimony of the beloved disciple as true.

Ad 3 – 21:23 does not necessarily imply that the beloved disciple is already dead. In this Hoskyns is quite correct.[128] [John 21:21-24] Carson is nearer the mark when he says "As it is, it seems simpler to think that the circulating rumour is making the rounds while the beloved disciple is still alive, but advancing in years, and he is determined to stifle it as well as he can for fear of the damage that would be done if he died before the Lord's return".[129] The publication of the Gospel would also be most apt if the beloved disciple was near to death. As I proposed above, the beloved disciple could well therefore have compiled this last Chapter 21 after the main body of the work had already been written (which explains both the unity of style and the somewhat detached nature of the account) and published it in view of his imminent death, together with the Ephesian elders, who are the "we"[130] knowing that he, the beloved disciple's testimony, is true, apostolic, and not Gnostic or in any way heretical.

Ad 4 – Finally, in response to Zumstein's stress on the change of perspective in Chapter 21 from the Christological to the ecclesiological,[131] this may be freely admitted by those who argue for unity of authorship for 1-20 and 21. The emphasis throughout the first twenty chapters is on the person of Christ and on faith in him. The emphasis in 21 is on the specific roles of disciples post-resurrection. But this comes from the theological situation of Christ sending his disciples, represented in Peter and in the beloved disciple to mission, and does not demand a different redactor.

However, Zumstein gives an added reason for another hand in that there is a deliberate attempt to reinstate Peter, whose profile is rather low in Chapters 1-20. Zumstein argues that the role of the beloved disciple is above Peter in 13-20. The beloved disciple is in the bosom of Jesus [13:23-25] and, after the arrest of Jesus, it is the beloved disciple who is able to ensure Peter's entry into the courtyard because of his knowledge of the high priest:

> Simon Peter and another disciple followed Jesus. Since that disciple was known to the high priest, he went with

263

> Jesus into the courtyard of the high priest, but Peter was
> standing outside at the gate. So the other disciple, who
> was known to the high priest, went out, spoke to the
> woman who guarded the gate, and brought Peter in.
> [John 18:15-16]

The continuing verses tell of Peter's denial; yet the beloved
disciple stays around, and is present at the foot of the cross to
witness the death of Jesus [19:26-27]. Then, the beloved
disciple also comes to the fore as a witness to the resurrection
in Chapter 20:

> Then Peter and the other disciple set out and went toward
> the tomb. The two were running together, but the other
> disciple outran Peter and reached the tomb first. He bent
> down to look in and saw the linen wrappings lying there,
> but he did not go in. Then Simon Peter came, following
> him, and went into the tomb. He saw the linen wrappings
> lying there, and the cloth that had been on Jesus' head,
> not lying with the linen wrappings but rolled up in a
> place by itself. Then the other disciple, who reached the
> tomb first, also went in, and he saw and believed; for as
> yet they did not understand the scripture, that he must
> rise from the dead. [John 20:3-9]

These points are well made by Zumstein. But are they
contradictory, or supplementary? The author of the Fourth
Gospel, looking at his completed work, might well have
realised that some misunderstandings need to be corrected,
and some points clarified before his call from the Lord to
leave the world. All that is being emphasised in Chapters
13-20 is the priority of the beloved disciple as an eye-witness
and also the continuing fidelity of the beloved disciple
throughout the ministry of Jesus which was one reason why
the Lord had him as a special friend. This says nothing at all
about the *respective authority* of the beloved disciple vis à vis
Peter. It is worth noting that there is the use of the word
Cephas in John 1:42, "He (Andrew) brought Simon to Jesus,
who looked at him and said, "You are Simon son of John.
You are to be called Cephas (which is translated Peter)". The
name Cephas was unknown either in the Semitic or in the

Hellenistic world. The same parallel between Messiah (a title) and Cephas (presumably also a title) is in John 1:41 and 1:42 as there is in Matthew 16:

Jesus	Peter
[Matthew 16:16] Simon Peter answered, "You are the Messiah, the Son of the living God."	[Matthew 16:18] And I tell you, you are Peter, and on this rock I will build my church, and the gates of Hades will not prevail against it.
[John 1:41] He first found his brother Simon and said to him, "We have found the Messiah" (which is translated Anointed).	[John 1:42] He brought Simon to Jesus, who looked at him and said, "You are Simon son of John. You are to be called Cephas" (which is translated Peter).

There seems to be here a consistent intention of the part of the evangelist to explain Semitic words to his readers, which have a link with titles. The first occurs in 1:38, "When Jesus turned and saw them following, he said to them, "What are you looking for?" They said to him, "Rabbi" (which translated means Teacher)." Then, as we see above, there is a parallel between Messiah being translated as Christ, and Cephas being translated as Peter, Rock. Thus, in the early part of the main text of John, the author seems already to be aware of Peter's title of Rock, as named by Christ. As Brown says, "As is known from the OT, the giving of a new name has a direct relation to the role the man so designated will play in salvation history (Genesis 17:5, 32:28)".[132] He is not introducing something entirely alien in Chapter 21, when he emphasises the Shepherd role of Peter in the new community.

At the same time, in the main body of the text, that same author wishes to emphasise the role of the beloved disciple as an eye-witness, and as close to Jesus, even though at times this may seem to be at the cost of Peter's role. Thus the author himself could have quite easily have added the final chapter, in his own style, but focussing on ecclesiology rather than Christology, which was the burden of the main part, Chapters 1-20 of the Fourth Gospel.

We might allow Jülicher the final say here, who came down on the side of the integrity of Chapter 21 with the rest of the work. His views are an interesting reversal of the usual ideas about the closing of the Gospel:

> In xx.21-23, Jesus had imparted their mission to his disciples; what special charge had he to lay upon his most faithful pair? It is this question to which chapter xxi gives the answer; the testimony of the departing Son of God, that the beloved disciple should tarry till his return, sets the seal upon the witness borne by this disciple throughout the Gospel to the Son of God; nor are even vv. 24ff. written by a different hand, but by the same interpreter to whom we owe verse 19a. The last two verses of chapter xx were not originally intended as the ending of the Gospel, but, like xix.35, constituted a sort of editorial addition inserted into the body of the story, like the phrase 'He that hath ears to hear, let him hear' of the Synoptics and the Apocalypse.[133]

Conclusion and summary of part two

Our conclusion is that the Gospel of John was at least possibly, indeed more than likely written by an individual, without using any identifiable literary sources. Any editorial work was most likely done by the evangelist himself, or at least by a redactor imbued entirely with the ideas of the evangelist. There is no compelling evidence of redactional insertions with theological motivation (e.g. conflicting ecclesiastical groups of the late first century with their own theological agendas) that is not the work of the evangelist. If the writer used sources, nothing prevents those sources being his own.

Zumstein maintains that the Fourth Gospel is not the work of a single hand, but is of several redactors. He claims that this is one of the few points Johannine scholars actually agree upon.[134] As we have seen, this is not the case. Dissenting from this view would not only be those named as "conservative", accepting the traditional authorship by John the Son of Zebedee. It would also include Hengel, Barrett, and Brodie, who all maintain that the Fourth Gospel was written substantially by one hand, which author made his own redactions.

However, many Johannine scholars act on the presumption that such redaction theories have been proved. The fact, as we have demonstrated above, that they certainly have not been so proved, any more than have Brown's Stages, has great significance for our General Conclusions, as we shall now see.

NOTES – CHAPTER TEN

1 Hengel, 1989.
2 Brown, 1979.
3 Hengel, 1989, 1.
4 Kaistli, Poffet, CJH, 207. For summary of Wellhausen's position see Schnelle, 1987, 12-13.
5 "The term 'Pentateuch' is derived from the Greek *pentateuchos*, 'five containers', indicating the written leather or papyrus rolls that were kept in receptacles. In this case the five rolls are the first five books of the Bible: Genesis, Exodus, Leviticus, Numbers, and Deuteronomy, to use their Greco-Latin names." NJBC, **1:3**, 3.
6 Kraus, 1969, 260-69.
7 NJBC, **1:6**, 4.
8 UFG, 30.
9 Kaistli, Poffet CJH, 207-8.
10 Ashton, J., 1991.
11 UFG, 32.
12 UFG, 31.
13 UFG, 31, n. 70.
14 Robinson, 1976, 261, Cf. above, 133.
15 Kraus, 1969, 258.
16 NJBC, **46:4**, 773.

17 Kaestli, Poffet, CJH, 207-8.

18 Cf. Above, 43-52.

19 CJH, 209.

20 *La Redaction Finale de L'Évangile selon Jean (À L'Exemple du Chapitre 2)*, in CJH, 207-230.

21 Kaestli, Poffet, CJH , 209. "La conclusion que le savant de Marbourg tire do son étude est que l'ordre traditionnel et canonique de l'evangile est le fait d'une rédaction ultérieure, et non de l'évangeliste, rédaction qui vient pleinement au langage dans le Chapitre 21."

22 RGG, col. 841. "Das Johannesevangelium is also offenbar von einer Redaktion herausgegeben worden, die als kirchlich bezeichnet werden muss, weil sie den Sakarementglauben und die Zukunfts-Eschatologie in das Johannesevangelium hineinkorrigierte, die ihm ursprünglich fremd waren. Für die kirchliche Orthodoxie erschien das Evangelium offenbar als bedenklich oder gefährlich und musste entsprechend redigiert werden."

23 D. Moody Smith, 1984, 25, concludes, on the contrary that "the present form of the Gospel of John may represent neither anti-Gnosticism (Bultmann) nor pro-Gnosticism (Käsemann, Schottroff), but an early stage in the emergence of motifs that had a later flowering in Gnosticism". Intriguingly, Moody Smith's view would lend support to the conclusion that the Fourth Gospel was more likely to have been the origin of Gnosticism, rather than Gnosticism the origin of John.

24 Brown, I, XXIX.

25 Cf. Above 125, "The Mandaeans?…"

26 Brown I, XXXI.

27 See above, chapter 7, 144. "of what he calls this 'historical tradition', independent…"

28 Parker, 1956, 304.

29 Brown, I, XXXI-XXXII.

30 Brown, I, XXXII.

31 For a much fuller treatment of source theories, together with an exposition of his own, cf. UFG. Cf. also Smith, 1984.

32 Cf. Above, 218-223, "Wellhausen…".

33 In W. Ward Gasque and William Sanford LaSor (eds.) *Scripture, Tradition, and Interpretation.* Eardmans, 1978. Quoted in Carson, 45. Morris concludes "We have no need to posit a redactor".

34 Cf. CJH, 210-1.

35 CJH, 211-2."dans sa perspective, chaque action appelle une réaction symmétrique, et l'histoire se constitue dans cet enchaînement de contraires successif".

36 CJH, 212. "l'attribution d'une parfaite homogénéité theologique 'chaque stade, puis leur mise en perspective chronologique nous semblent problématiques".

37 CJH, 212, 1.3.

38 CJH, 212.

39 CJH, 212; 3. 1:14-18, 5:27-29, 6:22,48-58, 13:10b-17, 15-17.

40 UFG, 87.

41 Cf. BMG, 200, for Marguerat's strictures concerning the hypothetical Signs Source.

42 Hengel, in L.D. Hurst and N.T. Wright, ed.1987, 92.

43 Carson, 42.

44 UFG, 546.

45 Cf. John McDade's critique of "low to high Christology" in BMG,183.

46 For a summary of these views on the Johannine Community, cf. NJBC **61:9-10**, 945-946.

47 De Boer, 1996, 80.

48 Hengel, 1989, 89-90.

49 Barrett, 26.

50 BMG, 200-201.

51 Van Belle, 1994, 376.

52 De Boer, 1996, 80, accepts the literary unity of the Fourth Gospel as demonstrated by Ruckstuhl *et al*. But he attributes this literary unity to the Johannine Community. But is there any other example of a School producing a unified style? Even collective documents, e.g. the Code of Canon Law and the Catechism of the Catholic Church, will most frequently employ a single individual to write the final document, even if that document is anonymous in authorship. Communities generally do not write books, particularly great books.

53 Jülicher, 1904, 391ff.

54 Moloney, 259: "For sound textual reasons it is universally admitted that the account of Jesus and the woman taken in adultery (7:53-8:11) does not belong to the Fourth Gospel..."

55 Jülicher 1904, 395-6.

56 John 4:2 – although it was not Jesus himself but his disciples who baptized – For Brown, I, 164, this is clear evidence of a redactor. "*Not Jesus himself.* This is clearly an attempt to modify 3:22, where it is said that Jesus did baptise, and serves as almost indisputable evidence of the presence of several hands in the composition of John. Perhaps the final redactor was afraid that the sectarians of John the Baptist would use Jesus' baptising as an argument that he was only an imitator of John the Baptist. The unusual word for "however", (*katoi ge*) may be another indication of a different hand". However, a small subordinate clause is hardly evidence of a redactor of great influence on the Fourth Gospel, even if we admit with Brown that this subordinate clause was a redactor's gloss. Carson, 215, gives what is to me a more commonsense explanation: "In a parenthetical note typical of the Evangelist (cf. 3:24, 4:8, 9b), verse 2 points out that Jesus himself did not baptise, but his disciples did – or, more pedantically, Jesus baptised only by using his disciples as the agents (cf. 3:22). This distinction between preaching and baptizing was later to be emulated in large part by Paul (1 Corinthians 1:14-17)". Thus, in Carson's view, Jesus

baptised *through* his disciples, Jesus confining himself to preaching and performing the wonderful works of the kingdom. That seems to me to be a thoroughly sensible explanation, without the unnecessary complications of redaction theory. Barrett also makes the important point that here we are not concerned with the full theological implications of post-resurrection and post-pentecost baptism, Barrett, 230. Rather, Jesus through his disciples is using a Baptist style of baptism, of repentance for the forgiveness of sins, cf. Matthew 3:1-6, and Matthew 4:17. This is a preparation for post-pentecostal baptism, which is an actual outpouring of the Spirit, Acts 2:38. Thus Barrett quotes W.F. Flemington, *The New Testament Doctrine of Baptism* (1948), 30f.: (especially) "If... baptism were practised with the approval of Jesus, it becomes easier to explain why, immediately after Pentecost, baptism took its place as the normal rite of entry into the Christian community (31)".

57 Brown, I, 165.

58 Morris, 253.

59 Cf. our discussion of *oi iudaioi* in BMG, Chapter 15, 267-295. *"The Jews"* (hoi Ioudaioi*) and the Death of Jesus.* Re John 4:22, cf. BMG, 274, 284, 285.

60 Cf. Above, 139, "For instance C.K. Barrett presents..."

61 Cf. 64-65, where we discuss the whole purpose of the writing of the Fourth Gospel. Cf. BMG, 181-195

62 For Mark Stibbe, 1994, 21, "The sudden switch from the Temple to Galilee is there for a reason. It alerts the reader to a phenomenon which will recur throughout Chapters 5 to 10: the mysterious and elusive movements of the Messiah."

63 *entia non multiplicantur praeter necessitatem.* For a brief account of Occam's philosophy, cf. ODCC, 1483-4. For my use of the principle of Occam's Razor as a principle in historical Jesus research, cf. BMG, 116-7, 148.

64 Ruckstuhl, 1987, 98.

65 As for instance in the work of M.C. De Boer, 1996.

66 Brown I, XXXIV.

67 How does Brown reconcile this "different style" with the conclusions of Ruckstuhl, which he seems to accept, that there is unity of style throughout the Fourth Gospel?

68 Brown, I, XXXVIII-IX.

69 Carson, 42.

70 Carson, 42.

71 Dodd, 1965, 4. "For the more clearly the theological position of the Fourth Gospel is examined, the more clearly is it seen to involve a reference to history."

72 Dodd, 1965, 335-365.

73 Dodd, 1965, 366-387.

74 Brown, I, XXXV.

75 Hoskyns, 1948.

76 Ruckstuhl, 1987.

77 This complex methodology, of using the concept of Brown's stages along with Johannine source theories, is followed for example by M.C. de Boer, in his *Johannine Perspectives on the Death of Jesus.* De Boer finds "aporias", 72 in John, such as we have already outlined, e.g. the Chapters 4,5,6 and 7 problem, and in addition the fact that the first two signs narrated in 2:1-11 and 4:46-54 are numbered, but subsequent signs are not. De Boer, 1996, 73. But again, the theory of traditional authorship can go easily along with that author editing his own work, and indeed writing sometimes in an apparently clumsy way; yet, as all have agreed, the end result is not clumsy at all, but a literary as well as a spiritual masterpiece.

78 Quoted in Brown, I, XXXI-II. Parker, 1956, 304.

79 Barrett, 43.

80 Cf. Above, 221, "We must ask, furthermore, whether Wellhausen…"

81 Brown, I, XXXVI.

82 Cf. Above, 114-5 "But Robinson is highly sceptical of Brown's…" Robinson, 1976, 273-4.

83 Robinson, 1976, 273. Robinson quotes Hare, *The Theme of Persecuting Christians in the Gospel According to St. Matthew,* Cambridge, 1967, 48-56.

84 Moloney, 16.

85 Carson, 63.

86 Carson, 63-64.

87 Carson, 66.

88 QHJ, 84.

89 Brodie, 1993.

90 Brodie, 18.

91 Bultmann, 631. "The words *egeiresthe, agómen enteuthen* mark the end of the scene started in 13.2, and lead on to ch.18. Thus we arrive at the traditional Passion narrative."

92 Brodie, 19.

93 Westcott, 211: "We must suppose that after these were spoken the Lord, with the eleven, at once left the house and went on the way which finally led to Gethsemane; and consequently that the discourses which follow, xv-xvii, were spoken after He had gone from the upper room and before He crossed the Kedron (xviii.1)."

94 Brodie, 11.

95 Cf. Above, 141, "We would make a similar response…" for earlier reference.

96 Brodie, 1993, 145.

97 CJH, 109, "En deux mots, je formulerai ansi cette hypothèse: les écrits johanniques on été composes à l'interieur de la communauté johannique par un groupe de proches du disciple bienaimé… La literature johannique est le reflet de cet enracinement communautaire.

L'unité littéraire de l'évangile peut ainsi être expliquée à partir du travail créateur de l'évangéliste sur le materiel dont il disposait. Quant au rédacteur, ses perspectives devaient aussi être proches de celles de l'évangéliste. Les apories de l'évangile, tout comme les differences qui le séparent des épîtres, peuvent alors trouver leur explication dans la pluralité des auteurs impliqués dans la production du corpus johannique. Il peut certes y avoir divergence entre nous quant au role des collaborateurs de l'évangéliste ou du rédacteur, mais nous sommes parfaitement d'accord sur le point suivant: nous n'avons certainement pas affaire à un évangile qui aurait été compose à partir de sources sans relation entre elles et provenant de communautés diverses, évangile qui aurait ensuite été révisé par un rédacteur dont la théologie différait de manière tranchée de celle de l'évangéliste." This is part of Culpepper's article *L'Application de la Narratologie et L'Évangile À L'Étude de Jean*, 97-120.

98 Hengel, 1989, 86, quotes A.Hilgenfeld, A.von Harnack, W. Wrede, A. Jülicher, H.J. Holtzmann, Hans Windisch, M. Dibelius, and Walter Bauer. Hengel asserts "They certainly saw problems in the text of John very clearly, but they could not agree with the literary-critical hypotheses in the body of the Gospel (chs.1-20) which were already very numerous and – as still today – often mutually contradictory".

99 Brodie, 1993, 152.

100 Ruckstuhl 1987, pp.20-179.

101 Schnackenburg, I, 44-58.

102 Schnackenburg, I, 45-74.

103 Schnackenburg, I, 22.

104 Not all scholars agree that "sign" (*sémeion*) means "miracle" in John; but it is our position, BMG, 349-52, and Brown's, I, 503-4.

105 Barrett, 193.

106 Barrett, 248.

107 Schnackenburg, I, 72.

108 Above, 137-145 "Dependance on the Synoptic Gospels?..."

109 Schnackenburg, I, 32.

110 Barrett, 44.

111 BMG, 200-1.

112 Schnackenburg, I, 72-3.

113 Dodd, HTFG, 366-7.

114 Dodd, HTFG, 196-222.

115 Schnackenburg, I, 73.

116 Schnackenburg, I, 73.

117 Barrett, 151.

118 Brown, I, 285.

119 Schnackenburg, I, 73.

120 Schnackenburg, I, 73.

121 Cf. Above, 235, "the ordering of chapters..."

122 Schnackenburg, I, 73-74.

123 CJH, 215-219.

124 Hoskyns, 561-2.

125 Above, 230, "E.Ruckstuhl refined Schweizer's method further in 1951..." "Ruckstuhl developed his older investigation..."

126 Westcott, xxviii.

127 Manns, F.,1991, 509. "Pour Jean la communauté chrétienne ne doit pas s'enfermer dans un ghetto: au contraire, elle doit s'ouvrir à la mission, piusque Jésus envoyé par le Père a envoyé ses disciples. Lui-même a guéri le Centurion et a discuté avec la Samaritaine. Ayant purifié le monde par le sang de sa croix, Jésus a accompli l'attente d'Israel." 509.

128 Hoskyns, 559.

129 Carson, 682.

130 For discussion as to who are the "we", Above, 192, "4. Who are the 'We' Testifying?..."

131 CJH, 222.

132 Brown, I, 80.

133 Jülicher, 1904, 394.

134 CJH, 207. L'évangile selon Jean n'est pas l'oeuvre d'une seule main. Deux, voire plusieurs rédacteurs ont participé á l'éboration du texte qui a été accueilli dans le canon néotestamentaire. Cette conviction s'inscrit dans la plupart des travaux qui jalonnent l'exégèse johannique contemporaine. C'est même – ils convient de le noter – l'un des seuls points de consensus existant dans ce domaine de recherche si controversé.

GENERAL CONCLUSIONS

In Chapter 8 of the present work we quoted the conclusion of Raymond E. Brown regarding the authorship of the Gospel of John:

> Thus it is fair to say that the only ancient tradition about the authorship of the Fourth Gospel for which any considerable body of evidence can be adduced is that it is the work of John son of Zebedee. There are some valid points in the objections raised to this tradition, but Irenaeus' statement is far from having been disproved.[1]

Our conclusion at the end of this present work only confirms such a judgement which Brown expressed in his excellent Anchor Bible Commentary first published in 1966.[2]

Our first point must be one of methodology. If the traditional authorship has not been disproved, then it must surely stand, particularly if, as Brown says, there is a considerable body of evidence for it. Where ancient documents are concerned, if the early testimony of their authorship has such good evidence, and objections to it have been reasonably answered, that constitutes a valid proof of such a tradition.

It is not required that no difficulties whatever remain unanswered, or other possibilities as to authorship still remain contrary to such a testimony. Such absolute certainties are not in the nature of conclusions from historical research. All that is needed is the positing of a reasonable case for such a tradition, and then that tradition should stand, if the objections to that tradition do not completely undermine its credibility.

We may use the analogy of the works of William Shakespeare. There is still a small minority who contest that Shakespeare actually wrote the plays bearing his name. In response, we could never say that it is absolutely impossible that Bacon or Marlowe or some anonymous genius wrote Shakespeare's plays. But the vast majority of us are quite satisfied with the traditional ascription of the authorship of Shakespeare's plays, believing that the objections to Shakespeare being the author of the plays ascribed to him are not sufficiently weighty to overturn the presumption that he was.

Presumption is important as a principle in historical study. If we are told by contemporaries that a given work is by a given author, then we must presume that they are right unless we can clearly prove them wrong, or unless the evidence for their testimony is palpably weak.

That is why I have taken most seriously of all Bauckham's objection, namely that the "John" referred to by the tradition is not the apostle, one of the Twelve, John the Son of Zebedee, but "John the Presbyter" who himself was the beloved disciple, a High Priest contemporary with or just after the time of Jesus. In this view, the testimony of tradition itself would be of a different author, and the presumption then would shift to another John as the author of the Gospel.

What finally has persuaded me against Bauckham's view is the classical argument of Westcott, most of all as he argues from the Gospel narrative itself. Many commentaries refer to this argument, and even commend it, but few if any consider it in full, as it deserves. If we accept with Westcott that the beloved disciple is identical with the anonymous disciple mentioned earlier in the Gospel, then it seems to me that we have to agree with Westcott also that this disciple is none other than John the Son of Zebedee.

As Wescott carefully argues, the only disciple who is also one of the Twelve in a close relationship with Jesus who is not named is John the Son of Zebedee; and, correctly it seems to me Westcott again argues, the disciple is anonymous precisely because he is the author of the Gospel (not simply behind the Gospel tradition), as 21:24 says explicitly that he is.

The question as to why that "anonymous disciple" is not named as "the beloved disciple" will remain to some extent an enigma. Perhaps the term "beloved disciple" is not used until the Passion Narrative because that disciple was especially associated with the Commandment of Love [13:34]. But this question can remain to some extent at least unanswered because the evidence for the identity of the beloved disciple as being John the Son of Zebedee is, I believe, just as strong as Westcott argues.

This would mean that the primary evidence for John the Son of Zebedee being the author of the Fourth Gospel as the beloved disciple is from the Gospel itself. That means in consequence that this would be the genuine source of the tradition; and therefore that the presumption would be that when the early witnesses such as Papias or Irenaeus refer to "John the disciple of the Lord", they mean John the Son of Zebedee and not the hypothetical "John the Presbyter", *pace* Bauckham.

John the Presbyter/Elder?

The view that the author of the Gospel of John was John the Elder was called in the earlier days of criticism a "mediating theory", because it was as it were half way between claiming traditional authorship and denying authorship by an eye-witness. The Pope, in asserting that John the Son of Zebedee was the beloved disciple, but that the author was John the Presbyter, means by this to defend the fact that the Fourth Gospel was dependant on a reliable apostolic eye-witness source. This is of course highly commendable, and, as we have seen in our Part One, is a key principle underlying the Pope's writing of *Jesus of Nazareth*. As the Pope quotes Stuhlmacher approvingly, "the contents go back to the disciple whom Jesus (especially) loved. The presbyter understood himself as his mouthpiece".[3]

But here I must agree with Bauckham that it is very difficult to avoid the plain meaning of the statement of 21:24 that the beloved disciple "wrote these things", namely was the author of the Fourth Gospel. If words mean what they mean, that is what "wrote these things" does mean. As we have seen, there is no evidence in antiquity that "wrote these things" means anything else than precisely an author, except perhaps referring to a scribe.

If, therefore, as the Pope says, the Fourth Gospel was

written by one dependant on an eye-witness source, then why was it not written by an eye-witness? This is why the theory that John the Presbyter wrote the Gospel is perhaps correctly called a "mediating theory", because those who propose the theory do not for one reason or another accept that John the Son of Zebedee could himself have been the actual author of the Fourth Gospel. The Pope himself offers "the complexity of the Gospel's redaction"[4] as a reason why we must look beyond the simple identification of the author with the Son of Zebedee, and need to resort to an author other than the Apostle.

But if, as we have argued in the last chapter of this book, there is no real evidence of a redactor at all in the writing of the Fourth Gospel, then the way is once more open to authorship by the Son of Zebedee, and written as a "seamless robe" in Strauss' terminology. This would not deny that the author has used sources, or has written the Gospel in stages; but that those sources are now undetectable, and the stages are also undetectable, and that they are the author's own sources and the author's own stages. What we have coherently is a single work which we call a "Gospel" with a unified style and a sure narrative direction, which needs no cutting up in Bultmannian fashion into a patchwork quilt of imaginary sources and later additions with theological agendas.

I would suggest that my conclusions concerning redaction in my final chapter are perhaps the most important in my whole study. If the Gospel of John stands as it does actually written by an eye-witness, and there is no evidence of a redactor or redactors out of touch with that eye-witness, then it must be taken seriously as an historical work. It becomes then of secondary importance whether that eye-witness was John the Apostle, Son of Zebedee, or John the Presbyter, John Mark, Lazarus, or anyone else. My contention that the tradition that the author was John the Son of Zebedee would add the not-insignificant advantage that it was written by a member of the Twelve, indeed one of the three most intimate circle of the Twelve. This solution is preferable, and, as I have demonstrated, the most persuasive from the evidence. But any other eye-witness would do theoretically, or any other writer such as John the Presbyter in close touch with an eye-witness source.

Authorship and tradition

As we have made clear in *Bad, Mad or God?*,[5] the tradition that John the Son of Zebedee wrote the Fourth Gospel is not a matter of Catholic dogma. It is a "tradition" with a small "t". The Second Vatican Council's Dogmatic Constitution on Divine Revelation affirmed not the apostolic *authorship* but the *apostolic origin* of the Four Gospels.[6] Thus a John the Elder, or a Lazarus, or a John Mark could have been the author of the Gospel of John; or even an unknown author at the beginning of the Gospel tradition, ending with work by the "Johannine community". None of these proposed solutions would be against Catholic faith, but could be held as the end process of a tradition originating from the apostolic era.

I have argued in my earlier book that, whichever of these solutions we adopt, we can develop a legitimate methodology to examine the Fourth Gospel to find the historical Jesus. "even if there is only a possibility that the Fourth Gospel has its own historical tradition, then we are legitimately free to examine John to see whether in his narrative there are sayings and stories which could authentically emanate from the historical Jesus, and that, in such an instance at least, John is not simply a fictional rewrite of the Synoptic account".[7] We did this in particular authenticating historically the miracle of the *Walking on the Water,* and the claims of Jesus in John to be the absolute I AM, the transcendent Son of God.

But now, as a result of our present investigation, we can go much further. Authorship by John the Son of Zebedee, as we quoted Strachan affirming at the beginning of the previous century, is potentially most important for Christian theology and Christian apologetics. At the very least we have argued in this book that authorship by John the Son of Zebedee is fully worthy of serious consideration. If so, then we must consider the possibility that John's Gospel was either a work of deliberate fiction by one of the apostles – a conclusion from which even radical German criticism recoiled[8] – or it is a substantially historical narrative.

This would provide an even firmer foundation for the Pope's project of writing a Life of Jesus, two further volumes of which we eagerly await, than if we accept his view in *Jesus of Nazareth* that the author was basing the content of his narrative on an apostolic eye-witness, but that the Apostle himself did not write the Fourth Gospel. If the author was actually John the Son of Zebedee, then the solemn testimony of John 21:24 becomes in such a case the most solid historical basis for faith in Jesus as Son of God, written by one who actually observed the events concerning which he writes.

The possibility the author intended St John's Gospel to be theological myth rather than history was rightly dismissed both by the Pope in *Jesus of Nazareth*, by Bauckham in his *Jesus and the Eyewitnesses: The Gospels as Eye-Witness Testimony*, by Ridderbos in his Commentary, and by Brown, who defines seeing the glory in the Old Testament as "a *visible* manifestation of His majesty in *acts of power*".[9] The very doctrine of John 1:14, that the *logos* became flesh and dwelt among us means for the writer of the Fourth Gospel that he is writing about a supremely historical event, the entering into our history of the Word, full of grace and truth.

What we mean by "historical" of course is "substantially historical" in terms of paragraph 19 of the Dogmatic Constitution on Divine Revelation. As we concluded in our discussion with the view of J.G. Dunn above,[10] we do not mean that we have in John the *ipsissima verba Jesu* necessarily, nor the exact sequence of events necessarily. But we do have fact not myth[11].

If what I have concluded in this book is correct, then our conclusions will be of real service to theologians.

Catholic Theology and Scripture Exegesis

In 1962, the distinguished Catholic theologian Karl Rahner drew attention to the increasing alienation between the biblical and theological disciplines within academic Catholic theology.

In a symposium entitled *Exegesis and Dogmatic Theology*, he bemoaned this increasing division:

> within Catholic theology there obtains a certain estrangement between the representatives of these two disciplines. It appears to us that not a few representatives of these two fields of work in Catholic theology regard each other with a certain distrust, even exasperation. The dogmatic theologian seems at times to have the feeling that exegetes pay scant attention to the dogmatics to which the theologian is bound, and which pronounces upon matters which are the subject of exegesis (in the widest meaning of the word). Some exegetes, on the other hand, seem convinced that the theologians want to tie the Scripture scholar's hands in a way for which there is no objective justification, but simply because the theologians have not taken sufficient account of the progress Catholic exegesis has made in recent decades.[12]

Rahner was clear that the biblical scholar must be rigorously critical, using all the tools and the strict discipline of the historical method:

> You must be critical, inexorably critical. You must not seek to arrange any dishonest reconciliations between the results of research and the doctrine of the Church. You may propose a problem and expound it sincerely where necessary. You need not leave seen-in spite of all your efforts you may not yet see-how clear, positive solutions can be found which will harmonise church doctrine, or what one takes to be such, with the real or ostensible results of your research. In such cases you need have no misgivings.

But on that same page Rahner goes on to challenge the Catholic exegete thus: part of his or her task is precisely to see how Church doctrine is consistent with biblical research:

> But the climax of your research you must seek only in the accomplishment of your whole duty. And part of this, since you are Catholic exegetes, is the demonstration of the harmony between your results and Church doctrine.

You must show how your results, of themselves, point on to Church doctrine as to their genuine expression. Of course not every exegete is bound to do this every time. Without specialisation and division of labour, no one can get very far nowadays. But that such a demonstration is basically part of the exegete's task should show more often and clearly among you than seems to me to be the case.[13]

Rahner's challenge still is relevant. The division still exists between Catholic exegesis and any attempt towards dogmatic theological affirmations. Indeed, much more recently, Mark Bockmuehl has drawn attention to divisions within the broad base of New Testament study itself, without any specific reference to Roman Catholicism. In June, 1936, C.H. Dodd, as we have seen, one of the best New Testament exegetes of the twentieth century,[14] delivered the inaugural lecture as Norris-Hulse Professor of Divinity at Cambridge. Bockmuehl notes "the supreme ease and confidence of many of his methodological assumptions..."[15] But he immediately adds, "Professor Dodd would soon discover that his discipline no longer enjoys any agreement either about the methods of study or even about the criteria by which one might agree about appropriate methods and criteria. Only a small handful of (usually tenured) authors have the guts to admit this explicitly".[16]

Bockmuehl continues: "There is a widespread delusion among historical critics of every theological stripe that the results of their study are themselves self-evidently irrelevant to the meaning of the gospel of Christian faith. They assume that they may therefore continue to operate more or less in splendid isolation from considerations of Christian theology, or indeed from an understanding of the wider cultural and philosophical context in which their own work is carried out".[17]

Bockmuehl then says why such scholars are deluded: "in dealing with the New Testament's inalienably theological subject matter there can be no neutral history nor a neutral historian... Historical research at its best contributes vital and helpful clarification of the literal sense of the text, but its role can only be assessed as part of an overall approach to New Testament interpretation".[18] Bockmuehl then quotes the apparently cynical conclusion of David Clines:[19]

> If there are no 'right' interpretations, and no validity in interpretation beyond the assent of various interest groups, biblical interpreters have to give up the goal of determinate and universally acceptable interpretations, and devote themselves to producing interpretations they can sell – in whatever mode is called for by the communities they serve... Those who pay the piper get to call the tune. And biblical interpreters are... no more than pipers, playing their tunes in the service of some community or other that authorises their work and signs their salary cheques.[20]

Bockmuehl notes with approval new approaches such as narrative and genre criticism, which "are at least in principle amenable to a dialogue with the sort of allegorical and spiritual interpretation that was practiced in the patristic and mediaeval periods and which, despite its recent neglect even among Catholic exegetes, has begun to find renewed support in some circles".[21]

On the other hand, others such as Schmithals see the future of New Testament exegesis only as an "objective scientific" study, without reference to the faith communities who are usually interested in it: "On this reading, the future of New Testament studies as an academic discipline in the universities must lie in re-grouping around a strictly secular phenomenological study, in which a Christian theological interpretation can have no part".[22] With such a view, our exegesis cannot have any relevance to our faith, without the theologian himself or herself pulling out a subsequent subjective interpretation of those purely secular results from a body of learning in itself unrelated to it.

Exegesis: a cross-roads

In the light of this challenge, it seems to me, Catholic exegesis has a real contribution to make. In our Part One, we discussed how the Pope presents a new starting-point, which includes faith in the investigation, but does not lose contact with reason. We have used Newman's concept of Antecedent Probability rationally to justify an approach which begins with at least the possibility of revelation. Then we have begun to discuss the conditions of its probability, confirming such a presupposition by our investigation.

My own work in this study confirms and justifies still further the Pope's use of scripture as a foundation for the doctrine of the incarnation. A "Life of Jesus" can be written which is a positive basis for theology and apologetics, thus satisfying Rahner's plea. The Pope's book *Jesus of Nazareth* is doubtless such a foundation. I cherish the fond hope that in discussing still further the question of the relationship of history and faith in Part One, and in my discussion of the authorship of the Gospel of John, I have made my own contribution to strengthening such foundations. This is important because, after all, foundations once destroyed, what will the just man do?

NOTES – GENERAL CONCLUSIONS

1   Brown, I., XCII.
2   Remarkably, in Brown's 1997 *An Introduction to the New Testament*, he abandons this position without any substantial reasons given for such change of view. Commenting on the Irenaeus tradition, he asserts "Nevertheless, as pointed out above (p.109), it is now recognised that such late-2d-century surmises about figures who had lived a century before were often simplified; and that authorship tradition was sometimes more concerned with the *authority* behind a a biblical writing that with the physical writer. As with the other Gospels it is doubted by most scholars that this Gospel was written by an eyewitness of the public ministry of Jesus". INT, 368-9. This contrasts disappointingly with the careful and rational consideration of all opinions which characterised the earlier two-volume Anchor Bible

Commentary followed by his own well-considered judgement. To me, this seems a prime example verifying my comment in the Foreword of this present work, to the effect that recent Catholic scholarship has accepted the current scepticism without question.

3   JN, 226.
4   JN, 225.
5   BMG, 158-9.
6   DV 18.
7   BMG, 172.
8   Cf. BMG, 56.
9   Brown, I, 503. Quoted in BMG, 350.
10 Above, 74, "for the truth of the..."
11 Cf. BV, 125. For my clarification of the meaning of DV19 regarding the historicity of the Gospels.
12 Rahner, 1964, 31.
13 Rahner, 1964, 36.
14 Cf. above, 142. Our consideration of Dodd's *The Historical Traditions in the Fourth Gospel.*
15 Bockmuehl, 1998, 271.
16 Bockmuehl, 1998, 277.
17 Bockmuehl, 1998, 282.
18 Bockmuehl, 1998, 282-283.
19 Few are better placed than David Clines, for years editing the excellent biblical publications of the Sheffield University Press, to realise the variety of scope and method in current work on exegesis.
20 Clines, 1983, 79-80.
21 Bockmuehl, 1998, 284.
22 Bockmuehl, 1998, 289.

COMMENTARIES ON ST JOHN'S GOSPEL

The following are the commentaries on John to which I have had access in writing this book. Endnote references to commentaries on St. John's Gospel mention only the author's surname, the volume if more than one, and the page number (Brown, I, 233).

Barrett, C.K., *The Gospel According to St. John. An Introduction with Commentary and Notes on the Greek Text*. 2nd Edition. London, SPCK, 1978.

Brodie, *The Gospel According to John: A Literary and Theological Commentary*. Oxford University Press, 1993.

Brown, R.E., *The Gospel According to John*. Two Volumes, London, Chapman, 1971.

Bultmann R., *The Gospel of John*. Transl. G.R. Beasley-Murray *et al.* Oxford, Basil Blackwell, 1971. A translation of *Das Evangelium des Johannes*, Göttingen, Vandenhoeck and Ruprecht, 1941.

Bruce, F.F., *The Gospel of John: Introduction, Exposition, and Notes*. Michigan, Eerdmans, 1983.

Carson, D.A., *The Gospel According to John*. Leicester, Inter-Varsity Press, Michigan, Eerdmans, 1991.

Edwards, M., *John*. Blackwell Bible Commentaries, Blackwell, Oxford, 2004.

Haenchen, E., *A Commentary on the Gospel of John*. Vol 1 (Chapters 1-6), and Vol 2 (Chapters 7-21) Transl. R.W. Funk. Philadelphia, Fortress Press, 1984. Original German edition: *Johannesevangelium: Ein Kommentar*. Tübingen, J.C.B. Mohr, 1980.

Hoskyns, E.C., ed. Davey, F.N., *The Fourth Gospel*. London, Faber and Faber, 1947

Hunter, A.M., *According to John*. London, SCM, 1968.

Lightfoot, R.H., *St. Johns Gospel: A Commentary*. Oxford University Press, 1956.

Lindars, B., *The Gospel of John*. London, Marshall, Morgan and Scott, 1972. Grand Rapids, Eerdmans, 1981.

Marrow, S.B., *The Gospel of John: A Reading.* New York, Paulist Press, 1995.

Moloney, F., *The Gospel of John.* Sacra Pagina Series, Collegeville, Minnesota, The Liturgical Press, 1998.

Morris, L. *The Gospel According to John: with Introduction, Exposition, and Notes.* Grand Rapids, Eerdmans, 1971.

Ridderbos, H., *The Gospel of John: A Theological Commentary.* Transl. J. Vriend. Grand Rapids, Michigan, Eerdmans, 1991.

Schnackenburg, R., *The Gospel According to John.* Volume I. Transl. K. Smyth. London, Burns and Oates, New York, Herder and Herder, 1968. Volume II, Transl. Cecily Hastings, *et al.* London, Burns and Oates, 1980.

Westcott, B.F., *The Gospel According to John.* Originally published 1880. New Edition London, James Clark, 1958.

Zumstein, J., *L'Évangile Selon Saint Jean (13-21).* Commentaire du Nouveau Testament IVb, Deuxième Série, Genève, Labor et Fides, 2007.

BIBLIOGRAPHY

Footnote references only mention the author's surname, the date of publication of the work to which reference is made, and the page number (e.g. Brown, 1979, 22, would be a reference to his book *The Community of the Beloved Disciple*). References to commentaries other than on the Fourth Gospel mention only the author's surname, the name of the biblical book which is the subject of the commentary, and the page number (e.g. Taylor, Mark, 222). Commentaries on John and books whose title is abbreviated for convenience are listed separately.

Abbott-Smith, G., *A Manual Greek Lexicon of the New Testament.* 3rd Edition. Edinburgh, T. and T. Clark, 1921.

Alexander, D., *Rebuilding the Matrix: Science and Faith in the 21st century.* Oxford, Lion, 2001.

Allen, R.E. ed., *The Concise Oxford Dictionary of Current English.* 8th Edition, Oxford University Press, 1990.

Anderson, P.N., *The Fourth Gospel and the Quest for Jesus: Modern Foundations Reconsidered.* Library of Historical Jesus Studies, 321. London, T. and T. Clark, 2006.

Aquinas, Thomas, *Commentaire sur L'Evangile de Saint Jean. I Le Prologue, La Vie Apostolique du Christ.* Paris, Editions du Cerf, 1968.

Ashton, J., *Understanding the Fourth Gospel.* Oxford, Clarendon Press, 1991.

Ashton, J., *The Identity and Function of the Ioudaioi in the Fourth Gospel.* NT, 27 (1985), 40-75.

Bacon, B.W., *The Fourth Gospel in Research and Debate: A Series of Essays on Problems Concerning the Origin and Value of the Anonymous Writings Attributed to the Apostle John.* Yale University Press, 1918.

Ball, D.M., *'I am' in John's Gospel: Literary Function, Background and Theological Implications.* JSNTS, 124, Sheffield Academic Press, 1996.

Barker, Margaret, *The Older Testament.* London, SPCK, 1987.

Barker, Margaret, *The Gate of Heaven: The History and Symbolism of the Temple in Jerusalem*. London, SPCK, 1991.

Barker, Margaret, *The Great Angel: A Study of Israel's Second God*. London, SPCK, 1992.

Barker, Margaret, *The Risen Lord: The Historical Jesus is the Christ of Faith*. London, SPCK, 1996.

Barnhart, B., *The Good Wine: Reading John from the Centre*. New York, Paulist Press, 1993.

Barrett, C.K., *Essays on John*. London, SPCK, 1982.

Barrett. C.K., *The Gospel of John and Judaism*. Transl. D.M. Smith. London, SPCK, 1975.

Barrett, C.K., *The Lamb of God*. NTS 1(1955), 210-8.

Bauckham, R., *Jesus and the Eyewitnesses: The Gospels as Eye-Witness Testimony*. Cambridge, Eerdmans, 2006.

Becker, J. *Das Evangelium des Johannes*. (TKNT) Gütersloh, Mohn, 1979, 112-120.

Benoit, P., *The Passion and Resurrection of Jesus Christ*. Transl. B. Weatherhead. London, Darton, Longman and Todd, 1969.

Bernhart, B., *Good Wine: Reading John from the Centre*. New York, Paulist Press, 1993.

Bigg, C., *A Critical and Exegetical Commentary on the Epistles of St. Peter and St. Jude*. Edinburgh, T. and T. Clark, 1901.

Blanchard, Y.-M., *Des Signes pour Croire? Une Lecture de L'Evangile de Jean*. Paris, Editions du Cerf, 1995.

Blinzler, J., *The Trial of Jesus*. Cork, The Mercier Press, 1959.

Blomberg, C.L., *The Historical Reliability of St. John's Gospel: Issues and Commentary*. Leicester, Inter-Varsity Press, 2001.

Bockmuehl, M., *To Be or Not to Be: The Possible Futures of New Testament Scholarship*. Scottish Journal of Theology 51(1998), 271-306.

Bockmuehl, M., *This Jesus: Martyr, Lord, Messiah*. Edinburgh, T. and T. Clark, 1994.

Borgen, P., *Philo, John and Paul*. Brown Judaic Studies, 131, Atlanta, Georgia, Scholars Press, 1987.

Bousset, *Kyrios Christos: A History of the Belief in Christ from the Beginnings of Christianity to Irenaeus.* Transl. J.E. Steely, Nashville, Abingdon Press, 1970.

Bouyer, L., *Le Fils éternel: Théologie de la Parole de Dieu et Christologie.* Paris, Editions du Cerf, 1974.

Brandon, S.G.F., *Jesus and the Zealots,* Manchester University Press, 1967.

Brandon, S.G.F., *The Trial of Jesus of Nazareth,* London, B.T. Batsford Ltd., 1968.

Bridges, J.J., *Structure and History in John 11: A Methodological Study Comparing Structuralist and Historical Critical Approaches.* Distinguished Dissertations Series, Volume 4. San Francisco, Mellen Research University Press, 1991.

Brown, R.E., *After Bultmann, What? An Introduction to the Post-Bultmannians.* CBQ, 26 (1964), 1-30.

Brown, R.E., *The Birth of the Messiah. A Commentary on the Infancy Narratives in Matthew and Luke.* London, Chapman, 1977.

Brown, R.E., *The Community of the beloved disciple: The Life, Loves and Hates of an Individual Church in New Testament Times.* London, Chapman, 1979.

Brown, R.E., *The Critical Meaning of the Bible.* London, Chapman, 1981.

Brown, R.E., *The Death of the Messiah* (2 vols.), New York and London, Chapman, 1994.

Brown, R.E., Fitzmyer, J.A., Murphy, R.E. ed., *The New Jerome Biblical Commentary.* London, Geoffrey Chapman, 1989.

Brown, R.E., *How Much Did Jesus Know? A Survey of the Biblical Evidence.* CBQ, 29 (1967) 315-345. (9-39).

Brown, R.E., *An Introduction to the New Testament.* New York, Doubleday, 1997.

Brown, R.E., *Jesus God and Man.* London, Chapman, 1968.

Brown, R.E., *The Value of John in Reconstructing Jesus' Ministry.* In McArthur, H.K., ed. *In Search of the Historical Jesus.* London, SPCK, 1969.

Bruns, J.E., *John Mark: A Riddle within the Johannine Enigma.* Scripture 15 (1963) 88-92.

Bruns, J.E., *The Confusion between John and John Mark in Antiquity*. Scripture 17 (1965) 23-26.

Bruce, F.F., *The Acts of the Apostles: The Greek Text with Introduction and Commentary*. Michigan, Eerdmans, 1952.

Bruce, F.F., *New Testament History*. London, Oliphants, 1969.

Bultmann, R. *Existence and Faith. Shorter Writings of Rudolf Bultmann*. Ed. and Int. Schubert Ogden. London, Collins, 1961.

Bultmann, R., *Faith and Understanding*. Ed. Robert Funk and transl. Louise Pettibone Smith, New York, Harper and Row, 1969. This is a translation of most of the articles contained in *Glauben und Verstehen*, Vol.1.

Bultmann, R., *The History of the Synoptic Tradition*. Transl. J. Marsh, 2nd Edition. Oxford, Blackwell, 1968.

Bultmann R., *Jesus and the Word*. Transl. Louise Pettibone Smith and Erminie Lantero. London, Collins, Fontana Books, 1958. (Original English Edition 1934.)

Bultmann, R., *Jesus Christ and Mythology*. New York, Charles Scribner's Sons, 1958.

Carnley, P., *The Poverty of Historical Scepticism*. In Sykes, S.W., and Clayton, J.P., ed., *Christ, Faith and History*. CUP, 1972, 165-189.

Caron, G., *Qui sont les "Juifs" de l'Evangile de Jean?* Recherches 35, Quebec, Bellarmine, 1997.

Casey, M., *Is John's Gospel True?* London and New York, Routledge, 1996.

Casey, M., *From Jewish Prophet to Gentile God; The Origins and Development of New Testament Christology*. London and New York, Routledge, 1991.

Catchpole, D., *The Trial of Jesus*, Leiden, Brill, 1971.

Cazelles, H., *Johannes. Ein Sohn des Zebedäus. 'Priester und Apostel'*. Communio 31(2002), 479-84.

Charlesworth, J.H., *The Beloved Disciple: Whose Witness Validates the Gospel of John?* Valley Forge, Pennsylvania, Trinity International, 1995.

Clark, F., *On Reason, Faith, and Sacred Being*, London, St Pauls Publishing, 2000.

Clines, D., *Possibilities and Priorities of Biblical Interpretation in an International Perspective.* Biblical Interpretation 1, 67-87.

Cohn, H., *The Trial and Death of Jesus.* London, Weidenfeld and Nicolson, 1967.

Collingwood, R.G., *The Idea of History.* Oxford University Press, 1953.

Collins, J.J., *Daniel.* Minneapolis, Fortress Press, 1993a.

Collins, J.J., *The Son of God Text from Qumran.* In *From Jesus to John. Essays on Jesus and New Testament Christology in Honour of Marinus de Jonge,* ed. M.C. de Boer. 65-82. Sheffield, IOSOT Press, 1993b.

Collins, J.J., *The Sceptre and the Star: The Messiahs of the Dead Sea Scrolls and Other Ancient Literature.* New York, Doubleday, 1995.

Conway, C.M., *Men and Women in the Fourth Gospel: Gender and Johannine Characterization.* SBL Series 167. Atlanta, Georgia, Society of Biblical Literature. 1997.

Cross, F.L. & Livingstone, E.A., ed., *The Oxford Dictionary of the Christian Church.* Oxford University Press, 1974.

Crossan, J.D., *The Historical Jesus: The Life of a Mediterranean Jewish Peasant.* San Francisco, HarperCollins, 1991.

Cullmann, O., *The Johannine Circle: Its Place in Judaism, among the Disciples of Jesus and in Early Christianity.* London and Philadelphia, 1976.

Culpepper, R.A., *Anatomy of the Fourth Gospel.* New Testament Foundations and Facets. Philadelphia, Fortress Press, 1983.

Culpepper, R.A., ed., *Critical Readings of John 6.* Leiden, Brill, 1997.

Culpepper, R.A., *John, the Son of Zebedee. The Life of a Legend.* Studies on Personalities of the New Testament. Columbia, University of South Carolina Press, 1994.

Culpepper, R.A., *The Johannine School: An Evaluation of the Johannine School Hypothesis Based upon an Investigation of the Nature of Ancient Schools.* SBL.DS26. Missoula, Mont. Scholars, 1975.

Cupitt, D., *The Debate about Christ.* London, SCM, 1979.

Cupitt, D., *The Sea of Faith: Christianity in Change*. London, British Broadcasting Corporation, 1984.

Daly-Denton, M., *David in the Fourth Gospel: The Johannine Reception of the Psalms*. Leiden, Brill, 2000.

Daube, D., *The "I am" of the Messianic Presence* in *The New Testament and Rabbinic Judaism*. London, Athlone, 1956, 325-29.

Dauer, A., *Die Passionsgeschichte im Johannesevangelium. Eine traditionsgeschichtliche und theologische Untersuchung z. Joh. 18:1–19:30*. SZANT XXX. Studien zum Alten und Neuen Testament. München, Koesel Verlag, 1972.

Davies, B., *Thinking About God*. London, Chapman, 1985.

Davies, W.D., and Allison, D.C., *The Gospel According to St. Matthew: A Critical and Exegetical Commentary. Volume 1, Introduction and Commentary on Matthew I-VII*. Edinburgh, T. & T. Clark, 1988.

Davis, S.T., Kendall, D., and O'Collins, G. eds., *The Incarnation. An Interdisciplinary Symposium on the Incarnation of the Son of God*. Oxford University Press, 2002.

Day Lewis, C., *The Collected Poems of Wilfred Owen*. London, Chatto and Windus, 1963.

Dekker, C., *Grundschrift und Redaktion im Johannesevangelium*. NTS, 13 (1966/7).

De Boer, M.C., *Johannine Perspectives on the Death of Jesus*. Biblical Exegesis and Theology No. 17. Kampan, The Netherlands, 1996.

de Jonge, M., *God's Final Envoy: Early Christology and Jesus' Own View of his Mission*. Michigan, Eerdmans, 1998. Cf. Morna Hooker, Rev Theology 102, No. 89, Sept. Oct. 1999.

De la Potterie, I., *La Figliolanza Divina del Cristiano Secondo Giovanni*. Padovese, L., *Turchia: la Chiesa et la sua storia*. Atti del VI Simposio di Efeso su S. Giovanni Apostolo, Istituto Francescano di Spiritualità\Pontificio Ateneo Antoniano, Roma, 1996, pp.53-80.

De la Potterie, I., *The Truth in St. John*. IJ, 67-82.

De Vaux, R., O.P., *The Bible and the Ancient Near East*, Transl. D. McHugh. London, Darton, Longman and Todd, 1972.

Deissmann, A., *Light from the Ancient Near East*. New York, George H. Doran, 1927.

Denaux, D., ed., *John and the Synoptics*. BETL, C1. Leuven University Press, 1992.

Dewey, A., *The Eye-Witness of History: Visionary Consciousness in the Fourth Gospel* in *Jesus in Johannine Tradition,* ed. R.T. Fortna and T. Thatcher, Louisville, Westminster, John Knox, 2001, 59-70.

Dodd, C.H., *The Apostolic Preaching and its Development*. London, Hodder and Stoughton, 1936.

Dodd, C.H., *The Interpretation of the Fourth Gospel*. Cambridge University Press, 1953.

Dodd, C.H., *Historical Tradition in the Fourth Gospel*. Cambridge University Press, 1965.

Dodd, C.H., *The Present Task in New Testament Studies:* An Inaugural Lecture delivered in the Divinity School on Tuesday 2 June 1936. Cambridge University Press, 1936.

Dover, K.J., *Thucydides. Greece and Rome: New Surveys in the Classics No.7*. Oxford, Clarendon Press, 1973.

Dreyfus, F., *Jésus savait-il qu'il était Dieu?* Paris, Editions du Cerf, 1984.

Duke, P.D., *Irony in the Fourth Gospel*. Atlanta, John Knox Press, 1985.

Dulles, A., *Historians and the Reality of Christ*. In *First Things,* December 1992. 20-25.

Dungan, D.L., *A History of the Synoptic Problem. The Canon, the Text, the Composition, and the Interpretation of the Gospels*. New York, Doubleday, 1999.

Dunn, J.D.G., *Christology in the Making*. London and Philadelphia, SCM, 1980.

Dunn, J.D.G., *Jesus and the Spirit*. Philadelphia, Westminster, 1975.

Dunn, J.D.G., *Jesus Remembered: Christianity in the Making,* Volume 1. Grand Rapids, Michigan, Eerdmans, 2003.

Dunn, J.D.G., *Spirit and Fire Baptism*. NT 14(1972): 81-92.

Dupuis, J., *Toward a Christian Theology of Religious Pluralism*. Maryknoll, Orbis Books, 1997.

Eckhardt, K.A., *Der Tod des Johannes.* Berlin, de Gruyter, 1961. Cf. Review in CBQ 24(1962) 218-9.

Evely, L., *The Gospels without Myth.* Transl. J.F. Bernard. New York, Doubleday, 1971.

Farkasfalvy, Denis, *In Search of a "Post-Critical" Method of Biblical Interpretation for Catholic Theology.* Communio 13 (1986) Winter, Denis, pp. 288-307

Fekkes, J., *Isaiah and Prophetic Traditions in the Book of Revelation.* Sheffield, University Press, 1994.

Felder, *Christ and the Critics.* London, Burns Oates and Washbourne, 1942.

Feuillet, A., *Johannine Studies.* New York, Alba House, 1964.

Filson, F.V., *Who was the Beloved Disciple?* JBL 68 (1949) 83-88.

Finegan, J., *Encountering New Testament Manuscripts.* London, SPCK, 1975.

Fitzmyer, J., *Essays on the Semitic Background of the New Testament.* London, Chapman, 1971.

Fitzmyer, J., *The Biblical Commission's Document "The Interpretation of the Bible in the Church".* Text and Commentary. Subsidia Biblica 18. Rome, Pontifical Biblical Institute, 1995.

Flusser, David, *Judaism and the Origins of Christianity.* Jerusalem, The Magnes Press, Hebrew University, 1988.

Fortna, R.T. and Thatcher, T., ed. *Jesus in Johannine Tradition.* Louisville, Westminster, John Knox Press, 1989.

Fortna, R.T., *The Gospel of Signs: A Reconstruction of the Narrative Source underlying the Fourth Gospel.* Cambridge University Press, 1970.

Fortna, R.T., *The Fourth Gospel and its Predecessor: From Narrative Source to Present Gospel.* Philadelphia Fortress Press, 1988.

Fortna, R.T., *From Christology to Soteriology: A Redaction-Critical Study of Salvation in the Fourth Gospel.* Interpretation, 27 (1973), 31-47.

Freedman, D.N., *The Anchor Bible Dictionary,* New York, Doubleday, 1997. Logos Library System electronic version.

Fuller, R.H., *The Foundations of New Testament Christology.* London, Collins, 1969.

Funk, R.W., and the 'Jesus Seminar', *The Five Gospels. The Search for the Authentic Words of Jesus*, New York, Scribner, 1993.

Galot, J., *La Personne du Christ: Recherche ontologique*. Paris, Lethielleux, 1969.

Geering, L., *Resurrection; A Symbol of Hope*. London, Hodder and Stoughton, 1971.

Green, M. ed., *The Truth of God Incarnate*. London, Hodder and Stoughton, 1977.

Griffiths, B., *The Marriage of East and West*. London, Collins, 1982

Grillmeier, A., *Christ and Christian Tradition*. Vol. 2, 2. London, Mowbray, 1995.

Güttgemanns, E., *Candid Questions Concerning Gospel Form Criticism. A Methodological Sketch of the Fundamental Problematics of Form and Redaction Criticism*. Transl. W.G. Doty, Pittsburgh, Pickwick Press, 1979.

Hastings, J., *A Dictionary of the Bible*. 5 vols. Edinburgh, T. and T. Clark, 1900.

Hahn, F., *Die "Juden" im Johannesevangelium*, in Müller, P.-G., and Stenger, V., ed. *Kontinuität und Einheit. Zeitschrift für F.Mussner*. Fribourg, Herder, 1981, 430-438.

Hahn, F., *The Titles of Jesus in Christology. Their History in Early Christianity*. London, Lutterworth Press, 1969.

Haenchen, E., *The Acts of the Apostles*. Oxford, Basil Blackwell, 1971.

Harnack, A. von, *Das "Wir" in den Johanneischen Schriften*. 97n.4. SPAW phil.-hist. Kl., (1923) 96-113, with the review by J. Behm, TLZ 49 (1924), 252-5.

Harris, E., *Prologue and Gospel: The Theology of the Fourth Evangelist*. SNT Suppl. Series 107. Sheffield Academic Press, 1994.

Harvey, A.E., *Jesus on Trial: a Study in the Fourth Gospel*. London, SPCK, 1976.

Hasitschka, M., *Befreiung von Sünde nach dem Johannesevangelium: Eine bibeltheologische Untersuchung*. Innsbrucker theologische Studien, Innsbruck, 1989.

Heil, J.P., *Jesus Walking on the Sea: Meaning and Gospel Functions of Matthew 14:22, Mark 6:45-52 and John 6:15b-21* Analectica Biblica 87, Rome, Biblical Institute Press, 1981.

Hengel, M., *The Johannine Question.* Transl. J. Bowden. London, SCM, 1989.

Hengel, M., *Judaism and Hellenism.* Vol I. Transl. J. Bowden. London, SCM, 1974.

Hengel, M., *Studies in Early Christology.* Transl. R. Kearns. Edinburgh, T. & T. Clark Ltd., 1995.

Hengel, M., *Crucifixion.* Transl. J. Bowdon. London and Philadelphia, Fortress, 1977.

Hengel, M., *Was Jesus a Revolutionist?* Philadelphia, Fortress, 1971.

Hennecke, E., *New Testament Apocrypha.* Ed. W. Schneemelcher, transl. R. McL. Wilson. Vol. I, London, SCM, 1963. Vol. II, London, SCM, 1965.

Hick, J. ed., *The Myth of God Incarnate.* London, SCM, 1977.

Higgins, A.J.B., *The Son of Man in the Teaching of Jesus.* SNT 39. Cambridge University Press, 1980.

Hodgson, Peter C. ed., *David Friedrich Strauss. The Life of Jesus Critically Examined.* London, SCM, 1973.

Hofrichter, P.L., *Logoslied, Gnosis und Neues Testament.* Hildesheim, Georg Olms Verlag, 2003.

Hooker, Morna D., *Jesus and the Servant.* London, SPCK, 1959.

Hooper, W. ed., *Fern-Seed and Elephants and Other Essays on Christianity by C.S .Lewis.* London, Harper Collins, 1977.

Horman, J., *The Source of the Version of the Parable of the Sower in the Gospel of Thomas.* NT 21/4 (1976), 326-343.

Howard Marshall. I., *The Origins of New Testament Christology.* Inter-Varsity Press, 1990.

Howard Marshall. I., *The Gospel of Luke. A Commentary on the Greek Text.* The New International Greek Testament Commentary. Exeter, Paternoster Press, 1978.

Hughes, J.J., *John the Baptist: Forerunner of God Himself.* *Novum Testamentum,* 14 (1972), pp.190-218.

Hurst, L.D., and Wright, N.T., *The Glory of Christ in the New Testament.* Festschrift, G.B. Caird, Oxford, Clarendon Press, 1987.

Jackson, M.H., *Ancient Self-Referential Conventions and their Implications for the Authorship and Integrity of the Gospel of John.* Journal of Theological Studies 50(1999), 1-34.

James, M.R., *The Apocryphal New Testament.* Oxford University Press, 1924.

Juster, J., *Les Juifs dans l'Empire Romain* (2 vols). Paris, Geuthner, 1914.

Jülicher, A., *An Introduction to the New Testament.* Transl. J.P. Ward. London, Smith Elder and Co., 1904.

Kasper, W., *The God of Jesus Christ.* London, SCM, 1982.

Keating, James F. *The Invincible Allure of the Historical Jesus for Systematic Theology.* Irish Theological Quarterly 66(2001), 211-226.

Kelber W.H. ed., *The Passion in Mark.* Philadelphia, Fortress Press, 1976.

Kelly, J.N.D., *Early Christian Doctrines,* London, Adam and Charles Black, 1968

Kenyon, F., *Our Bible and the Ancient Manuscripts.* London, Eyre and Spottiswoode, 1958.

Kereszty, R., *Historical Research, Theological Inquiry, and the Reality of Jesus: Reflections on the method of J.P. Meier.* *Communio* 19 (Winter 1992), pp.576-600.

Kertelge K. ed., *Der Prozess gegen Jesus. Historische Rückfrage und theologische Deutung.* Q D 112, Freiburg, Basel, Wien, 1988.

Kilpatrick, G.D., *The Trial of Jesus.* London, Friends of Dr. William's Library, 1953.

Klijn, *An Introduction to the New Testament.* Transl. M. van der Vathorst-Smit. Leiden, Brill, 1967.

Knox, John, *The Humanity and the Divinity of Christ.* Cambridge University Press, 1967.

Kragerud, A., *Der Lieblingsjünger im Johannesevangelium.* (Oslo University, 1959). Cf. review by M.-E. Boismard RB 67 (1960), 405-10.

Kraus, H.-J., *Geschichte der historisch-kritischen Erforschung des Alten Testaments*. 2nd Edition. Neukirchener Verlag, 1969.

Kremer, J., *Zur Diskussion über "das Leere Grab"* in Dhanis, E., ed., *Resurrexit. Actes du Symposium Internationale sur la Résurrection de Jésus*. Libreria Editrice Vaticana, 1974, 137-168.

Kümmel, W.G., *The New Testament: The History of the Investigation of its Problems*. Transl. S. Mclean Gilmour and H.C. Kee. London, SCM, 1973.

Kuyper, L.J., *Grace and Truth: an Old Testament Description of God and Its Use in the Johannine Gospel*. Interpretation 181964), 3-19.

Kysar, R., *Anti-Semitism and the Gospel of John*. In Evans, A.E., and Hagner, D.A. ed., *Anti-Semitism and Early Christianity. Issues of Polemic and Faith*. Minneapolis, Fortress Press, 1993, 113-127.

Lagrange, M.-J., *Le Messianisme chez les Juifs*. Paris, Gabalda, 1909.

Lampe, G.W., *The Resurrection*. Cf. EJ, 97. n.4.

Latourelle, R., *The Miracles of Jesus and the Theology of Miracles*. Transl. M.J. O'Connell, New York, Paulist Press, 1988.

Légasse, S., *The Trial of Jesus*. London, SCM, 1997.

Lehmann, J., *The Jesus Report*. Transl. M. Heron. London, Souvenir Press, 1971.

Leibig, J.E., *John and the Jews: Theological Anti-Semitism in the Fourth Gospel*. JES, 20 (1983), 209-234.

Letourneau, *Jesus, Fils de L'Homme et Fils de Dieu: Jean 2:23-3:36 et la double Christologie Johannique*. Recherches Nouvelle Série 27. Les Editions Bellarmin, Editions du Cerf, Montreal, Paris, 1993.

Lidzbarski, *Ginza, der Schatz oder das Grosse Buch der Mandäer*. Göttingen, Vandenhoeck und Ruprecht, 1925.

Lindars, B., Ruth B. Edwards and John M. Court, *The Johannine Literature*. Sheffield Academic Press, 2000.

Lohse, E., *The History of the Death and Suffering of Jesus Christ*. Transl. M.O. Dietrich. Philadelphia, Fortress Press, 1967.

Lonergan, B., *A Second Collection*. London, Darton, Longman, and Todd, 1974.

Lowe, M., *Who Were the Ioudaioi?* NT, 18(1974), 101-130.

Lowther Clarke, W.K., *Concise Bible Commentary*. London, SPCK, 1952.

MacRae, G.W., *The Ego Proclamation in Gnostic Sources*. In Bammel, E. *The Trial of Jesus*. London, SCM, 1970, 129.

MacQuarrie, J., *An Existentialist Theology. A Comparison of Heidegger and Bultmann*. London, SCM, 1955.

MacQuarrie, J., *Christology Revisited*. London, SCM, 1998.

Machen, J.G. *The Virgin Birth of Christ*. London, James Clarke, 1958. First Edition 1930.

Mack, B., *A Myth of Innocence*. Philadelphia, Fortress Press, 1988.

McNamara, M., *Targum and Testament: Aramaic Paraphrases of the Hebrew Bible : A Light on the New Testament*. Irish University Press, Shannon, 1972.

Malatesta, E., *St. John's Gospel 1920-65: A Cumulative and Classified Bibliography of Books and Periodical Literature on the Fourth Gospel*. Analectica Biblica 32, Rome Pontifical Biblical Institute, 1967.

Malavez, L., *The Christian Message and Myth. The Theology of Rudolf Bultmann*. London, SCM, 1958.

Manns, F., *L'Evangile de Jean à la Lumière du Judaïsme*. Jerusalem, Franciscan Printing Press, 1991.

Marguerat, D., *"La Source des Signes" existe-t-elle? Réception des Récits de Miracle dans L'Evangile de Jean*. CJH, 68-93.

Martin, M., *Jesus Now*. London, Collins, 1975.

Martyn, J.L., *History and Theology in the Fourth Gospel*. Nashville, Abingdon, 1979. First published in 1968.

Martyn, J.L., *Source Criticism and Religionsgeschichte in the Fourth Gospel*. In Ashton, J., ed., *The Interpretation of John*. 121-146.

Mascall, E.L., *Theology and the Gospel of Christ: An Essay in Reorientation*. London, SPCK, 1977.

McArthur, Harvey K., ed. *In Search of the Historical Jesus*. London, SPCK, 1969.

McDade, J., *Jesus in Recent Research. In The Month,* Second New Series, 31/12, December 1998, 495-505.

McGrath, J.F., *John's Apologetic Christology: Legitimation and Development in Johannine Christology*. Society for New

Testament Studies, Monograph Series 111. Cambridge University Press, 2001.

McLeish, K. and Unwin, S., *A Pocket Guide to Shakespeare's Plays.* London, Faber and Faber, 1998.

Meier, John P., *A Marginal Jew: Rethinking the Historical Jesus. Volume I. The Roots of the Person and the Problem.* Anchor Bible Reference Library. New York, Doubleday, 1987.

Meier, John P., *A Marginal Jew: Rethinking the Historical Jesus. Volume II Mentor, Message, and Miracles.* Anchor Bible Reference Library. New York, Doubleday, 1994.

Meier, John P., *A Marginal Jew: Rethinking the Historical Jesus. Volume III. Companions and Competitors.* Anchor Bible Reference Library. New York, Doubleday, 2001.

Moloney, F., *The Johannine Son of Man.* Rome, Libreria Ateneo Salesiana, 1976.

Montefiore, H. and Turner, H.E.W., *Thomas and the Evangelists.* SBT 55, London, SCM, 1962.

Morris, L., *Studies in the Fourth Gospel.* Exeter, Paternoster Press, 1969.

Moule, C.F.D., *The Origins of Christology.* Cambridge University Press, 1977.

Moule, C.F.D., *Jesus and the Politics of His Day.* Cambridge University Press, 1984.

Mounce, W.D., *The Analytical Lexicon to the Greek New Testament.* Grand Rapids, Zondervan, 1993.

Mowinckel, S., *He That Cometh.* Transl. G.W. Anderson. Oxford, Basil Blackwell, 1956.

Murphy-O'Connor, J. *The Holy Land: an Archaeological Guide from Earliest Times to 1700.* Oxford University Press, 1980.

Mussner, Franz, *The Historical Jesus in the Gospel of John.* Quaestiones Disputatae 19, Freiburg, Herder, 1967.

Neirynck, F. et al., *Jean et les synoptiques: Examen critique de l'exégèse de M.-E. Boismard.* BETL, XLIX. Leuven University Press, 1971.

Neumann, J., *Historischer Jesus und Altes Testament. Hellenistische Quellen der Juedischen Bibel und die Angst der Theologen vor dem wissenschaftlichen Fortschritt.* Radebeul, Johannes Neumann Fachverlag, 2000.

Newman, J.H., *An Essay in Aid of a Grammar of Assent*. New Edition edited and introduced by C.F. Harold. New York, Longmans, Green and Company, 1947.

Neville, G., *Lay Theology: The case of Dorothy L. Sayers*. Theology. 102, 809 Sept, Oct 1999.

Nicol, W., *The Semeia in the Fourth Gospel. Tradition and Redaction*. (New Testament Studies 32), Leiden, 1972.

Nineham, D.E., *Eye-Witness Testimony and the Gospel Tradition, III*. JTS 11 (1960), 254-264.

Nineham, D.E., *The Gospel of Mark*. London, A. and C. Black, 1963.

Nunn, H.P.V., *The Authorship of the Fourth Gospel*. Oxford, Blackwell, 1952.

O'Collins, G., *The Easter Jesus*. London, Darton, Longman and Todd, 1973.

O'Collins, G., *The Resurrection – What Actually Happened and What Does it Mean?* London, Darton, Longman and Todd, 1987.

O'Collins, G., *Incarnation*. New Century Theology, London, Continuum, 2002.

O'Collins, G., *The Resurrection of Jesus: Some Contemporary Issues*. Marquette University Press, 1993.

O'Connell, M.J., *The Concept of Commandment in the Old Testament*. TS 21 (1960).

O'Day, G.R., *Revelation in the Fourth Gospel*. Philadelphia, Fortress Press, 1986.

Odeberg, H., *The Fourth Gospel Interpreted in its Relation to Contemporary Religious Currents in Palestine and the Hellenistic-Oriental World*. Chicago, 1928.

O'Neill, J.C., *Who Did Jesus Think He Was?* Leiden, Brill, 1995.

Orwell, G., *1984*. London, Penguin Books, 1954.

Pailin, D.A., *The Way to Faith: An Examination of Newman's Grammar of Assent as a Response to the Search for Certainty in Faith*. Library of Ecumenical Studies. London, Epworth Press, 1969.

Painter, J., *The Quest for the Messiah: The History, Literature, and Theology of the Johannine Community*. Edinburgh, T. and T. Clark, 1991.

Painter, J., *John: Witness and Theologian*. London, SPCK, 1979.

Pancaro, S., *The Law in the Fourth Gospel: The Torah and the Gospel, Moses and Jesus, Judaism and Christianity According to John*. NT Suppl. XLII Leiden, Brill, 1975.

Parker, P., *John and John Mark*. JBL 79 (1960), 97-100.

Parker, P., *Two Editions of John*. JBL 75 (1956), 303-14.

Peers, E. Allison, transl. and ed., *The Complete Works of Saint John of the Cross*. From the Critical Edition of P. Silvero de Santa Teresa, C.D. Three volumes in one Edition, Wheathampstead, Anthony Clarke, 1964.

Pesch, R., and Schnackenburg, R., ed. *Jesus und der Menschensohn*, Freiburg, Herder, 1975.

Peter, J., *Finding the Historical Jesus*. London, Collins, 1965.

Podechard, E. *Psaume 110*. In *Etudes de critique et d'histoire religieuses. Lyon, Facultés Catholiques*, 1984. 7-24.

Polythress, V., Novum Testamentum 26 (1984), 312-340. *Idem* Westminster Theological Journal, 46 (1984), 350-369.

Rahner, K., *Exegesis and Dogmatic Theology*. pp.31-65 in H. Vorgrimler, ed., *Dogmatic Versus Biblical Theology: Essays in Two Disciplines*. Transl. K. Smyth. Wheathampstead, Anthony Clarke, 1964.

Rahner, *Visions and Prophecies*. Questiones Disputatae No. 10, London, Burns and Oates, 1963.

Ratzinger, J., *Truth and Tolerance: Christian Belief and World Religions*. Transl. H. Taylor. San Francisco, Ignatius Press, 2004.

Redford, J. ed., *Hear, O Islands: Theology and Catechesis in the New Millennium*. Dublin, Veritas, 2002.

Ruether, R., *Faith and Fratricide. The Theological Roots of Anti-Semitism*. New York, Seabury, 1974.

Richter, J., *Ani Hu and Ego Eimi*, Unpublished Dissertation, University of Erlangen, 1956.

Ricoeur, P., *Essays on Biblical Interpretation*. Ed & int. Lewis S. Mudge, London, SPCK, 1981.

Robert, A., and Feuillet, A., *Interpreting the Scriptures*. Transl. P.W. Skehan *et al*. With an Appendix on *The Dogmatic Constitution on Divine Revelation* by W. Harrington and L. Walsh. New York, Desclée, 1969.

Robinson, J.A.T., *The Destination and Purpose of St. John's Gospel.* NTS 6 (1959-60), 21-38.

Robinson, J.A.T., *Elijah, John and Jesus: an Essay in Detection.* NTS 4 (1957-81). Also in TNTS, 28-52.

Robinson, J.A.T., *Honest to God.* London, SCM, 1963. Cf. Edwards, D.L. Ed., *The Honest to God Debate: Some Reactions to the Book "Honest to God".* London, SCM, 1963.

Robinson, J.A.T., *Redating the New Testament.* London, SCM, 1976.

Robinson, J.A.T., *The Priority of John.* London, SCM, 1985.

Roberts, C. Robert, *Rudolf Bultmann's Theology: A Critical Interpretation.* London, SPCK, 1977.

Roloff, J., *Das Kerygma und der irdische Jesus.* Göttingen, Vandenhoeck und Ruprecht, 1970.

Ruckstuhl, E., *Die literarische Einheit des Johannesevangeliums.* NTOA 7, Göttingen, 1987.

Ruckstuhl, E., Dschulnigg, P. *Stilkritik und Verfasserfrage im Johannesevangelium. Die johanneischen Sprachmerkmale auf dem Hintergrund des Neuen Testaments und des zeitgenoessischen hellenistischen Schrifttums.* NTOA 17, Göttingen, 1987.

Sanday, W., *Outlines of the Life of Christ.* 2nd Edition. T. and T. Clark, Edinburgh, 1911.

Sanday, W., *The Criticism of the Fourth Gospel.* Eight Lectures, Union Theological Seminary, New York, Nov 1904. Oxford, Clarenden Press, 1905.

Sanders, E.P., *Jesus and Judaism.* London, SCM, 1985.

Sanders, J.N., *St. John on Patmos.* NTS 9 (1960), 97-110.

Sanders, J.N., and Mastin, B.A., *The Gospel According to John.* Black's New Testament Commentaries, London, Adam and Charles Black, 1968.

Sayers, D.L., *The Man Born to be King.* London, 1943, pp.33f. Bruce says 'See also her comments, quoted on page 409 (on John 21:24) with regard to the eyewitness claim of this Gospel'.

Schillebeeckx, E., *Jesus: An Experiment in Christology.* Transl. H. Hoskins. London, Collins, 1979.

Schnackenburg, R., *Zur Traditionsgeschichte von Johannes 4:46-54*. BZ 8 (1964).

Schneiders, Sandra M., *Because of the Woman's Testimony... Reexamining the Issue of Authorship in the Fourth Gospel*. NTS 44 (1998) 513-535.

Schneiders, Sandra M., *A Case Study: A Feminist Interpretation of John 4:1-42*. IJ, 235-259.

Schoonenberg, P., *The Christ*. Transl. D. Couling. London, Sheed and Ward, 1972.

Schram, T.L., *The Use of Ioudaios in the Fourth Gospel, An Application of some Linguistic Insights to A New Testament Problem*. State University of Utrecht, Th.D., 1974, Xerox University Microfilms.

Schrer, *The History of the Jewish People in the Age of Jesus Christ. (175 B.C. TO A.D.135)*. Rev. and ed., M. Black, G. Vermes, F. Millar, and M. Goodman. 3 vols. Edinburgh, T. and T. Clark, 1973-87.

Schweizer, E., *The Good News According to Mark. A Commentary on the Gospel*. Transl. D.H. Madvig. London, SPCK, 1970.

Selman, F., *From Physics to Metaphysics*. London, The Saint Austin Press, 2001.

Sheed, F., *What Difference does Jesus Make?* London, Sheed and Ward, 1971.

Sherwin-White, A.N., *Roman Society and Roman Law in the New Testament*. Oxford, 1963.

Smalley, *John, Evangelist and Interpreter*. Exeter, Paternoster Press, 1978.

Smith, D.M., *The Composition and Order of the Fourth Gospel: Bultmann's Literary Theory*. Yale University Press, 1965.

Smith, D.M., *Johannine Christianity: Essays on its Setting, Sources, and Theology*. University of South Carolina Press, 1984.

Smith, D.M., *John Among the Gospels: The Relationship in Twentieth Century Research*. Minneapolis, Fortress Press, 1992.

Smith, G.D. ed., *The Teaching of the Catholic Church: A Summary of Catholic Doctrine.* London, Burns Oates and Washbourne, 1952.

Stauffer, E., *Jesus and his Story.* London, SCM, 1960.

Stibbe, M.W.G., *John as Storyteller. Narrative Criticism ad the Fourth Gospel.* SNTS, 73, (Society for New Testament Studies) Cambridge University Press, 1992.

Stibbe, M.W.G., *John's Gospel,* London and New York, Routledge, 1994.

Stolz, H.-H., *History and Criticism of the Marcan Hypothesis.* Transl, and ed. D.L. Niewyk. Edinburgh, T. and T. Clark, 1980.

Sykes, S.W., and Clayton, J.P., *Christ Faith and History.* Cambridge University Press, 1972.

Taylor, V., *The Gospel According to St. Mark: The Greek Text, with Introduction, Notes and Indexes.* 2nd Edition London, MacMillan, 1966.

Temple, S., *The Core of the Fourth Gospel.* London, Mowbrays, 1975.

Thatcher, T., *John's Memory Theatre: the Fourth Gospel and Ancient Memo-Rhetoric.* CBQ 69/3, July 2007, 487-505.

Theissen, G. and Merz, A., *The Historical Jesus: A Comprehensive Guide.* London, SCM, 1998.

Theissen, G., *Urchristliche Wundergeschichten.* (StNT 8), Gütersloh 1974.

Van Belle, G., *The Signs Source in the Fourth Gospel: Historical Survey and Critical Evaluation of the Semeia Hypothesis.* Leuven University Press, 1994.

Van Daalen, D.H., *The Real Resurrection.* London, Collins, 1972.

Vincent, M.R., *The Epistles to the Philippians and to Philemon.* International Critical Commentary. Edinburgh, T. & T. Clark, 1897. Vincent, 1897, 58-9.

Von Wahlde, U.C., *The Gospel of John and the Presentation of Jews and Judaism.* In Efroymson, E.J., Fisher and L. Klenicki, ed., *Within Context: Essays on Jews and Judaism in the New Testament.* Minnesota, Collegeville, The Liturgical Press, 1993.

Wansbrough, H. *Risen from the Dead.* Slough, St Pauls
    Publications, 1978.
Watson, F. *Text, Church, and World.* Edinburgh, T. and
    T. Clark, 1994.
Wedderburn, A.J.M., *Beyond Resurrection.* London, SCM,
    1999.
Wells, G.A., *Did Jesus Exist?* New York, Buffalo, 1975.
Whitacre, R.A., *Johannine Polemic: The Role of Tradition and
    Theology.* SBL Dissertation Series 67, Chico, California,
    Scholars Press, 1982.
Whitacre, R.A., *John.* The IVP New Testament
    Commentary Series. Leicester, Inter-Varsity Press, 1999.
Williams, R., *Christ on Trial: How the Gospel Unsettles our
    Judgment.* London, HarperCollins, 2000.
Wilson, A.N. *C.S. Lewis: An Autobiography.* London, Harper
    Collins Ltd, 1990.
Winter, P., *On the Trial of Jesus.* SJ 1, Berlin and New York
    1961, 1974.
Wojtyla, K., *The Acting Person.* Dordrecht, D. Reidel
    Publishing Company, 1979.
Woll, D.B., *Johannine Christianity in Conflict: Authority,
    Rank, and Succession in the First Farewell Discourse.* SBL
    Dissertation Series 60, Chico, California, Scholars Press,
    1981.
Wrede, W., *The Messianic Secret.* Transl. J.C.G. Greig.
    Library of Theological Translations. London, J. Clarke,
    1971. German Edition *Das Messiasgeheimnis in den
    Evangelien. Zugleich ein Beitrag zum Verständnis des
    Markusevangeliums.* Göttingen und Ruprecht 1901.
Zimmerman, H., *Das Absolute "Ego Eimi" als die
    neutestamentliche Offenbarungsformel.* BZ (1960), 54-69,
    266-76.

ABBREVIATIONS

ABC   Dulles, A., *Apologetics and the Biblical Christ*. London, Collins, 1963.

ALGT   Mounce, W.D., *The Analytical Lexicon to the Greek New Testament*. Grand Rapids, Zondervan, 1993

AS   Abbott-Smith, *A Manual Greek Lexicon of the New Testament*. 3rd Edition. Edinburgh, T. and T. Clark, 1937.

BI   Megivern, J.J., *Bible Interpretation. Official Catholic Teachings*. Consortium Books. North Carolina, McGrath.

BETL   Bibliotheca Ephemeridum Theologicarum Lovaniensium.

BMG   Redford, J., *Bad, Mad or God? Proving the Divinity of Christ from St. John's Gospel*. London, St Pauls Publications, 2004.

BV   Redford, J., *Born of a Virgin: Proving the Miracle from the Gospels*. London, St Pauls Publications, 2007.

CBQ   Catholic Biblical Quarterly.

CCC   *Catechism of the Catholic Church*. London, Geoffrey Chapman, 1994.

CJH   Kaestli, J.-D., Poffet, J.-M, and Zumstein, J. *La Communauté Johannique et son Histoire. La Trajectoire de L'Évangile de Jean aux Deux Premiers Siècles*. Labor et Fides, Geneva, 1990.

CM   Dunn, J.D.G., *Christology in the Making*. London and Philadelphia, SCM, 1980.

COD   Allen, R.E. ed., *The Concise Oxford Dictionary of Current English*. 8th Edition. Oxford University Press, 1990.

Davis   Davis, Stephen T., Kendall, D. and O'Collins, G. ed., *The Incarnation. An Interdisciplinary Symposium on the Incarnation of the Son of God*. Oxford University Press, 2002.

DCG   Hastings, J., *A Dictionary of Christ and the Gospels*. Vol. I. Edinburgh, T. and T. Clark, 1906.

DFT   Latourelle, R. and Fisichella, R. *Dictionary of Fundamental Theology*. English Language Edition, ed. R. Latourelle, Slough, St Pauls Publishing, 1994.

DV   *Dogmatic Constitution of the Second Vatican Council on Divine Revelation Dei Verbum ("The Word of God")*. The version used in this book is in Tanner, II, 971-981 (for Tanner, cf. below.)

EBT   Bauer, J. ed., *Encyclopaedia of Biblical Theology*. London, Sheed and Ward, 1970.

ECD   Kelly, J.N.D., *Early Christian Doctrines*. London, Adam and Charles Black, 1968.

EF   Bultmann, R., *Existence and Faith. Shorter Writings of Rudolf Bultmann*. Ed. and transl. S. Ogden. London, Collins, 1961.

EJ   O'Collins, G., *The Easter Jesus*. London, Darton, Longman and Todd, 1973.

ENTM   Finegan, J., *Encountering New Testament Manuscripts*. London, SPCK, 1975.

ET	Benoit, P., *Exégèse et Théologie*. Editions du Cerf, Paris, 1961.
FU	Bultmann, R., *Faith and Understanding*. Ed. R. Funk and transl. Louise Pettibone Smith. New York, Harper and Row, 1969. This is a translation of most of the articles contained in *Glauben und Verstehen,* Vol.1.
FG	Funk, R., and Hoover, R.W., and the *"Jesus Seminar"*, *The Five Gospels. The Search for the Authentic Words of Jesus.* Scribner, New York, 1993.
GEAT	Kraus, H.-J.*Geschichte der historisch-kritischen Erforschung des Alten Testaments.* 2nd Edition. Neukirchener Verlag, 1969.
GA	Newman, J.H., *An Essay in Aid of a Grammar of Assent: Introduction by Nicholas Lash.* University of Notre Dame Press, 1979.
GEL	Bauer, W., *A Greek-English Lexicon of the New Testament and Other Early Christian Literature.* Transl. W.F.R. Arndt and F.W. Gingrich. 2nd Edition, 1958. Chicago University Press, 1979.
HDB	Hastings, J., *A Dictionary of the Bible.* 5 vols. Edinburgh, T. and T. Clark, 1900.
HJCG	Theissen G., and Merz, A., *The Historical Jesus: A Comprehensive Guide.* London, SCM, 1998.
HST	Bultmann, R., *The History of the Synoptic Tradition.* Transl. J. Marsh. 2nd Edition. Oxford, Blackwell, 1968.
HTFG	Dodd, C.H., *Historical Tradition in the Fourth Gospel.* Cambridge University Press, 1965.
IAM	Ball, D.M., *'I am' in John's Gospel: Literary Function, Background and Theological Implications.* JSNTS, 124, Sheffield Academic Press, 1996.
IB	Laymon, C.M. ed., *Interpreters' One Volume Commentary on the Bible.* London, Collins, 1972.
IFG	Dodd, C.H., *The Interpretation of the Fourth Gospel.* Cambridge University Press, 1953.
IJ	Ashton, J. ed., *The Interpretation of John.* Edinburgh, T. and T. Clark, 1986.
INC	O'Collins, G., *Incarnation.* New Century Theology, London, Continuum, 2002.
INT	Brown, R.E., *An Introduction to the New Testament.* London, Doubleday, 1997. [INT Brown]. Klijn, *An Introduction to the New Testament.* Transl. M. van der Vathorst-Smit. Leiden, Brill, 1967 (INT Klijn).
ITQ	Irish Theological Quarterly.
JCM	Bultmann, R., *Jesus Christ and Mythology.* New York, Charles Scribner's Sons, 1958
JEC	Schillebeeckx, E., *Jesus: An Experiment in Christology.* Transl. H.Hoskins. London, Collins, 1979.

JN	Ratzinger, J. Pope Benedict XVI, *Jesus of Nazareth: From the Baptism in the Jordan to the Transfiguration.* Transl. A.A. Walker. London, Bloomsbury, 2007.
JPGG	Casey, M., *From Jewish Prophet to Gentile God; The Origins and Development of New Testament Christology.* London and New York, Routledge, 1991.
JQ	Hengel, M., *The Johannine Question.* Transl. J. Bowden. London, SCM, 1989.
JR	Dunn, J.D.G., *Jesus Remembered. Christianity in the Making,* Vol.1. Eerdmans, Grand Rapids, 2003.
JTS	*Journal of Theological Studies.*
JUIF	Caron, G., *Qui sont les "Juifs" de l'évangile de Jean?* Recherches 35, Quebec, Bellarmine, 1997.
JSD	Dreyfus, F., *Jésus savait-il était qu'il Dieu?* Paris, Editions du Cerf, 1984.
JVG	Wright, N.T. *Christian Origins and the Question of God. Volume II, Jesus and the Victory of God.* London, SPCK, 1996.
JTS	*Journal of Theological Studies.*
JW	Bultmann R., *Jesus and the Word.* Transl. Louise Pettibone Smith and Erminie Lantero. London, Collins, Fontana Books, 1958.
LJCE	Hodgson, P.C. ed., *David Friedrich Strauss. The Life of Jesus Critically Examined.* London, SCM, 1973.
LVT	Zorell, F., *Lexicon Hebraicum et Aramaicum Veteris Testamenti.* Roma, Pontificium Institutum Biblicum, 1968.
MGI	Hick, J., *The Myth of God Incarnate.* London, SCM, 1977.
MJ1	Meier, J.P., *Rethinking the Historical Jesus. Volume One: The Roots of the Problem and the Person.* New York, Doubleday, 1991.
MJ2	Meier, J.P., *Volume Two: Mentor, Message, and Miracles.* New York, Doubleday, 1994.
MJ3	Meier, J.P., *Volume Three: Companions and Competitors.* New York, Doubleday, 2001.
MJTM	Latourelle, R., *The Miracles of Jesus and the Theology of Miracles.* Transl. M.J. O'Connell. New York, Paulist Press, 1988.
MLM	Bockmuehl, M. *This Jesus: Martyr, Lord, Messiah.* Edinburgh, T. and T. Clark, 1994.
ND	Neuner, J. and Dupuis, J., *The Christian Faith in the Doctrinal Documents of the Catholic Church.* London, Collins, 1983.
NJBC	Brown, E., Fitzmyer, J.A., Murphy, R.E. ed., *The New Jerome Biblical Commentary.* London, Geoffrey Chapman, 1989. (The system of numbering of this commentary we adopt in this book will be the article number, followed by a colon and the paragraph number of that particular article (all in bold), followed finally by the page number in ordinary type, e.g. NJBC, **42:75**, 653).

NRSV   *The New Revised Standard Version Bible; Catholic Edition.*
        Copyright (c) 1993 and 1989. Division of the Christian
        Education of the National Council of the Churches of Christ
        in the United States of America. Electronic edition, *Catechism
        and Scripture Disk for Windows,* London. Chapman.
NT   *Novum Testamentum.*
NTA   Hennecke, E., *New Testament Apocrypha.* Transl. R. McL.
        Wilson. Vol. I, London, SCM, 1963. Vol. II London, SCM,
        1965.
NTH   Bruce, F.F., *New Testament History.* London, Oliphants,
        1969.
NTHIP   Kümmel, W.G., *The New Testament: The History of the
        Investigation of its Problems.* Transl. S. Mclean Gilmour and
        H.C. Kee. London, SCM, 1973.
NTI   Wickenhauser, A., *New Testament Introduction.* New York,
        Herder and Herder, 1958.
NTS   *New Testament Studies.*
ODCC   Cross, F.L. & Livingstone, E.A. ed., *The Oxford Dictionary of
        the Christian Church*, Oxford University Press, 1974.
OC   Moule, C.F.D., *The Origins of Christology.* Cambridge
        University Press, 1977.
PCB   Black, M. and Rowley, H.H., *Peake's Commentary on the
        Bible.* Revised Edition. London, Nelson, 1962.
QHJ   Schweitzer, A., *The Quest of the Historical Jesus. A Critical
        Study of its Progress from Reimarus to Wrede.* Transl. W.
        Montgomery. 3rd Edition. London, A. and C. Black, 1954.
PJ   Robinson, J.A.T., *The Priority of John.* London, SCM, 1985.
RNT   Robinson, J.A.T., *Redating the New Testament.* London,
        SCM, 1976.
RGG   Religion in Geschichte und Gegenwart.
RSG   Wright, N.T., *The Resurrection of the Son of God. Vol. 3,
        Christian Origins and the Question of God.* London, SPCK,
        2003.
SHJ   McArthur, Harvey K. ed., *In Search of the Historical Jesus.*
        London, SPCK, 1969.
Tanner Tanner, N. P. ed., *Decrees of the Ecumenical Councils.* II Vols.
        London & Washington, DC, Sheed & Ward and Georgetown
        University Press, 1990.
Taylor Taylor, V., *The Gospel According to St. Mark: The Greek Text,
        with Introduction, Notes and Indexes.* 2nd Edition. London,
        MacMillan, 1966.
TGI   Green, M. ed., *The Truth of God Incarnate.* London, Hodder
        and Stoughton, 1977.
TJC   Hahn, F., *The Titles of Jesus in Christology. Their History in
        Early Christianity.* London, Lutterworth Press, 1969.

TROC   Trocmé, E., *The Formation of the Gospel According to Mark.* Transl. Pamela Gaughan. London, SPCK, 1963.

UFG   Ashton, J., *Understanding the Fourth Gospel.* Oxford, Clarendon Press, 1991.

V2AP   R. Latourelle, ed., *Vatican II Assessment and Perspectives, Twenty-Five Years After (1962-1987).* Volume One. New York, Paulist Press, Mahwah, 1988.

VGT   Moulton, J.H. and Milligan G., *The Vocabulary of the Greek Testament. Illustrated from the Papyri and Other Non-Literary Sources.* Michigan, Eerdmans, 1930.

YHWH   A transliteration of the divine name, often now designated *Jahweh.* In the Hebrew Bible, the consonants *yhwh* appear with the vowel pointing of *Adonai,* Lord, because the Jews would not pronounce the divine name.

\\   If a Synoptic Gospel, e.g. Matthew, has instances of the same narrative in the other two Synoptists, i.e. Mark and Luke, then we will follow the convention to abbreviate by backslash lines \\, indicating synoptic parallels. E.g. Matthew 26:26-29\\ = Matthew 26:26-29, Mark 14:22-25, Luke 22:19-20.

315

OLD TESTAMENT

NEW TESTAMENT

317

318

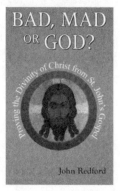 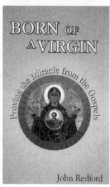